# A BRIEF HISTORY OF MEXICO

## FOURTH EDITION

## LYNN V. FOSTER

Checkmark Books®
*An imprint of Infobase Publishing*

*To Lawrence Foster,*

*husband and best friend*

**A Brief History of Mexico, Fourth Edition**

Copyright © 2009, 2007, 2004, 1997 by Lynn V. Foster

Checkmark Books
An imprint of Infobase Publishing
132 West 31st Street
New York NY 10001

**Library of Congress Cataloging-in-Publication Data**

Foster, Lynn V.
  A brief history of Mexico / Lynn V. Foster. — 4th ed.
      p. cm.
  Includes bibliographical references and index.
  ISBN 978-0-8160-7405-1 (hc)
  ISBN 978-0-8160-7406-8 (pb)
  1. Mexico—History. I. Title.
  F1226.F67 2009
  972—dc22                              2009018298

Checkmark Books are available at special discounts when purchased in bulk quantities for businesses, associations, institutions, or sales promotions. Please call our Special Sales Department in New York at (212) 967-8800 or (800) 322-8755.

You can find Facts On File on the World Wide Web at http://www.factsonfile.com

Cover design by Semadar Megged/Alicia Post
Graphs by Dale Williams
Composition by Hermitage Publishing Services
Cover printed by Yurchak Printing, Landisville, Pa.
Book printed and bound by Yurchak Printing, Landisville, Pa.
Printed in the United States of America

This book is printed on acid-free paper.

# CONTENTS

# LIST OF ILLUSTRATIONS

# LIST OF MAPS

# LIST OF TABLES

# ACKNOWLEDGMENTS

The illustrations in this book result from the generous assistance of many individuals and organizations, acknowledged next to their corresponding photographs. The majority of photographs, however, are the works of personal friends who requested no such recognition, foremost among them Donnelly Marks, whose contributions to the book are immeasurable. The new illustrations in the revised editions result from the persistent efforts of Manuel Ramirez and the generosity and talents of Erik Boot, Michele Gibbs, Diana Ricci, Barry Scheinberg, and Cherra Wyllie.

Two editors deserve special thanks: Randy Ladenheim Gil, who encouraged me to write the book, and Claudia Schaab, who guided the updated editions into print.

# INTRODUCTION

Only five years have passed since the first revised edition of *A Brief History of Mexico* was published; however, these few years have been filled with surprisingly numerous twists and dramatic turns of events, as Mexico attempts to forge a new political and economic order. In 2004 it was believed the reforms sweeping over Mexico after the 2000 presidential election would bring a new era of democracy and prosperity. With the 70-year-old Partido Revolucinario Institucional ([PRI] Institutional Revolutionary Party) dictatorship removed, corruption would decrease too, and there would be a "bonus" to help the nation eliminate poverty. A more open society would see the end of privileged elites controlling the nation's resources, and free-trade agreements would modernize the economy.

The optimism wavered during the 2006 presidential election when two major candidates, neither from the PRI, represented opposite poles of the political spectrum, giving the voters a real choice and demonstrating what was best about the new democracy. Many were convinced, however, that the election, decided by the slimmest fraction of votes, was fraudulent, leading to two months of protests and delays before Felipe Calderón Hinojosa of the conservative Partido de Acción ([PAN] National Action Party) was officially declared the winner. The election crisis was resolved peacefully, but it also left a legacy of political polarization and doubt. The new president tried to unite the nation through a declaration of war against the cartels transshipping drugs through Mexico into the United States. The war, conducted with U.S. aid, seems to be failing, as it unleashes levels of violence that have undermined national morale and worried many across the border in the United States. Now, in 2009, a more collaborative solution is being implemented, encouraged by U.S. president Barack Obama and the Mexican government.

The drug war is only one example of an area of common interest between Mexico and the United States. Equally important is the North American Free Trade Agreement (NAFTA) that has intertwined the economies of the two nations since 1991. NAFTA has also led to another important exchange between the nations, as it contributed to a phenomenal increase in migration to the United States when it undermined the survival of millions of subsistence farmers. In fact, migration and free trade have created such profound cultural and economic links between the two countries in the past decade that it has been given a special name: "transnationalism." Mexicans re-create their culture in communities in the United States and bring their resources to bear on their homes in Mexico. Some Mexican Americans even return to their villages to run for political office; many others vote in local elections, bringing U.S. political values with them. Unfortunately, these ties that have brought the two nations closer have also caused hostility in the United States, where a 600-mile fence along the border neared completion in 2009.

Despite the increasing familiarity of Mexican culture in the United States, Mexico remains something of an enigma to its neighbors north of the border. Yet Mexico is vital to the United States, both as a good neighbor and an economic partner. Knowledge of Mexico's distinctive heritage is indispensable for continued cooperation and understanding. Fortunately for the reader, Mexican history is fascinating. It is rooted in a sophisticated indigenous civilization that in its heyday built some of the largest cities in the world. When the Spanish conquerors arrived, they encountered a densely settled land, not the wilderness that marked much of what is now known as the United States. The drama of Hernán Cortés's conquest ushered in three centuries of Spanish colonization as well as the first hospital and university in the Americas. This early history laid the foundation for modern Mexico, one that is predominantly mestizo, a mixed race and culture of Indians and Spaniards. It is the formation of this modern nation, with its revolutionary struggles against a legacy of Spanish feudalism and its proud contribution of artists and Nobel laureates, that holds the key to understanding the Mexico of today.

This history begins with the peopling of the Americas and gives broad coverage to Mexico's pre-Columbian civilizations that thrived from at least 1200 B.C.E. until the Spanish conquest in 1519 C.E. Even though much of this past is not recorded in writing and so is not technically "history," it is integral to understanding contemporary indigenous culture as well as Mexico's pride in its unique past. It even clarifies popular political gestures and expenditures—such as President Calderón's support for current excavations in Mexico City that may lead to the lost tomb of the great Aztec emperor Ahuitzotl. So much progress has been made in the last decades toward understanding the values and beliefs of these ancient societies that a close examination is well rewarded.

This history also lingers over the early exchanges between the Spaniards and Indians. Not only is it fascinating to examine the unexpected encounter of two civilizations, but the period is critical for the future course of events in Mexico. The Spanish Empire left its mark in language and art, in religion, politics, and the economy. When Mexico gained its independence, it found itself without a political center and with an economy and social system that would hold it back for decades longer.

Mexico's struggle for political stability and independence was not achieved until the 20th century. It was a hard-fought effort that had to overcome centuries of colonial occupation by Spain followed by nearly a century of internal strife and regional factionalism. In the end, it took the upheaval and devastation of the Revolution of 1910 to set it on its modern course. These historic events defined Mexican national identity, providing it not only with a modern constitutional government but also heroes and icons that have made their way into school primers as well as art and literature. In the 21st century, Mexico is undergoing another revolution, the so-called democratic revolution that is opening up its politics to vigorous dialogue and speeding the country along the path of economic globalization.

Accounts of political and cultural events too often give a monolithic and dehumanized impression of society. But many individuals do not walk in step with the main course of political events, especially not in a country of such regional and ethnic diversity. And many political events have an unexpected impact on the fabric of society and the ecology of the land. To provide more contrasts and a deeper understanding of the variety of human responses to events, this history attempts to elaborate various epochs with contemporary quotations and illustrations of period art. It also provides asides in photo captions or boxed "close-ups" about everything from religious icons to the sacredness of corn, from the decipherment of ancient hieroglyphs to life in the capital during a military coup.

The close-ups also are intended to amplify the unusual backgrounds of some important individuals in politics. Just as often they give voice to those who are not usually represented in the official histories: a Spaniard preferring life in a Maya village to rejoining his fellow conquistadors; a poet choosing the nunnery over the viceregal court; a successful mulatto painter in a racist society. This history also uses the close-ups to overcome a tendency in Mexican histories to abandon the fate of the indigenous people a century after the Spanish conquest. The Indians become numbing statistics about impoverished peasants. Yet many native peoples (estimated to constitute 10 to 30 percent of the populace) have struggled to preserve to this day their separate cultural identity and ancient traditions. Their growing resurgence captured world attention in the Zapatista uprising of 1994 and forced an amendment to the Mexican constitution in 2001. A number of the close-ups spotlight their diverse methods of survival. Others follow the fortunes of some Mixtec Indians in Oaxaca through the centuries after the conquest to their migration to the United States in the 21st century.

As this fourth edition of *A Brief History of Mexico* is prepared for press, presidents Calderón and Obama are making headlines as they discuss solutions to their mutual problems of drug violence, migration, and trade. Within Mexico, the global financial crisis overshadows the nation's ongoing debate about poverty and development, and the wave of drug violence undermines the nation's discussion of human rights and greater government accountability. But these problems have also spurred Mexicans to participate more in their democracy, resulting in louder demands for more open institutions and greater government investment in the economy to alleviate joblessness and poverty. How President Calderón responds may decide the future direction of Mexico's fledgling democracy and its political stability. It is hoped that this book, however brief, will shed light on the challenges Mexico faces in creating a new political and social order for the 21st century.

# 1

# THE FIRST PEOPLES: PRE-COLUMBIAN MEXICO

*They had always known within themselves*
*the lengths of their days.*
*The moon, the year, the day, and the night,*
*The breath of life were fulfilled and they passed.*

■

Maya Book of the Chilam Balam of Chumayel
*(translated by Ralph Roys)*

Mexico contains the ruins of more than 10,000 ancient cities dating from before the Spanish conquest. Some dominate the countryside in sublime isolation; others are mostly obscured by urban sprawl except for their too-grand-to-hide pyramids supporting monumental 16th-century Spanish churches. Others have yet to be discovered: new ones, some surprisingly large but in remote regions, are found practically every year.

These ruins represent the great pre-Columbian civilizations that flourished for 3,000 years. The earliest civilization, the Olmec, dates to 1200 B.C.E.—around the time in which Egypt was ruled by the dynasty of Ramses the Great but western Europe had yet to achieve a civilization, much less produce a great ruler. Pre-Columbian cities ranked among the largest in the world: Teotihuacán, known for its pyramids of the Sun and Moon that still stand outside modern Mexico City (SEE page 30), had a population of more than 200,000 in 600 C.E., a time in which the most populous city in the world, Constantinople, had only 500,000 inhabitants. In the early 16th century, the Aztec capital of Tenochtitlán was five times larger than London. Although massive, Mexico's great metropolises were constructed without pack animals and with only stone-age technology:

I

obsidian (volcanic glass) and stone tools, not metal ones; wheels were used, but for toys, not pulleys and carts.

The descendants of the people who built these pre-Columbian cities live on in Mexico today, a country named after the ancient Mexica, the Aztecs' name for themselves. Mexico's population is primarily mestizo, or mixed Indian and European extraction, but at least 10 million Mexicans are Indian—perhaps three times that number according to more generous estimates. Mexico's most traditional citizens preserve the mythologies of their ancestors, farm the land for the maize and beans that have sustained American Indians for thousands of years, and speak the Nahuatl, Yucatec Mayan, and other languages of this pre-Hispanic land. Their legends and artistic heritage are an integral part of the national identity, inspiring modern artists and writers and infusing every aspect of life from political rhetoric to haute cuisine, not to mention the pyramid-shaped hotels at beach resorts, such as Cancún. Their demands for indigenous rights are part of 21st-century politics. No understanding of Mexico can be complete without an examination of its prehistoric indigenous past.

## Origins of the First Americans

*The words of the song arrived*
*When there wasn't heaven and earth*
*There, then, it was born . . .*

■

Maya Book of the Chilam Balam of Chumayel
*(translated by Peter Keeler)*

In the 15th century when Europeans set out on their search for a sea route to Asia, they expected to sail their way to the East Indies unimpeded. Coming upon the land masses now known as the American continents, they assumed they had reached some islands off the coast of the Indies and forever perpetuated their mistake by calling the people they encountered "Indians." They had sailed into an entirely new world, one previously unknown to Europeans. Living in an age of romance novels, they wondered whether they had stumbled upon the fabled lands of Amazonian women and fountains of eternal youth.

Upon coming to Mexico, the Spaniards were awed by the sheer number of people in this unexpected land. In battle, as the Europeans soon learned, these Americans were "demonic-looking" with their tattooed

Mexico before the Conquest *(1945), Diego Rivera's mural of the Aztec capital Tenochtitlán, in the National Palace, Mexico City*

faces and jaguar capes. They marched to a cacophony of tortoise-shell drums, conch-shell horns, and shrill whistles. The stone cities of pre-Columbian Mexico were just as otherworldly: There was nothing so large in 15th-century Spain. Some of the soldiers had traveled to Constantinople and Rome, but even they never had seen anything like the Aztec capital of Tenochtitlán. The Aztecs were equally perplexed by the Europeans, whom they found terrifying with their clanging metal armor, snorting horses, and snarling attack dogs.

The curiosity concerned more than appearances: Each wondered about the origin of the other. The Aztec emperor Moctezuma was uncertain whether the Spaniards were gods or humans. He ordered all the archives in the land to be searched for paintings of creatures such as these. Not one was found. While the foreign ships, described by the Aztecs as floating mountains, were still anchored in the Gulf of Mexico, he sent his prophets and wise men to the coast to observe the strangers. These messengers carried two kinds of food to the ships to see which would be eaten: the food of the gods, sprinkled with sacrificial blood, was repulsive to the Europeans; they opted, instead, for the tortillas, turkey, guavas, and avocados, revealing their humanity in the process.

The conquistadores were curious, too. Christopher Columbus, like Moctezuma, reflected on the nature of the people he first encountered. Without a tortilla test, however, he decided the Americans were *hombrecillos*—almost, but not quite, humans. His compatriots in Europe found such questions more compelling. The Catholic church, especially, needed to determine whether these were beings capable of salvation. Once answering "yes," a more perplexing issue remained: if all humans descended from Adam and Eve, as taught by the Bible, how did the Indians arrive in the New World? Even scientists would later be forced to ask similar questions, because no pre–*Homo sapiens* skeletal remains have ever been discovered in the New World. Who were these previously unknown people? Survivors of Alexander's shipwrecked fleet? Descendants of legendary lost Atlantis? Egyptians?

Such questions, and some fantastic answers, would preoccupy thinkers for centuries to come, often with a passion that is unimaginable today. Some idly speculated free of any cumbersome evidence; it mattered little, for example, that ancient Egypt possessed no seafaring boats capable of reaching the Americas. Others studied illustrated reports on the New World looking for clues as to the true identity of the ancient people. Lord Kingsborough of Ireland, for instance, collected and published at his own expense everything he could find about the

New World. He bankrupted himself and died in debtors' prison without ever proving his belief that the Indians were descendants of the Lost Tribe of Israel. (Yet he did preserve a wealth of material for future scholars, including copies of those precious few pre-Columbian books that miraculously survived the devastation of the conquest.)

# GONZALO GUERRERO

Today, the scientific view that the Americas were peopled by Ice Age migrants from Asia has quieted most other speculation as to the origins of the first Americans. Many remain fascinated, however, by ideas of exotic, even extraterrestrial, cultural contacts with the Americas. Such ideas about the origin of civilization certainly are more dramatic than the reports archaeologists provide on the gradual evolution of native civilizations. Erich von Daniken's *Chariots of the Gods* is a case in point: he claimed that other planetary beings landed in the Americas, bringing civilization with them. He just never explained why the space age jets left behind only Stone Age tools.

The accidental shipwreck is often advanced as another means of bringing advanced civilization to the New World. A critical question seldom is asked by such theorists: how might strange-looking, storm-lost seafarers be received? One answer is recorded in history. In 1511, when Spain had yet to venture as far as Mexico, a hurricane destroyed one of its ships on the way from Panama to the Dominican Republic. Twenty men managed to grab on to a lifeboat. Just over half survived two weeks without food and water before a current tossed them onto the Mexican coast south of the modern resort of Cancún, a region occupied then, as now, by Maya Indians. Five of these bearers of European iron-age civilization were immediately killed in a sacrificial rite, according to one of the two survivors, Jerónimo de Aguilar. The others escaped from their pens and fled into the arms of more benign Maya, who only enslaved them. Aguilar himself, rescued eight years later by Hernán Cortés, lived as a servant within Maya society. The only Spaniard to thrive was Gonzalo Guerrero who completely integrated himself into Maya life, marrying a Maya noblewoman, tattooing his body, and piercing his nose and lips with gold plugs. Unlike Aguilar, he refused Cortés's offer of escape. Maybe Guerrero made a European mark on Maya civilization, but all that is recorded is his tactical advice on fighting the Spaniards. He died on the battlefield with his fellow Maya.

The only indisputable legacy from the Old World left by the shipwreck survivors was smallpox.

Although some contemporary writers toy with ideas about strange voyagers peopling and civilizing the Americas, scientists believe that the first peoples in the Americas arrived by land and by sea in coast-hugging canoes from northern Asia across what is now the Bering Strait. Comparative studies of DNA support this view. During the Pleistocene, or late Ice Age that began around 40,000 B.C.E., the sea level was reduced by 300 feet, converting the strait into a 1,000-mile-wide land bridge connecting Siberia and Alaska. Many thousands of years before Alexander the Great built his fleet in the fourth century B.C.E., big-game hunters stalked bisons and mammoths, some 13 feet in height, across the tundra of this land bridge, and other nomads exploited the marine resources along its coast. Exactly when they started arriving in the Americas remains uncertain—some argue humans arrived during an earlier Ice Age, 100,000 years ago. There is more convincing evidence for settlements from as early as 15,000 years ago along the Pacific coast of the Americas. However, the first clear evidence of peoples in Mexico dates a few thousand years later and is associated with a massive mammoth kill in the highland plateau of central Mexico. The earliest known human skeletal remains in the Americas may turn out to be from Mexico as well, but the dating of the fossil bones called Eva of Naharon to 13,600 years ago is controversial. If the dating proves correct, the 20-year-old Eva would belong to this same period of big-game hunters. The first peoples, then, filtered into the Americas from Asia in Paleolithic times, possibly continuing to arrive until around 10,000 B.C.E., when melting glaciers submerged the land bridge and isolated the American continents from the rest of the world.

## The Land

The first known Mexicans were big-game hunters. Over the millennia, the rainfalls and grasslands diminished; the hairy mammoths and giant armadillos and Ice Age horses became extinct around 5000 B.C.E. Some argue that overhunting from indiscriminate mass kills contributed to their extinction. Humans survived, but out of necessity they evolved into seminomadic hunters of deer, rabbit, and peccary; trappers of iguanas, turtles, shellfish, and birds; and gatherers of wild plants, roots, and seeds. Then, around 3000 B.C.E. after maize (or corn) was domesticated in Mexico, they became farmers.

By 2000 B.C.E. the first Mexicans—unlike their neighbors to the north—had become sedentary villagers, relying on cultivated crops. As surplus crops of corn, beans, chile peppers, and squash produced a wealthier and more complex culture, the villagers changed from sub-

*Mexico's major topographic features*

sistence survivors to citizens of the first American civilizations. The cultures that evolved were unique to the New World—even the basic foods were distinct from the wheat, barley, and rye of the Old World civilizations. And these cultures were unusual in their independence from outside influence: the nearest center of Old World civilization was 7,000 miles away in China, a distance greater than from London to Beijing and made more formidable by the barrier of the sea.

The land provided a richly diverse setting for the evolution of these cultures. Most often pictured as the cactus desert of western movies, Mexico also is the tropical rain forest of Chiapas with howler monkeys, jaguars, and brilliantly colored macaws. It is a highland plateau dominated by snowcapped volcanic peaks, like that of Orizaba (18,700 feet), one of the three highest peaks in North America. It is the tangled green tropical lands of the coasts and riverine lowlands, as well as the cool, pine-forested regions of the Sierra Madre.

The mountainous land contrasts with its largest flat area, the Yucatán peninsula, a limestone shelf barely above sea level. Other coastal lowlands are found along the Gulf of Mexico and the Pacific Ocean. Not all

7

level areas are in the lowlands, however. Many highland plateaus, such as the central basin surrounding today's Mexico City (a city 7,349 feet in altitude), are cut off from each other by the various chains of the Sierra Madre. In this land, altitude determines the climate as much as season: really only two seasons exist, one with rains and one without. Half the year most vegetation dies from lack of rain, and the other half it is miraculously reborn by torrential downpours. There are lakes, rivers, natural springs, 3,000 miles of coast, and geysers—and deserts.

## Mesoamerica

The territory occupied by the great cultures of Mexico did not coincide with the country's present political borders. The northern deserts, rarely hospitable to the agriculture necessary to sustain the settled lifestyle of urban civilization, formed a natural buffer zone with the cultures in what is currently the U.S. Southwest. To the south, the Maya civilization spilled into what are the modern states of Belize, Guatemala, and parts of Honduras and El Salvador. This ancient cultural region, covering about 400,000 square miles, is called Mesoamerica by archaeologists.

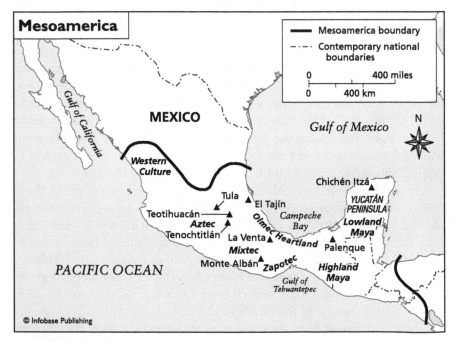

The pre-Columbian civilizations covered a somewhat different territory than modern Mexico. Less northern in its reach, Mesoamerica did extend farther south into Central America.

Throughout the millennia the farthest points of Mesoamerica were in contact, primarily through trade. Although there were no wheeled vehicles or pack animals, canoes trafficked the rivers and coasts. Sea trade, in fact, was quite extensive. Christopher Columbus reported intercepting some canoes off the coast of Honduras that belonged to Maya traders from Yucatán, a people and land unknown to him. In 1984 archaeologists discovered a port, with massive masonry docks, for the ancient inland Maya city of Chichén Itzá. The large dugout canoes must have pulled into port laden with the many objects excavated at that Yucatec city: gold leaf from as far away as Panama as well as green obsidian from north of Mexico City and turquoise from near what is now Cerillos, New Mexico—almost 3,000 miles away. And there is evidence of pre-Columbian trade along the 2,000 miles of Pacific coast between Mesoamerica and faraway Peru.

For land transport, human carriers, as onerous as their burdens must have been, more efficiently maneuvered the mountain passes and scrub jungles than carts ever could, given the technology. From the southern cloud forests they carried quetzal bird feathers and from the tropical ranges, cacao beans for making chocolate—the favorite drink of Moctezuma when spiked with vanilla, brought from the rainy slopes of Veracruz. Cacao was so valued it also was used as currency. From coastal regions like Yucatán came cotton, salt, and honey. From the highlands was traded much needed obsidian, essential for tools and weapons as well as shamans' mirrors, and textiles woven from feathers and maguey, a cactus-looking plant also used to make alcoholic *pulque*. As told by a Spanish conquistador, all these objects, and much more, could be bought in the great marketplace of the Aztec capital:

> ... *gold, silver, and precious stones, feathers, mantles, and embroidered goods. Then there were other wares consisting of Indian slaves both men and women ... in another part there were skins of tigers and lions, of otters and jackals, deer and other animals and badgers and mountain cats, some tanned and others untanned ... Let us go on and speak of those who sold beans and sage and other vegetables ... fowls, cocks with wattles, rabbits, hares, deer, mallards, young dogs ... let us also mention the fruiterers, and the women who sold cooked food ... then every sort of pottery made in a thousand different forms from water jars to little jugs ... But why do I waste so many words in recounting what they sell in that great market?—for I shall never finish ...*
> ■
>
> Bernal Díaz del Castillo (1928, 215–216)

## Fundamental Traits of Mesoamerica

Mesoamerican cultures were extremely diverse in their political and artistic attainments. Between the time of the earliest Olmec civilization in 1200 B.C.E. and the Spanish conquest in 1521 C.E., the Classic Maya city-states flourished (250–900 C.E.) in the southern lowlands, and the great city of Teotihuacán (150 B.C.E.–650 C.E.) dominated the central highlands. In the tropical valleys and fertile basins of the Sierra Madre that separated these famous Mesoamerican cultures, many other groups, such as the Zapotecs, Mixtecs, and Totonacs, built their own distinctive cities. Such regional diversity continued throughout the final phase of Mesoamerican civilization, which was dominated by the Aztecs (1345–1521 C.E.). Before looking at these regional cultures individually and examining the conditions and remaining mysteries surrounding their rise to power and collapse, it is important to consider what unifies them and makes them distinctively Mesoamerican.

### Maize

The Aztec emperor chose from among 30 dishes for his dinner each day. The ordinary citizen, however, was sustained primarily by maize and beans—a perfect protein complex. Ground on a stone mortar, called a *metate,* and mixed with water to make cornmeal, the maize was consumed as a thick gruel called atole or was cooked with various ingredients (such as beans and chile peppers) for tamales (very Mayan), or patted into flat maize cakes called tortillas (very central Mexican).

Maize was so essential for survival that the Mesoamerican worldview parallels its recurring agricultural cycle of harvesting (death) and sprouting (rebirth). In the Maya creation myth from the surviving book of the *Popol Vuh,* the maize god is central to the birth of the sun and the dawning of the world of the Maya where the first humans were shaped out of cornmeal (SEE page 18).

> the making the modeling of our first mother-father, with yellow corn, white corn alone for the flesh, food alone for the human legs and arms for the first fathers, the four human works.
>
> ■
>
> Popol Vuh *(translated by Dennis Tedlock 1985, 164)*

For the Aztecs, too, cultivated corn was "precious, our flesh, our bones" (Sahagún 1950–82, 11:279). Moreover, the world created in the *Popol Vuh* myth is a "cosmic corn field" (Taube 1993, 54), measured and dedicated in the same manner as a *milpa* (cornfield) was prepared centuries ago and just as it is in Yucatán today.

Despite the cultural upheavals experienced by the indigenous peoples of Mexico, corn remains venerated—there are hundreds of varieties in Mexico, from blue husked to yellow, white speckled with black to reddish. The three-stone hearth for cooking cornmeal is the same as it has been for millennia, and it is held sacred. According to contemporary Maya of Chiapas, the mistreatment of maize is one of the greatest offenses against the ancestors and may cause soul loss and, sometimes, death. The *milpa* demands such respect that 19th-century rebel Maya, who had just about driven all Europeans from Yucatán, abandoned their very successful war because it was time to tend to their fields. Contemporary poet Homero Aridjis believes that a change in the quality of tortillas would seriously indicate a deterioration of Mexican life. From its Mesoamerican beginnings to the present, maize has been a symbol of life itself.

## Calendars, Computations, and Celestial Events

*The sciences which they taught were the computations of the years, months and days, the festivals and ceremonies, the administration of the sacraments, the fateful days and seasons, their methods of divination and their prophecies, events and cures for diseases ...*

■

*Bishop Diego de Landa, 16th century*

By measuring the days and years and by studying the seasons and movement of celestial bodies, the ancient Americans hoped to understand and to influence, if not totally control, the most important events of their world. The study of the planets and stars, believed to be manifestations of the gods, led to the development of calendars for guiding people through the agricultural and ritual cycles of their lives.

Naked eye astronomy was aided by building alignments and window. slats. Sometimes entire complexes were constructed for observatories, such as the Caracol at the Yucatec city of Chichén Itzá. Mesoamerican skywatchers plotted the movements of the stars in the night skies so skillfully they could predict the positions of Venus for over 500 years with only a two-hour margin of error. Entire cities could be aligned with an astronomical event, such as the heliacal set of Pleiades—known

# MAYA BOOKS

The great Mesoamerican civilizations were the only ones in the Americas that created writing and used it to compose books: books of poetry and ritual, books of astronomical cycles (and associated astrological events), books of history, and books that told the legends of world creation.

*A page from the* Dresden Codex, *one of only four surviving Maya hieroglyphic books* (Courtesy of the American Philosophical Society)

*A Maya scribe paints a book, pictured on a late classic-period vase in the National Museum of the American Indian, New York. With the decipherment of Maya hieroglyphics, scholars now know that scribes belonged to the nobility; some were women and some signed their works. Drawing by Cherra Wyllie* (after Persis Clarkson, © Foundation for Latin American Anthropological Research)

THE FIRST PEOPLES: PRE-COLUMBIAN MEXICO

as "the rattlesnake" by the Mesoamericans—that divided the year into rainy and dry seasons. Or a sacred building, such as a great ruler's tomb, might be designed to glow in the setting sun at solstice, a symbolic moment when the sun was believed to enter the Underworld, the realm of the dead.

These astronomers excelled in their mathematics. Neither ancient Greeks or Romans had the concept of zero. The Maya did, and they used it in computations that took them thousands of years backward into mythic time when the original ruler-gods were born and the sun first dawned. While Europe tried to calculate with unwieldy Roman numerals, the Mayas used a positional system comparable to our decimal system; theirs had a base of 20, however, not 10.

These sophisticated scientific innovations resulted from a fatalistic view of the universe. Mesoamericans viewed the world as repeating cycles, repeating prophecies. What had happened in the past, surely would happen again—in its right time. For the Yucatec Maya, for example, every period called "Katun 13 Ahau" was a period when "things fall to ruin." Perhaps they felt no surprise in seeing Spanish ships on the horizon during just such a *katun* period. Many centuries before, according to their books of the Chilam Balam, the great city of Chichén Itzá had been abandoned during the same cycle of time. All was determined by the "divine mandate" of the ever recurring calendrical cycles. Whether the ancient Maya had such prognostications for their 5,000 year "long count" (SEE page 15) is unknown. The long count calendar reaches the end of its mathematical cycle in 2012, more than 1,000 years after the Maya abandoned its use. Today, however, New Age proponents argue that the Maya ended their calendar on December 21, 2012, because they foresaw a cataclysm on that day—bringing doom, according to some, or an era of spiritual renewal, according to others. Unfortunately, ancient Maya are silent on the matter.

Knowing when to expect the worst and when to perform rituals and sacrifice to avert calamity was essential. For the learned ones, the priests, there was no distinction between astronomy and astrology. They studied the calendars and sky and predicted dangerous times, like eclipses, and times of war, like Venus stations. They read the omens and understood when there would be good crops and when not. Using books as accurate as any astronomer's chart, as indispensable as a farmer's almanac, and as prophetic as an astrologer's table, the priests advised rulers and commoners alike. All was based on the calendars and celestial cycles; all was done to please the gods who could be as menacing as they could be beneficent and for whom perfect ritual performance counted. Good intentions were not enough.

> They [Yucatec Maya] had a high priest ... the lords made him
> presents and all the priests of the towns brought contributions
> to him ... In him was the key of their learning.
>
> ■
>
> Bishop Diego de Landa, 16th century

There were many cycles and calendrical correlations. The most important were the following:

**Solar Calendar**   The Mesoamericans devised a solar-year calendar as accurate as our Gregorian calendar, and more accurate than the calendar used by their contemporaries in Europe. The solar calendar was composed of 18 months of 20 days each; an additional five-day period occurred at the end of each year, a period believed to be fraught with danger.

**Sacred Round**   Another calendar, used for divinations, was the 260-day sacred round. Archaeologists speculate this calendar may have been based on the nine-month agricultural cycle and the nine months of human gestation. Probably the oldest system of measured time in the New World, the earliest known example of a sacred round was found in highland Oaxaca and dates from about 500 B.C.E. The origin of the calendar, however, may very well have been in the Olmec lowlands because some of the days are named after tropical creatures such as crocodiles, jaguars, and monkeys. The nature of a king's rule was determined by the day he acceded to power, and people's destinies were determined by their birthdays in this calendar, the name of the day becoming part of their own name—the clever could manipulate their fate, however, by choosing another day for "christening." In the sacred round, numbers 1 through 13 rotate consecutively with 20 day names, then begin at 1 again with a new order of the same day names so that there is an unrepeating cycle of 260 numbered days.

**Calendar Round**   Throughout Mesoamerica, religious festivals and dynastic events were dated by the sacred round combined with the solar calendar. In this calendar round, any given day had two names, one in each cycle—something like saying, "January 10th, the second Tuesday." It took 52 years before the dual name of any day would repeat, a period of time in the Mesoamerican system comparable in significance to our century. During the final five days, though, instead of a blow-out centennial new year's celebration, the Aztecs extinguished all fires, broke all their pottery, sacrificed, fasted, and prayed for the gods to permit the cycle to begin anew and their world to continue.

**The Long Count**  Mesoamerican history is difficult to reconstruct using the 52-year calendar round: the dates yielded are like '92, with no distinction made between 1292 and 1992 or any other century. An additional cycle of time, most often associated with the Maya but used in the Mesoamerican lowlands from Veracruz in Mexico to Copán, Honduras, has permitted archaeologists to date Mesoamerican history with far greater accuracy. Called the "long count," the system begins with zero (August 11, 3114 B.C.E. in our calendar) and counts forward without repeating for over 5,000 years—enough time to cover the flourishing of Mesoamerican civilization 1,500 years before the arrival of the first Europeans. While many archaeological techniques, such as radiocarbon dating, are accurate within only a few hundred years, the long count dates that were carved into stone monuments from 36 B.C.E. to 909 C.E. have enabled archaeologists to reconstruct the chronology of ancient Mesoamerica in unusual detail.

### Creation Myths and Worldview

*And here is the beginning ... Whatever might be is simply not there: only murmurs, ripples, in the dark, in the night.*

■

Popol Vuh *(translated by Dennis Tedlock)*

There was never a Garden of Eden in the Mesoamerican worldview. The first people, molded out of ground maize dough, never sinned, they never fell from grace. They were, instead, the most recent efforts by the gods to create creatures to speak and pray to them and honor them through sacrificial offerings. In return, the people of maize would be fed and, as the Aztecs thought, given the gift of laughter and sleep "so that [they] would not die of sadness" (Sahagún 1950–82, 6:93).

The gods previously had tried to create appropriate earthly companions. They had always been disappointed, however, by the inability of these earlier races to nourish them through prayers and offerings and, at times, by their overweening arrogance. So the gods had destroyed their own creations. According to the Aztecs, the very first creatures were giants that the gods had devoured by fierce jaguars; the most recent were transformed into fish when floods destroyed the mountains and the sky crashed to the earth.

# THE FIRST BALL GAME

**M**esoamerica produced the first rubber ball; the rubber came from the milky sap found in the *guayule* trees of the tropical zone, which was occupied by the earliest civilization, that of the Olmecs. The Aztecs later imported 16,000 rubber balls a year from this Gulf coast region. The ball was used in any number of games, from a hockey-like stick ball (seen in the murals of the city of Teotihuacán, near Mexico City) and a baseball version (seen in ceramic figurines from Western Mexico) to the more prevalent hipball game in which the ball—solid and packing a wallop—was bounced off hip protectors, not the hands or feet. Aztec hipball matches, according to Spanish witnesses, were accompanied by considerable betting. A team could lose by allowing the ball to hit the ground or go out of bounds. Scoring in one version of hipball required the ball to pass through narrow stone rings; this was so rarely achieved that when it happened spectators showered the scoring ballplayer with their jewelry. Fascinated by the game, the conquistador Hernán Cortés took two teams back to Spain on his first trip to report to Emperor Charles V, thereby introducing ball games to the Old World. Others simply tried to describe to the uninitiated exactly what was so remarkable about a rubber ball:

> *Jumping and bouncing are its qualities, upward and downward, to and from. It can exhaust the pursuer running after it before he can catch up.*

■

*Friar Diego Durán, 1579*

*Toniná Stone Monument 171. This Late Classic Maya sculpture, now in the National Museum of Anthropology, depicts two ballplayers with hip protectors flanking a ball. The hieroglyphic texts name the players as King K'inich Baaknal Chaak of Toniná (on the left) and King Yuknon Took' K'awiil of Calakmul and suggest the sculpture dates to October 30, 727.* (Courtesy Erik Boot)

The competitive games played today, however, have none of the cosmic significance the ancient Americans attached to ball games. Most of the great pre-Columbian cities had stone ball courts in their very center next to the most sacrosanct buildings. In the Aztec origin myth, the patron god Huitzilopochtli (weet-zee-loh-POACH-tlee) slays the forces of night in a ball court. The Maya story of creation as told in the *Popol Vuh* involved ballplaying hero twins who, through self-sacrifice and cleverness, defeated the gods of evil and prepared the world for the birth of the Sun, the dawning of the ancients' universe. When rulers took the throne in the seventh century C.E. at the beautiful Maya city of Palenque, they assumed the title of "ballplayer," just like the hero twin gods they were believed to embody. And when the game was played, creation was reenacted: decapitation of the losers paralleled the sacrifice of the creator gods in the Underworld ball game; the arching ball signified the movement of the Sun. The game had agricultural significance, too: Central Mexican kings were said to play the rain god for bountiful crops. Momentous matters of state—alliances, border disputes, and ruler legitimization rituals—were decided on the sacred ball court.

*The Great Ball Court at the Maya city of Chichén Itzá. The scoring ring is visible on the right wall.* (Courtesy Peter Selverstone)

According to the Maya *Popol Vuh*, the gods continually tried to create a more perfect world, looking for a race that could speak in order to pray, that could remember the gods in order to be thankful. After their previous attempts (four for the Aztecs; three for the Maya), the gods finally created this one, the world of the true Sun and Moon, of maize and humans.

Lifting the sky from the sea, where it had crashed in the floods, and naming the mountains and caves and places of the land, they created the middle world of earthlings. The world of the maize people was ordered into four directions and centered by the world tree that reached into the earthly Underworld with its roots and raised up to the heavens with its branches. For all Mesoamericans this world was created through the ultimate self-sacrifice of the gods. To create the Sun and Moon, two Aztec gods had thrown themselves onto a raging fire; and Maya ancestral deities had entered the Underworld where they were defeated and decapitated in a game of hipball by the gods of death and disease. Eternal night was banished, and the world was ordered and perfected for humans only through the blood sacrifices of the central Mexican god Quetzalcoatl ("feathered serpent") and the Maya hero twins, all of whom traveled to the Underworld to find the skulls and bones of their ancestors in order that they could be magically reborn in the sky. It was from these sacrifices that maize sprouted and the primordial ancestors ground the kernels to shape the first humans out of cornmeal.

*Enthroned Death God presiding over the Underworld. This life-size terra-cotta sculpture, dating from the Late Classic period, was entombed inside a pyramid at the Veracruz site of El Zapotal and surrounded by other figures representing both death and rebirth. (Drawing courtesy Cherra Wyllie)*

The creation myths provided a metaphor for proper human behavior. The gods had sacrificed themselves in order to be reborn as the Sun and Moon; so the Sun required human sacrifice before it would dawn again after a night in the Underworld. The gods went into the Underworld to defeat the lords of death and to honor their ancestors; so all Mesoamericans must sacrifice in order to honor their gods and ancestors. To keep the people of maize from becoming too arrogant and believing themselves godlike, the gods invented alcoholic *pulque* to blur their vision like "breath on a mirror": Modesty and a sense of one's place in the cosmos were imperative.

The myths also infused the world with spiritual meaning. Nature itself was animate and willful, the winds and rains and storms and drought were godly expressions. The stars represented an aspect of the gods, caves were portals to the frightening Underworld, mountains were home to ancestral deities.

The myths justified the political order. Rulers embodied the creator gods, their deified ancestors. They wore god emblems on their costumes and communicated with the ancestors during shamanistic trances brought on by autosacrifice and hallucinogens. Their cities often were constructed as cosmograms, or replicas of places of creation—pyramids represented the sacred ancestral mountains and the place where corn was born; the small temple interiors represented caves or entrances to the Underworld, places where rulers communicated with the gods.

Like the Bible, the creation myths of Mesoamerica explained the genesis of the world and prescribed correct social and political behavior. Irreverence would result, not in hell, but in the destruction of the maize world, by earthquake according to the Aztecs. Although a few late versions of these myths have been preserved through the Spaniards' contact with the last Mesoamerican civilizations, older ones have recently been deciphered in the hieroglyphic texts of the ancient Maya. Even earlier, these myths can be identified in the art of the Olmec, dating from three millennia ago. And the myths continue to infuse the worldview of many indigenous peoples today: From Maya communities in highland Guatemala to Nahuatl ones near Mexico City, ancestral mountains are still worshiped and the skies are watched for the activities of the old gods.

## Human Sacrifice

*...when they sacrifice a wretched Indian they open the chest with stone knives and hasten to tear out the palpitating heart and blood, and offer it to their Idols, in whose name the sacrifice is made.*

■

*Bernal Díaz del Castillo (1928, 213)*

Grisly tales of human sacrifice permeated the conquistadores' reports to Europe. Atop the towering pyramidal platforms, in front of the most sacred temples, priests stretched their still-living victims over sacrificial stones and cut out their hearts. Sometimes they cut out the entrails, too, and flayed the skin in order to make "cloaks" worn by priests in honor of Xipe Totec, a god of spring. The remaining corpse would be rolled down the steps of the Aztec Great Temple where the captors of the prisoner had the right to take home various parts for a cannibalistic corn stew.

The Spaniards reported that thousands of victims at a time were dispensed in this manner. Twenty thousand war captives were sacrificed just to dedicate the temple to the Aztec patron deity, Huitzilopochtli. Over 100,000 skulls of victims were displayed in the sacred center. Or so it was said.

Other early civilizations are known to have practiced human sacrifice—even in the Bible, Abraham vows to sacrifice Isaac, and the ancient Romans subjected gladiators and slaves to torturous deaths simply for sport. Likewise, cannibalism has been identified as ritual behavior in various tribes. The massive scale of ritual sacrifice reported for the Aztecs, however, has often been considered unique in world history.

Time-motion computer simulations have cast doubt on the actual number of sacrificial victims reported by the conquistadores. Scholars now emphasize that at the time of their reports, the Spaniards were mistreating the Aztecs and had much to gain by portraying them as despicable. Careful studies of the reports made by the first missionaries on the native religion indicate there were really not a great number of human sacrifices performed for the annual rituals and that cannibalism was extremely rare, more a kind of religious sacrament. How many sacrifices were performed remains a matter of controversy. But they were performed, and with considerable variety, depending on the feast day.

Until recent decades, archaeologists believed the Aztecs had a barbaric streak that made them more bloodthirsty than their predecessors in ancient Mexico. Now human sacrifice is recognized as a religious practice in all Mesoamerican cultures. Exactly why their worldview evolved to demand such behavior remains obscure, but the land itself, with its stark seasonal contrasts of drought and rain, desiccation and verdure, deprivation and abundance, surely reinforced any tendency to believe that from hardship and sacrifice and death came the rebirth of maize and life itself. Although the details of Mesoamerican resurrection cosmology are unique, human sacrifice is far from unusual in early

20

*Carved stone skull rack excavated from the Aztecs' Great Temple in Mexico City*

civilizations—large numbers of sacrificed individuals have been found in ancient tombs in both Mesopotamia and China.

The Mesoamerican world was created by sacrifice of the gods, according to native myths. For that world to continue, humans had to reenact the original sacrifice. Nobles sacrificed their own blood, spattered and burned it on paper and sent the smoke as food for the gods. Men perforated their genitals with stingray spines or obsidian in order to let blood. Both men and women pulled ropes of thorns through their lips; priests pricked their tongues and lips so often they barely could speak. Commoners marched into holy wars to capture sacrificial victims, or to become victims themselves. These sacrifices of Mesoamericans provide compelling evidence of their faith. However, few willingly gave their lives or those of their loved ones to the temple priests: most sacrificial victims were, at the time of the Spanish conquest at least, prisoners of war, orphans, or slaves.

Sacrifice was necessary to keep the sun on its course, to bring on the rains, to assure order by maintaining the cycles of human existence. The world was particularly at risk during the completion of a cycle of time or a transition between seasons or rulerships. At such times, human sacrifice was especially demanded: Hearts were needed to feed

21

the sun and guarantee its cyclical renewal; small children were offered to bring on the rains—the worse their cries, it was said, the more Tlaloc, the rain god, was pleased.

For the Mesoamericans, their world could continue only by sacrifice. Such was the unremitting fate of the New World inhabitants, a tragic fate that infused every aspect of their lives.

# 2

# DIVERSITY OF MESOAMERICAN CIVILIZATION

**M**esoamerican civilization survived 2,500 years. Mesoamerican trade goods and trade patterns changed over these many centuries, as did the environmental and political setting. And with those changes, cities achieved moments of greatness, then expired. Vast regions sometimes were bypassed by new political and economic arrangements, until they, too, passed away. As a result, the variety in Mesoamerican art and architecture is extremely rich.

Archaeologists have identified these different cultural and temporal horizons. The Preclassic period was dominated by the earliest Olmec culture from 1200 to 400 B.C.E.; and during the Protoclassic period from 400 B.C.E. to 250 C.E. many cities first made their appearance throughout Mesoamerica, from the great city of Teotihuacán near modern Mexico City to the many southern cities, such as Izapa near the Guatemalan border, Monte Albán in Oaxaca, and the earliest Maya sites. During the Classic period from 250 to 900 C.E. many of the Protoclassic cities achieved their greatest heights, from Teotihuacán and Monte Albán to Maya cities like Palenque in Chiapas and Uxmal in Yucatán. Then, during the Early Postclassic period from 900 to 1200 C.E. many of the Classic cities were forever abandoned while others, such as Tula in central Mexico and Chichén Itzá in Yucatán, flourished. Finally, during the Late Postclassic period much of Mesoamerica was dominated by the Aztecs. This last Mesoamerican horizon came to a calamitous end with the Spanish conquest.

The contrasts in geography, not just in time, also influenced the different regional cultures. The art of Mesoamericans of highland central Mexico tends toward geometric and abstracted figures, hard-cut and deeply shadowed sculpture (SEE page 40). The art is powerful and awesomely expressive, if often impersonal. By contrast, the lowland areas of the Gulf coast and the Maya region concentrate far more on portraiture (SEE pages 16 and 35) and Maya art often has the soft, curved forms and lush foliate designs of the tropical environment that surrounded those people.

## The Preclassic and the Olmec (1200–400 B.C.E.)

Not until the 1950s, when radiocarbon tests were developed to date excavated materials, did archaeologists realize how old Mesoamerican civilization was. Equally surprising, at least to some archaeologists, was that the earlier dates belonged to the Olmec culture (1200–400 B.C.E.), not to the more famous peoples of the central highlands and not to the Maya of the southern lowlands. Some had thought the Olmec culture might be a provincial branch of Maya civilization. Instead it was proven older, much older.

The Olmec culture had been discovered only in the late 19th century, when a farmer clearing his field had found a colossal basalt head (SEE page 27)—the first of 17 that would be uncovered in southeastern

### Chronology of Ancient Mexico

| Period | Date | Central Mexico | Oaxaca | Gulf Coast | Chiapas | Yucatán Maya | Michoacán/Mexico West |
|---|---|---|---|---|---|---|---|
| Postclassic Period | 1520 C.E. / 1200 | Aztec | Mixtec | Zempoala | CHIAPA DE CORZO | Tulum / Mayapán | Tarascan |
| | 900 | Toltec | Monte Albán IV | | | Chichén Itzá | |
| Classic Period | 600 | Xochicalco | Monte Albán III | El Tajín | Palenque | Uxmal / Edzná / Cobá / Kohunlich | Shaft Tombs |
| Protoclassic Period | 250 C.E. / 100 B.C.E. | Teotihuacán | Monte Albán II | Tres Zapotes | Izapa | DZIBILCHALTUN | |
| Preclassic Period | 500 / 900 / 1200 B.C.E. | Cuicuilco / Tlatilco | Monte Albán I / San José Magote | OLMEC / La Venta / San Lorenzo | | | Chupícuaro / Guerrero Olmec |

The Great Goddess, one of the three patron deities of Teotihuacán, is frequently depicted in murals, such as this one, painted on palace walls.

Veracruz, the most recent one just in 1994. These bodyless basalt heads, found at many Olmec sites and now thought to be portraits of Olmec rulers, are 5 to 11 feet high and weigh up to 20 tons.

By the time of their rediscovery, the largest Olmec cities of La Venta and San Lorenzo Tenochtitlán had been abandoned for 2,500 years. No subsequent cities had been built over them to link them with later times and later peoples. The Aztecs, Mayas, and Zapotecs had been encountered by Spanish conquistadores and written about by evangelizing friars, but it was unclear if the Mixe-Zoque residents of the region were the Olmec themselves or later settlers. Too much time had lapsed. The region, no longer densely populated, seemed rather abandoned—and mysterious.

The first civilization arose in one of the wettest and most bountiful regions of Mesoamerica. Many rivers, including the Coatzalcoalcos and Papoloapan, cut through tropical rain forests and mangrove swamps on their way to the sea. Jaguars, monkeys, crocodiles, wild turkeys, boar, and deer thrived. Shellfish, turtles, and fish abounded in the estuaries. Heavy rains and mists made the dry season practically unknown and allowed crops to grow year-round. Even without cultivated crops, the region was rich and had evolved into sedentary villages well before 1200 B.C.E. With the introduction of maize from the highlands, it became a land of plenty, and the villages grew into important political and religious centers.

With extra crops and goods, the Olmec set about spending their surpluses. They traded their crops and rubber balls for central highland obsidian to make tools and southeastern lowland green-blue jade to create magnificently polished objects. They exchanged their magnificently carved ornaments and worked shells for Oaxacan iron-ores in order to make polished mirrors—mirrors known to be used later in Mesoamerica by shamans and rulers for communicating with the gods and ancestors.

At home, the Olmecs constructed the first monumental buildings. The buildings were earthen, not stone like later cities, but while other areas of Mesoamerica were mere villages of wattle and daub (interwoven poles plastered with clay), the Olmecs of San Lorenzo (1200–900 B.C.E.) reconstructed a natural salt mound into an immense plateau, 3,000 feet long and almost 2,000 feet wide. On top were 200 earthen mounds for residences and ceremonial buildings and an elaborate drainage system connecting artificial ponds. At La Venta (900–400 B.C.E.), the local population, numbering 18,000, constructed a great pyramid, 100 feet high. Here they buried, perhaps as offerings to the Underworld gods, immense deity masks (16.5 × 20 feet), stone mosaics, and colored clays, 3,022 pieces of precious polished jade and, in one burial alone, 1,000 tons of serpentine stone imported from the Pacific coast!

The Olmec built their great centers and carved their delicate bas reliefs with the stone age kit that would persist until the Spanish conquest. What they undertook with such limited technology is often astonishing. The nearest basalt to San Lorenzo was 30 miles away and from La Venta, 80 miles. Yet vast quantities of this stone were imported for carving colossal heads of rulers and 50-ton thrones showing their divine descent. The stone had to be cut without metal (probably rope-and-water abrasion assisted by drilling) and transported without wheeled cart or pack animal. Most likely the basalt was dragged to a river then floated on rafts to the centers. Some estimate these monumental stones required crews of 1,000 people to move them.

It remains unknown why the Olmec civilization ended. Their hallmark art style—jade bas-reliefs of snarling jaguar-human figures (probably part of a shamanistic cult) and more portrait-like freestanding sculptures of rulers with slanting eyes, flaring noses, and thick lips—gradually disappeared. The monolithic sculptures were ritually mutilated, then carefully buried. Olmec political centers were abandoned one by one. The power centers of Mesoamerica shifted elsewhere.

But the Olmecs left a legacy. Their trade into Honduras and across Mexico to the Pacific coast, and the spread of their art and ideas, geographically defined Mesoamerica. Olmec trade stimulated the devel-

*More than seven feet high, this portrait head of an Olmec ruler dates between 1200 and 900 B.C.E.* (Photo: Michael Edwards)

27

opment of other emerging cultures into more complex societies. Their religious and artistic symbols were borrowed by new elites as badges of social prestige and authority—burial sites as far away as Honduras have been found to contain Olmec jades and pottery. And the inherited shamanistic power of the rulers created a rigid class structure that was maintained even after the Spanish conquest.

As archaeologists dig deeper into the long-held secrets of the earth, they may find other civilizations as important or more ancient than the Olmec. Current evidence suggests, however, that it was the mother culture of Mesoamerica. Most of the traits that characterize later pre-Columbian societies can be identified in this earliest period of civilization, from shamanism and rulership to Underworld offerings and pyramid construction, from the rubber ball game and human sacrifice to the feathered serpent deities and, of course, the gods of maize, rain, earth, and fire.

Before the end of the Olmec culture, other cultures flourished throughout Mesoamerica—calendrical dates were recorded in the Zapotec highlands of Oaxaca, and the pyramids were built by the Maya and central Mexicans. During the Protoclassic period (400 B.C.E.–250 C.E.) writing was carved into stone monuments; some of the earliest examples come from the Olmec heartland. The region shifted into second-class status, however, with newer, more urban centers taking control elsewhere.

## The Classic Period: Teotihuacán, Monte Albán, and Maya Cities

The Classic period was first named for those centuries when cultures flourished throughout Mesoamerica, from the Maya and Zapotec to the highland Mexican and Gulf coast cities. This was a period of urbanization. And it was a period of widespread literacy; a period when the Maya used the exact long count system of dating. There was also a great diversity of city-states—hundreds in the Maya area alone, quite a number with populations of 50,000 to 100,000. The richness and variety in art was never greater.

Until recently it was believed these classic cultures were peace-loving, theocratic states that engaged in neither war nor human sacrifice. Such notions have been forever dispelled by the work of archaeologists as recently as the 1980s. At Teotihuacán, archaeologists discovered a ritual burial of over 200 sacrificed individuals symmetrically arranged inside the base of the Pyramid of the Feathered Serpent; most of them, including the women, were outfitted as warriors. In the Maya area, archaeologists have uncovered signs of devastating warfare, and epigraphers have translated hieroglyphs about battles between cities.

The Classic period then, was not an especially stable time. By its end, entire cities were abandoned, and power and trade alliances had shifted to new sites on the periphery of the classic regions—such as Chichén Itzá in northern Yucatán, El Tajín in Veracruz, and Cacaxtla and Xochicalco on the edges of the basin of Mexico. Some Maya regions were depopulated, not to recover until the 20th century. The possible causes of these various collapses have been the subject of considerable archaeological study.

Near the Gulf coast, cities, which may have been very large, have been rediscovered in the 1990s. At the same time, the Pacific coast is being more closely examined for sites and cultural affiliation. Excavations in these areas will surely change archaeologists' understanding of Mesoamerica. For now, it is only the better excavated and better understood cities that can be described. As a sample of the diverse settings and cultures of Mesoamerica, it is worth examining some of the most important: Teotihuacán, the Maya, and Monte Albán.

## Teotihuacán (150 B.C.E.–650 C.E.)

Once the sixth largest city in the world, the ancient city of Teotihuacán was one of the greatest powers in the 2,500-year span of Mesoamerica. Located near Lake Texcoco, about 30 miles from modern Mexico City, Teotihuacán still proclaims its mighty presence with its monumental Pyramid of the Sun and Pyramid of the Moon. It once controlled a region about the size of Belgium: Its influence was felt in cities as far as away as in Honduras; its trade reached to northern Mexico and the Pacific coast. Its emissaries—warrior merchants, most likely—can still be seen depicted in the art of foreign cities, such as the Maya site of Tikal in Guatemala and the Zapotec city of Monte Albán.

So much prestige was invested in Teotihuacán, "the place where the gods were made," according to one myth, that the Aztecs venerated it at the time of the conquest when Emperor Moctezuma made regular pilgrimages there—900 years after Teotihuacán's fall. The Aztecs believed they lived in the age of the Fifth Sun, which was created when the Sun and Moon were born at Teotihuacán. Teotihuacán's rise to power may have been related to just such a religious belief about its cosmic importance. Archaeologists have discovered a sacred cave, a place of emergence for Mesoamericans, beneath the Pyramid of the Sun; astronomers now argue that the alignment not only of the pyramid but

# NEW WORLD PYRAMIDS

**P**yramids in the New World, such as the Pyramid of the Moon at Teotihuacán shown below, are unlike those in Egypt in that, rather than coming to a peak, they are level atop, forming platforms for temples. American pyramids often achieved their monumental proportions because their builders, rather than starting from scratch, would envelope old structures as fill. The Cholula pyramid, with a volume of 3 million meters, a base covering 46 acres, and a height of 198 feet, has been said to be the largest preindustrial building ever erected on earth. Yet its final bulk was achieved by various building projects over the centuries that incorporated earlier pyramids—larger than the Pyramid of the Moon. Like their Egyptian counterparts, however, the pyramids sometimes contain royal tombs painted with murals and accompanied with precious jades and, in the Postclassic period, gold ornaments. Although many have speculated about burials inside Teotihuacán's Sun and Moon pyramids, the first evidence suggestive of a royal tomb in the Pyramid of the Moon was discovered only in 2002.

*Pyramid of the Moon, Teotihuacán*

of the entire city may correlate with ancient beliefs about the creation of the Mesoamerican world.

More than religion propelled Teotihuacán into power. Located near the highland lake where the Aztecs would eventually build their island capital, Teotihuacán had access to fish and fowl as well as to the agricultural potential of the central basin. Teotihuacanos also controlled vast quantities of precious obsidian, the glass "iron" from which Mesoamerican tools were made and their major item of trade. Teotihuacanos' wealth paid for the Pyramid of the Sun, completed by 150 C.E., and covering about the same area as the Great Pyramid in Egypt, but with only half its height. That great effort of human construction was followed by others, including the Pyramid of the Moon and a 48-acre administrative and market complex, larger than the Pentagon in Arlington, Virginia (34 acres).

Yet for all of Teotihuacán's recognized greatness, its rulers remain anonymous: nowhere in the art of the city are their portraits discovered, and nowhere on the monuments and great buildings were any writings inscribed about their achievements. Yet their presence is felt in every element of the city's design. A rigid grid plan prevails for over eight square miles. No natural feature was permitted to interfere with the layout: the San Juan River was canalized to conform to the grid as it passed through the city. Symmetry was the aesthetic mandate, from the composition of paintings in palaces to the urban plan for the city.

The urban plan invaded even private homes. The population—who, based on depopulation studies of the surrounding countryside, were probably coerced into living in the city—resided in 2,000 apartment complexes for 60 to 100 individuals each. These complexes could vie with modern housing projects in the uniformity of their plan: one-story, windowless buildings with rooms constructed around interlocking, open courtyards. These complexes included a semipublic space for worship, especially of the city's patron, the Great Goddess, from whose yellow hands flowed streams of jades and shells and other symbols of fertility and wealth (SEE page 25). Of course, the elite classes lived in grander complexes decorated with bas relief sculptures and murals. There were warrior enclaves as well as neighborhoods of potters and obsidian workers. Archaeologists have identified foreign neighborhoods, too: residences with cultural traces from the Zapotec, Gulf coast, and Maya regions that may have housed traders and artisans.

Many aspects of life in Teotihuacán remain mysterious. Some Mesoamericanists wonder whether the objects in the precious stream flowing from the Great Goddess's fingers are in fact signs that constitute a form of writing. If not, then there is no writing known from this great city despite the fact that the Teotihuacanos were exposed to the hieroglyphs of other Mesoamerican cultures, such as the Maya. Could they have consciously rejected literacy? Many believe records were kept, but on perishable bark paper rather than stone. Because there is no written record from this period, the language, and ethnic identity, of the Teotihuacanos is unknown.

Sometime around 650 C.E. Teotihuacán's elite lost control. The sacred center of the city was burned and sacked and never again occupied. The city never recovered its farflung trade or prestige. Archaeologists remain uncertain as to whether the populace rose up in rebellion against oppressive ruling powers or whether other city-states, competing for the lucrative trade of Teotihuacán, invaded the city. What is certain is that after 800 years, Teotihuacán ended cataclysmically.

### Southern Lowland Maya (600 B.C.E.–900 C.E.)

In contrast to highland Teotihuacán, the Maya flourished in the southern lowland rain forests of Mexico, Guatemala, and Belize (SEE map, page 8) where colorful bird feathers and jaguar pelts were valued trade items. They also thrived in the northern scrub jungles of Yucatán where cotton and salt were items of exchange as well as in the highlands of Guatemala where obsidian was a resource. Although the Maya built large cities, quite a number with populations from 50,000 to 100,000, they built too many of them, perhaps, for any one to achieve the kind of centralized control that occurred at Teotihuacán.

The aesthetic sensibilities of the southern lowlands and central Mexican highlands could not be more different. The Maya cities were never built to a grid plan; more often they conformed to the irregularities of the natural landscape. Their buildings were constructed with a corbel arch (the closest Mesoamerica ever came to using the true arch), permitting greater height. Splendid tombs of rulers and other nobility have been found incorporated into the pyramidal platforms of temples; some are connected to the temples by ceramic tubes, or what have been called "psychoducts"—the Maya may have used them to communicate with venerated ancestors. Maya art is never anonymous, but full of portraiture, whether a ruler or ballplayer or tormented captive is the subject (SEE pages 16 and 35). Even Maya gods have faces, and many of them are deified ancestors and former rulers.

Another major contrast with Teotihuacán is the use of writing on stone monuments that have preserved their texts till this day. Although archaeologists have uncovered sizable Maya cities dating back to middle Olmec times (600 B.C.E.), the earliest known Maya hieroglyphic text with an exact long count date (SEE page 15) occurs in 292 C.E., and the last long count date known to archaeologists is 909 C.E.:

These dates have been used to define the temporal limits of the Classic period. Most of the dated Maya monuments are found in the southern lowlands, called the Maya heartland. Here are the most famous ancient cities of classic Maya civilization, such as Palenque in Mexico, Tikal in Guatemala, and Copán in Honduras.

Other Mesoamerican cultures, such as the Zapotecs in Oaxaca and the Aztecs, recorded brief hieroglyphic statements in stone; many also had bark-paper books, but few of these survived. Pottery shards and artifacts are all that can be pieced together to tell us about the Olmec and Teotihuacán civilizations. The Maya, however, developed a partially phonetic writing system and left long enough texts for the hieroglyphic statements to be deciphered by today's scholars. In recent decades, epigraphers have made enormous strides in translating these hieroglyphs. They have revealed the first written history of the Americas—a very biased history, one based on rulers' proclamations and boasts, but a brief history nonetheless of the classic period Maya world. Archaeologists now can enhance their understanding of the Maya with these deciphered writings. Rulers, a few of them women, now have names. In addition to the names, a system of governance has been revealed through the deciphered texts. The rulers' inherited right to rule is asserted through dynastic lists; their divine right to rule is proclaimed by associating the gods with royal ancestors. Political and marriage alliances are recorded, wars and noble captives boasted about, and religious ceremonies with royal bloodletting described.

Despite the remarkable contrasts between the lowland Maya and Teotihuacán, there was considerable contact between them. The Maya presence is clear at Teotihuacán in one of the apartment complexes and in trade items, such as carved jades. Teotihuacán-style buildings, ceramics, and obsidian are found at numerous Maya sites, and Teotihuacán symbols were adapted by Maya rulers as part of their war costume. Some archaeologists have argued that Teotihuacán conquered some Maya cities or even founded them; others believe the evidence equally supports mere trade and political alliances. Whatever influence Teotihuacán had, there is major growth in the number and size of Maya cities after the fall of that central Mexican state.

The collapse of Classic period Maya civilization has been one of the great Mesoamerican mysteries. Drought, disease, and incessant warfare have all been suggested as causes. The collapse was most likely caused by a combination of such factors. But one additional element of the collapse cannot be overlooked, that of the environment.

*Eighth-century C.E. palace at the Maya ruins of Palenque*

# K'AN XUL II, MAYA KING

The unusual tower of the palace at the ruined Maya city of Palenque in Chiapas, Mexico, is believed to have been built by Lord K'an Xul who ruled the city from June 3, 702 to August 30, 711. Considerable historical knowledge, such as K'an Xul's name (now known to be more accurately spelled phonetically as K'an Hok' Chitam) and his royal lineage, has resulted from rapid advances in interpreting Maya hieroglyphs. Scholars have known for the past century how to translate the Maya long count into our Gregorian calendar, but the rulers' names, their births, accession, and other events in their lives have been translated through phonetic decipherments only in the past few decades.

In the Palace Tablet K'an Xul sits between his deceased parents who legitimize his right to rule Palenque from the otherworld. This scene is part of a beautiful hieroglyphic panel that begins on the left with a long count date after which it states the royal ancestry of K'an Xul and tells of events before his accession to the throne of Palenque. The glyphs in the top scene name the actors and events.

Even after many of the texts at Palenque had been deciphered, scholars were not able to determine when K'an Xul died. He simply fell out of the written history of Palenque. The discovery of the carving at the

*Palace Tablet, Palenque* (Drawing by Merle Greene Robertson; used with permission)

nearby site of Toniná revealed the historical truth that Palenque scribes had avoided telling. The scene depicts a lord, his arms bound, who has been captured by Toniná. Identified by the hieroglyphs on his thigh, this victim is none other than K'an Xul of Palenque. The hieroglyphs to the right state that a war occurred on a certain date.

*Toniná Monument 122* (Drawing by Ian Graham, courtesy Peabody Museum, Harvard University)

The Classic period Maya radically altered their rain forest environment. Two hundred cities replaced the forest. Palaces and temples and ball courts covered the most fertile land. More forest had to be cut for farming, and trees were needed to burn limestone for the stucco the Maya used to plaster their buildings both inside and out—20 trees with all their branches, it is estimated, produce only a small 3-foot-high pile of stucco. Still more trees had to be felled for wood-fired pottery kilns. The result, based on pollen studies, was massive deforestation that caused soil erosion and environmental degradation.

It is not difficult to imagine that the lowland Maya may have outstripped the carrying capacity of the lowlands. Some archaeologists have argued that overpopulation and deforestation caused the collapse of their civilization. Examination of skeletal remains at some sites suggests malnutrition among the poorer classes and, in some instances, among the elite as well. The fact that the southern lowlands were abandoned by the end of the Classic period certainly suggests problems with the environment. The degradation of the ecosystem, even if not the sole cause of the collapse of the lowland Maya, could have rendered them vulnerable to other pressures, including prolonged warfare and drought.

From 800 to 900 C.E., cities gradually stopped erecting monuments and an increasing number were abandoned. Some were surrounded by defensive walls. After the year 909, not a single ruler is proclaimed anywhere in the long count calendar. The Maya continued to thrive in northern Yucatán, parts of Belize and highland Guatemala—all regions where they live today—but not in the southern lowlands. By the time of the Spanish conquest, the southern lowlands had reverted to tropical rain forest, and the Classic period cities of stone, once so numerous, were hidden under the jungle growth. Hernán Cortés, marching through the region in 1525, considered it a wilderness.

## Monte Albán (500 B.C.E.–750 C.E.)

The Zapotec city of Monte Albán never was large compared to Teotihuacán—its entire ceremonial center would fit under the Pyramid of the Sun. It was not large compared to the great cities of the Maya either. But Monte Albán, set atop a mountain, required a herculean effort to construct. First the mountain was flattened and the city laid out symmetrically, but not in a Teotihuacán-style grid. Then building materials were carried up the mountainside—without pack animals or wheeled vehicles. Stone for columns, the first known in Mesoamerican architecture, were hauled up for the construction of a colonnaded hall. And, finally, the city of 26,000 people was continually supplied with food and water.

Located in the middle of a series of narrow valleys created by two converging chains of the Sierra Madre, Monte Albán may have been chosen for its central, easily defensible position. Archaeologists have argued that a confederacy of the nobles from the valleys jointly chose the site as their capital for ruling highland Oaxaca. Although people continued to populate the valleys (unlike the basin surrounding Teotihuacán), there is evidence that the elite no longer did. The only city-state in Oaxaca with any concentration of power (unlike the Maya region), Monte Albán dominated a vast region, at least according to the hieroglyphic proclamations of conquest carved into its buildings.

In its earliest history, the Oaxaca valley had close cultural contacts with the Olmecs with whom they traded magnetite for mirrors, and, later, with the Maya to the south. Throughout the Classic period, the Zapotec followed the Maya practices of erecting sculptures carved with hieroglyphic texts extolling the military exploits of their rulers, and building stone ball courts in their most sacred centers. Great tombs were built for their rulers and the nobility, and there is evidence of ancestor worship, just as there is in the Maya region.

But Monte Albán's most important contact during the Classic period was with Teotihuacán. Whether that contact was always peaceful is unclear, given the defensive position of Monte Albán. Yet there was an enclave of Oaxaqueños at Teotihuacán, and archaeologists have found remnants of a Teotihuacano-style palace at Monte Albán from the Early Classic period. The two cities certainly traded, but whether this trade was in the form of tribute or exchange remains uncertain. Although Monte Albán differed from the central Mexican city in its artistic preference for portraiture and its use of writing on public monuments, the warrior dress of its rulers and the mural art of its elaborate stone tombs shows borrowing from that great city.

Monte Albán's power gradually eroded after the collapse of Teotihuacán. The grand carvings dedicated to its leaders' war victories were replaced with less grandiose ones about marriage alliances and lineages. Numerous, competing city-states appeared in the Oaxaca valleys. Monte Albán was abandoned until a new group made its appearance: the Mixtecs.

## Postclassic Mixtec and Aztec

The deepest understanding we have of Mesoamerican culture comes from its final phase. A few of the codices painted on bark paper have survived from this time. The conquistadores left eyewitness accounts of the peoples they conquered, and after the conquest, the Catholic friars recorded many of the myths and oral histories of the peoples they converted, such as the Yucatec and highland Guatemalan Maya, the Mixtecs of Oaxaca, and the Nahuatl-speaking groups of central Mexico, especially the Aztecs. Ironically, this phase is often poorly known archaeologically because the Spaniards usually built over the cities they conquered, including the Aztec capital at Tenochtitlán, which now lies beneath modern Mexico City.

Preceding the final phase of Mesoamerica, there was a decided shifting of power and movement of peoples throughout the Mexican region. From the collapse of the Classic period cultures rose new cities in Veracruz (El Tajín), northern Yucatán (Chichén Itzá), the northern basin of Mexico (Tula), as well as other areas. The inhabitants of these cities borrowed from both their Maya and Teotihuacán predecessors to create a more eclectic, more pan-Mesoamerican art style: they carved hieroglyphs on stone monuments, but only short texts; their art was naturalistic like that of the Maya, but stylistically was more sharp-edged and rectilinear like that of Teotihuacán. Their political and religious cults placed special emphasis on the ball game; and their ball-court art elaborately depicted human sacrifice and was associated with skull racks. They created a trade route more expansive than that of even the Classic period, and searched far and wide for turquoise and gold and cacao beans, which were used for money as well as chocolate. The Aztec would build on the foundation laid by these earlier cultures.

By 1200 C.E., most of the Early Postclassic cities were either abandoned or greatly diminished in power. The Aztecs moved into the cultural void that ensued—they may even have had something to do with the collapse. According to their origin myths, they were nomadic barbarians at this time and only ended their migrations from the north a century later when they settled in the central Valley of Mexico and received the veneer of civilization by marrying into more noble groups.

The Aztecs' historic myths indicate that in 1345 their nomadic ancestors witnessed an eagle devouring a serpent (a symbol borrowed for the Mexican flag); the sign, according to their patron deity, meant their wanderings had ended, their promised land had finally been reached. Archaeologists, however, believe the Aztecs settled on an isolated island on Lake Texcoco much earlier, forced there by other groups in the central valley.

It would take the Aztecs more than a century before they even achieved independence as a city-state. In the meantime they expanded their island by heaping mud from the lake bottom on rafts; plants anchored their roots to the mud, and the landfill became rich farmland. Through considerable engineering ingenuity, they built dikes to control flooding and aqueducts to carry freshwater. In the exact center of this five-square-mile artificial island was the Templo Mayor (Great Temple), the double-temple pyramid to Tlaloc, the rain god, and Huitzilopochtli, the Aztec sun god of war. Slightly askew from true north, the great

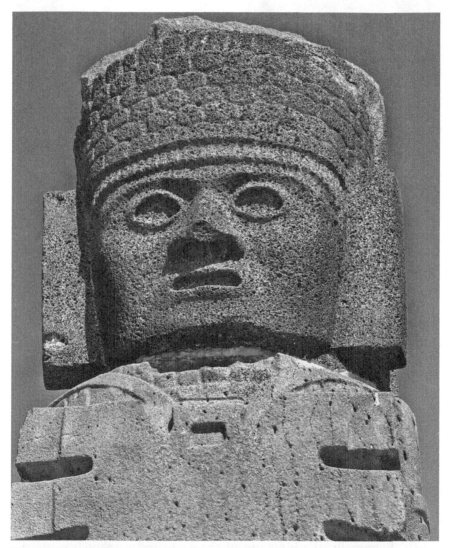

*Warrior column (15 feet in height) from the Postclassic city of Tula in central Mexico* (Colman Lerner Gerardo)

*Aztec stone sculpture of a jaguar* (National Museum of Anthropology, Mexico City)

temple was instead aligned with sacred mountains on the mainland and astronomically aligned with the rising Sun at equinox. From this holy center four avenues divided the city into Mesoamerican divine order.

Despite their humble beginnings, the Aztecs flourished and evolved into a highly complex state based on rigid class distinctions—commoners were severely punished for emulating noble dress, for example—and ruled by a divine king. They created and built Tenochtitlán, the center of a 19-island lake kingdom, crisscrossed by canals and reached from the mainland by three monumental cause-ways. From their islands, the Aztecs forced a triple alliance with their most powerful neighbors and imposed tribute, not just trade, on conquered regions as far away as Guatemala. Their commerce was so great that some estimate nearly 100,000 canoes trafficked the lake and canals. Eventually, the kingdom of the eagle and serpent became the capital of Mesoamerica's strongest empire.

As archaeologists now know, the Aztecs were not the first militant culture in Mesoamerica. Nor did they introduce personal bloodletting and human sacrifice to the pre-Columbian world. Rather, they incorporated the religious practices of the cultures that had preceded them—perhaps embellishing them in the process—in order to appease their gods (and, probably, intimidate their enemies). Ritual wars, called "flowery wars," were imposed on their Tlaxcalan neighbors so the Aztecs could capture sacrificial victims—certainly a gruesome practice and a grim worldview, but one not unique to the Aztecs.

Aztec art was interregional, particularly so because artists were brought to Tenochtitlán from all other parts of Mesoamerica, especially from Oaxaca and Veracruz. Aztecs sculpted in a rectilinear and often fearsome style that also could be exceptionally realistic, whether depicting nature or human sacrifice (SEE page 20). They produced

# NEZAHUALCÓYOTL: POET KING

Out of the native histories compiled by the early Franciscan friars emerges a portrait of a king who could rival Lorenzo the Magnificent of Renaissance Florence in his learning and support for the arts. Almost 50 years before the Spanish, Nezahualcóyotl (nay-zah-wahl-KOH-yohtl; meaning Hungry Coyote) ruled Texcoco, part of the Aztec Triple Alliance. He codified Aztec law, studied astronomy, engineered elaborate aqueducts, and designed his garden to include fountains and a zoo. A war captain, he battled for Aztec supremacy while also setting aside part of his palace for poets, philosophers, and historians to gather and teach. This most learned man was also a poet whose name and work has been preserved for us from the pre-Columbian world. He died in 1472, but is a culture hero in modern Mexico, with streets and even a neighborhood named after him.

> We are not here forever,
> But pause only for a moment in time.
> Though it be of jade it will shatter,
> Though it be of gold it will break,
> Though it might be of quetzal feathers it will decay.
> Nothing endures for eternity on this earth,
> But is here only fleetingly.
>
> ■
>
> Nezahualcóyotl (Davis 1973, 117)

three-dimensional sculptures that were among the greatest artistic works of Mesoamerica.

The Aztec empire was so powerful it rendered other regions weaker. After the collapse of Mayapán in 1446 C.E., for example, the Yucatec Maya no longer built grand cities of stone and plaster, but rather lived in the older ones of their ancestors or built smaller shrine-like centers, such as Tulum. Although never conquered by the Aztecs, these Maya seemed diminished and peripheral to the main course of Mesoamerican events.

The Mixtecs of Oaxaca, however, flourished during the Late Postclassic period. The longtime occupants of the mountainous regions of Oaxaca, they had been overshadowed by both Monte Albán and Teotihuacán in the Classic period. In the Postclassic, however, they may very well have dominated the Zapotec area. Mixtec pictographic codices (SEE pages 76 and 77) boast of marriage alliances, probably achieved through military conquest, with the Zapotecs; Mixtec murals and zigzag fret designs are found on many Oaxacan valley buildings, such as at Mitla. The Mixtec warlords demanded, and received, tribute from the Zapotecs.

Just before the conquest, the Mixtecs were subjugated by the Aztecs and forced to pay tribute themselves. The Aztecs left the region to itself, however, and so failed to influence the local art style. Mixtec wealth is

*Mixtec gold pendant from a tomb in Zaachila, Oaxaca*

reflected in the tribute paid to the Aztecs: 40 sacks of cochineal (used to make purplish red dye), 20 bowls of gold dust, two strings of precious green stones, 800 bundles of quetzal feathers, and thousands of bundles of finely woven and decorated mantles and loincloths.

Mixtec polychrome pottery and exquisite gold jewelry were prized possessions, and often were imitated throughout Mesoamerica in the Late Postclassic period. Some of the finest examples of Mixtec jewelry were excavated from tombs at Monte Albán, which the Mixtecs reused when burying their own lords.

In 1519 Mesoamerica was a checkerboard of cultures, just as it always had been. Unprecedented, however, was the Aztecs' domination of most of the land and their onerous demands for tribute. Their enemies soon would find an opportunity to fight back.

# 3

# THE AGE OF CONQUEST

*They came in battle array, as conquerors, and the dust rose in whirlwinds on the roads, their spears glinted in the sun, and their pennons fluttered like bats. They made a loud clamor as they marched, for their coats of mail and their weapons clashed and rattled . . . they terrified everyone who saw them*

■

An Aztec account (translated by Miguel León-Portilla)

*The greatest thing after the creation of the earth, excepting the incarnation and death of he who created it, is the discovery of the Indies.*

■

Francisco López de Gómara, 16th century

One of the most gripping events in world history is the Spanish conquest of Mexico, that collision of two totally foreign civilizations, each previously unknown to the other. For Mexico, the conquest defines the beginning of the modern mestizo nation of mixed indigenous and European peoples, a defining event commemorated with a singularly Mexican twist: not one statue in the land honors the captain of the conquistadores, Hernán Cortés, yet many recall the heroism of Cuauhtémoc, the last Aztec emperor. For Spain, the Aztec conquest would eventually lead to an empire strewn across the two New World continents and 40 times its own size.

## Moctezuma's Empire

On the eve of the conquest, the Aztec emperor Moctezuma II, grandson of an Aztec king, ruled an empire the size of modern Italy—and it was still expanding. The capital of this realm, Tenochtitlán, with a population approaching 250,000, was one of the largest cities in the world. The empire dominated central Mexico, which may have had as many as 25 million inhabitants. Spain in its entirety had less than 8 million people.

Tenochtitlán, an independent state since just 1427, had achieved legitimacy through marriage alliances (Moctezuma had four wives) into the older, more noble cities of central Mexico. Its expansion from a small island city to an empire had been achieved through the Triple Alliance with neighboring city-states and through trade, but above all through military conquest. The Aztecs' major concern in expanding beyond Tenochtitlán and the central basin of Mexico was tribute, tribute that included not only prestige items and wealth for the ruling classes, but basic foodstuffs for subsistence as well.

The Aztec empire was only loosely held together. Tenochtitlán had no large standing army to maintain the empire; it often left local, conquered rulers in office. But it kept itself well informed: long-distance merchants were known to be state spies, and relay runners were positioned every few miles throughout the empire for rapid communication. And the Aztecs were intimidating. Every adult male received military training and military success was a means to social advancement for both commoners and nobles. From this pool of half a million trained citizens (the Spaniards found them sophisticated and brave in battle), the Aztecs frequently mobilized armies of 7,000 or more. When necessary, Aztec governors were installed in trouble spots, accompanied by a small Aztec garrison.

During his 16 years of rule, Moctezuma put down numerous rebellions and maneuvered his partners in the Triple Alliance into subordinate positions. In 1515, the death of one of the rulers in the alliance resulted in a struggle for the Texcoco throne. The loser never forgot Moctezuma's role in his defeat; in exile, he remained a constant threat to Tenochtitlán. The Aztecs had many enemies, and war with remaining independent states, such as Tlaxcala, intensified in the final years of the empire as the Aztecs tried to gain more control and more tribute.

## Aztec Omens

The last 10 years of Moctezuma's reign were troubled by a series of disturbing events, all taken as signs of divine displeasure. A drought in 1505 created a severe shortage of maize. An unusual lightning bolt, without thunder, destroyed a temple in Tenochtitlán's sacred precinct. In 1517, the very year the Spaniards landed briefly in Yucatán, a comet flamed over the land and showered it with red hot sparks.

For Moctezuma, who was not merely a political and military leader but also the spokesman for the gods (as for all Aztec rulers, his title was *tlatoani*, or speaker), such messages from the gods required careful translation and consultation with priestly advisers and shamans.

> *Tell the magicians to say what they believe: whether sickness is going to strike, or hunger, or locusts, or storms on the lake, or droughts ... If war is threatening Mexico, or there will be sudden deaths ...*
>
> ■
>
> Crónica mexicana *(León-Portilla 1962, 14)*

One noble sage interpreted the omens as proof the empire was soon to end in violence. Refusing to believe such an apocalyptic prophecy, the emperor challenged the sage to a game of ball; the winner—chosen by the gods, the Aztecs believed—would determine the truth. Moctezuma lost.

Amid such internal stresses and ill omens, the Spaniards appeared along the Gulf coast of Moctezuma's empire. Their arrival, like that of Juan de Grijalva's expedition the previous year, brought all the evil portents to a climax.

## Spain's War Machine

> *Our Spaniards in sixty years of conquest have discovered, explored, and conquered so much land ... Blessed be God who gave them such grace and power.*
>
> ■
>
> Francisco López de Gómara, 16th century

The conquistadores off the coast of Moctezuma's empire were the product of a country that had the greatest war machine in all of Europe. For several centuries Spain had fought to rid itself of the Moorish infidels. Anarchy had ruled the land until 1492, when the last Islamic outpost surrendered at Granada. In recognition of the defeat of the Muslims, the pope granted Spain's rulers the extraordinary privilege of heading the church in all their dominions. In the very year Christopher Columbus set sail, Spain was unified as a Christian nation under the Catholic despots, Ferdinand and Isabella, and soon thereafter under Holy Roman Emperor Charles V.

At the time Christopher Columbus proposed his voyage, Spain was in an unusually strong position to consider overseas expansion. Isabella was captivated by the promise of new souls for the church as much as Ferdinand was interested in a new trade route for exotic spices and silks from the Orient. After so many centuries of war, the nation had a ruined economy and little standing among European trading nations. Fighting holy wars, however, had become a Spanish specialty. When Columbus did discover the West Indies for the Crown, it was taken as a sign that God had chosen Spain over all other nations to civilize the New World. The pope concurred.

Returning to Spain with proof of his discoveries, Columbus presented to the court six kidnapped Indians, an iguana, 40 parrots, and a pile of gold. His announcement excited many Spaniards, who took the divine mandate as an excuse to enrich themselves. Centuries of crusading battles had made warriors, not merchants, out of them. Years of plundering farms and pillaging villages had done much to hurt the economy and little to promote industriousness. Get-rich-quick dreams associated with new lands, Indian slaves, and untapped gold mines appealed to impoverished aristocrats and unemployed soldiers of fortune alike.

## Hernán Cortés

Hernán Cortés, unusual in his cunning and leadership, was otherwise typical of many Spaniards who joined the ships to the New World. A member of the bankrupt lesser aristocracy, he could make his fortune only through the military. He learned soldiering from his father, who had fought at Granada. At the age of 18 he was on his way to fight in the Italian wars, but when he heard of Columbus's discovery, he headed for Seville instead. Delayed nearly a year by an injury from an amorous escapade in which he fell from a window, he sailed for the New World in 1504—along with other penniless nobles, debtors, and criminals.

On reaching the island colonies, Cortés discovered, like so many others, how meager the prospects really were for wealth. It is said that he initially refused the offer of land, preferring gold mining to dirtying his hands like a peasant. Eventually he owned a sugar plantation as well as some gold mines in Cuba, and he held minor positions in the local government where he was well known as a convincing speaker. He remained poor, however, spending the money he gained on finery, entertainment, and gambling. For someone who had once proclaimed he wanted either to dine triumphantly to trumpets or die on the scaffold, colonial life must have been disappointing indeed.

There was too little gold to satisfy any of the colonists' grand dreams. Their own brutality, whether soldier or settler, eventually exterminated

# BARTOLOMÉ DE LAS CASAS

In 1516, it was reported that the Taino Indians of Hispaniola (the island comprising the Dominican Republic and Haiti) would soon be extinct (which came to pass), because their numbers had been reduced to as "few as grapes after the harvest." Such statistics on the native death rate in the New World speak only too plainly about the exploitation of the Indians. Yet not all Spaniards, or even Spanish policy, condoned such brutality. No one better exemplified the struggle to protect the Indians than Father Bartolomé de Las Casas. Himself a colonist in Cuba, his father a companion of Columbus and a colonist of Hispaniola, Las Casas witnessed the suffering of the Indians. In order to protect them, he became a priest. His book, *Historia de las Indias,* and his decades of tireless lobbying in Spain, eventually led to the reform laws of 1542 governing the treatment of Indians in Mexico and all of Spain's New World dominions.

the native population—the very pagans they were supposed to save, not to mention the only available labor supply. When the Crown sent a commission to investigate Indian abuses, it found the villages tragically empty of natives to interview. Around this time in the early 16th century, explorations started once again for slaves and gold, for new lands and, perhaps, a passage to Asia, which was thought to be quite near.

## Spaniards Land in Yucatán

In 1517, Hernández de Córdoba landed on the Yucatán peninsula and reported an entirely new level of civilization; one that had not been encountered in the previous 25 years of exploration. In Yucatán the natives wore finely woven textiles and gold ornaments in their noses and ears. Their cities were larger than Seville, and their homes and temples were well constructed in stone. And they were fierce. Armed with bows and arrows and obsidian-pointed spears and clubs, they successfully routed Córdoba—more than a quarter of his men were killed, the rest were wounded, and Córdoba himself suffered 30 wounds from which he eventually died.

Excited by Córdoba's report, Diego Velázquez, governor of Cuba, sent his nephew, Juan de Grijalva, to learn more while he himself applied to Spain for a license to colonize Yucatán. Grijalva sailed around the tip of

Yucatán and continued up the Gulf coast to what is now Veracruz. On his travels he traded glass beads and pins and needles for 20,000 pesos in gold. At Veracruz, he heard about a great city in the interior of the land. He did not venture to look for it, however. He claimed that his men were tired of the year-long journey and had convinced him to turn back to Cuba. His chaplain thought him simply too timid to attempt a conquest. At the very least, if Grijalva had lingered a bit longer, he would have received the feathered headresses and gold bracelets Moctezuma was preparing for him. Moctezuma's messengers had kept him well informed of the foreign presence.

## The Cortés Expedition

With no prior experience commanding soldiers, much less an expedition, Cortés would nonetheless succeed where his predecessors had failed. His gambling instincts, his audacity, his intelligence, and his consuming desire for glory would enable him to defeat a nation of millions with soldiers numbering in the hundreds.

If Governor Velázquez had suspected the greatness of the land, he would not have sent so few. On the other hand, if he had realized the historic importance of the expedition, he would have appointed no one but himself to conquer "the island" of Yucatán. In fact, Cortés's first challenge was to escape Cuba with his ships fully outfitted before Velázquez could retract his commission; to do so, his men stole the entire meat supply of the town of Santiago. And because Cortés was authorized only to trade with, but not colonize, the new land, his actions throughout the conquest were of questionable legality. Cortés gambled that Spain's new king, the Holy Roman Emperor Charles V, would not be punitive when offered a conquered kingdom, especially if it turned out to be a rich one.

In the year 1519, the Aztec year of One Reed, Cortés landed on the Maya island of Cozumel. Accompanying him were 550 Europeans, 16 horses, attack dogs, and some small cannon. The conquistadores were mostly foot soldiers and sailors, a few were crossbowmen, carpenters, and artillery officers. There was also a chaplain and four other priests, a doctor, a few women housekeepers, so it is said, and hundreds of slaves (a few from Africa, the majority from Cuba). The conquistadores were predominantly poor, young, and Spanish—although others joined, a few Portuguese, African freemen, and Italians among them. All were hellbent on making their fortune in the name of God and country.

*Hernán Cortés, portrait from the Hospital de Jesús, which he founded, in Mexico City*

# HERNÁN CORTÉS (1485–1547)

From the bounty and honors bestowed on him, Hernán Cortés became one of richest men in Spain and married into a noble family. He was later reviled in Mexico, however, as a symbol of foreign domination. During Mexico's War of Independence, his remains had to be hidden so they wouldn't be destroyed. Diego Rivera's malicious portrait of the conquistador—a notorious womanizer—as the syphilitic destroyer of native civilization captures the nationalistic spirit following the Revolution of 1910.

*Hernán Cortés (left), from a detail of Diego Rivera's mural* Mexico of Yesterday *(1945) in Mexico City's National Palace*

From reports of the previous expeditions, Cortés knew that ship-wrecked Spaniards were rumored to live on the mainland across from Cozumel (SEE "Gonzalo Guerrero," page 5). Only one, Jerónimo de Aguilar, responded to the messengers offering refuge with their countrymen. Aguilar, by then a fluent speaker of Yucatec Mayan and a nine-year observer of local manners, became a translator for Cortés. Then, after a skirmish on the Gulf coast, Cortés received a peace offering that included the slave girl, Malinalli, who was baptized "Marina" by the conquistadores. Having grown up in a Nahuatl-speaking area of central Mexico, but sold by her mother to a Maya cacique (chief), Marina was bilingual. With Aguilar and Marina able to speak to each other in Mayan, Cortés could communicate extensively with the native populations; he could flatter and threaten not only the Nahuatl-speaking Aztec but their enemies as well.

Cortés rapidly distinguished himself from the preceding expeditions by actually starting battles—and successfully finishing them. He often bullied even friendly people with cannon shots and skirmishes. This created a fearsome aura of indestructibility, especially when his small force easily won battles against forces 10 times its size.

An astute observer, Cortés noted the native reaction to European weaponry. Although he found the local cotton armor provided adequate protection against obsidian-tipped arrows and spears, Cortés realized the awesome psychological impact steel armor made on the Indians and so continued to use it. Horses "as tall as a roof" (León-Portilla 1962, 30) and cannon with an odor that "penetrates even to the brain" (León-Portilla 1962,30) created understandable confusion in the ranks of Indian soldiers: mounted horses initially were thought to be strange centaur-like creatures, and the power of the awful cannon to rip holes in mountains was "unnatural." As Cortés sailed along the Gulf coast toward the central region where Grijalva had heard so much about a great city in the mountains, Moctezuma's messengers carried the terrible news to Tenochtitlán: "the strangers brought arms which could shoot fire, and wild animals on leashes" (from an Aztec account, translated by León-Portilla).

## Moctezuma and Cortés

Believing the conquistadores represented the fulfillment of the ill omens reported throughout his empire, Moctezuma faltered. Instead of moving to destroy the strangers with his armies, he sent magicians and shamans to cast spells. When these failed, he became all the more indecisive.

# WOMEN IN MESOAMERICAN SOCIETY

**M**arina was Hernán Cortés's translator, mistress, and loyal companion. Without her, he could not have negotiated with the Tlaxacalans, his allies against the Aztecs. Known as Malinche in Mexican histories, her very name has come to mean "traitor." Marina bore Cortés a son, Martín, but she eventually married another conquistador. About the 19 other female slaves accompanying Marina, nothing is known. That Marina, along with other slaves, would be handed over to the conquistadores as gifts leaves us with a dispiriting view of the importance of women in ancient Mesoamerica. In pre-Columbian society rulers are known to have had many wives and noble mistresses and to have used such relationships to form political alliances. In just such a symbolic gesture, Moctezuma later gave Cortés his daughter Tecuichpo (baptized "Isabel"), with whom Cortés also had a child. Women were not merely chattels, however. They had essential roles in religious rituals and were integral to the economy: Textiles were a valued trade item, for example, and women were the master weavers. Marina's own mother was cacique of a small town, and women are known to have ruled Classic Maya cities, such as Palenque.

*A mural by D. H. Xochitiotzin (1967–68) in the Tlaxcalan town hall pictures Marina as central to the meeting of Tlaxcalan chiefs and Spanish invaders.*

Then his messengers relayed the news that Cortés, still on the coast, wanted to meet the great ruler. Moctezuma attempted to buy more time by sending excuses. He was too ill to travel so far. Moreover, the Spaniards should not come to Tenochtitlán either; the 200-mile journey was too rugged and climbed from the tropics up through deserts and snowy passes, from Moctezuma's friendly subjects on the coast to dangerous enemy territories in the Tlaxcalan highlands.

Moctezuma sent his discouraging words tempered with gifts of gold embellished with emeralds from Colombia and turquoise from northern Mexico, quills of precious feathers filled with gold dust, and yet more gold—one piece Cortés described as "a large gold wheel with a design of monsters on it and worked all over with foliage. This weighed 3,800 *pesos de oro*" (Cortés 1986, 40). Of course, this gold dispelled any qualms the conquistadores might have had about their venture to "Yucatán"; as the Aztecs soon learned, "they hungered like pigs for gold." (León-Portilla 1962, 51). These gifts, shipped to Charles V, emboldened Cortés who included with them his first letter to the Spanish emperor asking for his sanction.

> *And, trusting in God's greatness and in the might of Your Highness's Royal name, I decided to go and see [Moctezuma] wherever he might be ... I assured Your Highness that I would take him alive in chains or make him subject to Your Majesty's Royal Crown.*
>
> ■
>
> *Hernán Cortés (1986, 50)*

## The March to Tenochtitlán

Before marching to Tenochtitlán, Cortés needed to attend to his enemies within the Spanish camp. A mutiny among his own men, followers of Governor Velázquez, was quashed and the culprits treated harshly: Two Spaniards were executed and one had his feet cut off. In addition, agents of the Cuban governor had secretly landed near Veracruz: Cortés captured them and incorporated an extra 60 Spanish men and nine horses into his forces. And in his boldest act, he destroyed his own ships to banish any thought of retreat among his men. He told the Spaniards that one ship remained for those who wished to leave; after noting those who showed interest in escaping, he sunk that one, too.

On August 16, 1519, leaving a contingent behind to build a fortress in Veracruz, Cortés set out with 15 horsemen, 300 Spanish foot soldiers, 1,000 Indian carriers, numerous Indian hostages from among the nobility of Spain's newest allies, and an undetermined number of native warriors. Even with local guides to show him the best route, Cortés's march to Tenochtitlán was plagued by lack of water and firewood, hailstorms and bone-chilling cold, just as Moctezuma had warned. He was attacked by indigenous peoples and nearly routed. But on the whole he traveled with a certain degree of security. His allies on the coast were tired of the tyrannical Aztecs who "took their children to sacrifice," and they encouraged him to expect that other enemies of the Aztecs would embrace him in the interior, at Tlaxcala.

Along his route, Cortés was constantly observed by Moctezuma's messengers and allies. It took Cortés and his forces three months to reach Tenochtitlán; it took Moctezuma's messengers one and a half days by relay runners. At each advance, Moctezuma sent more gold, more precious feathers, more gifts, in the hope that the strangers would go away. He offered to pay tribute to Cortés's king, if only Cortés would turn back. When Cortés rested in Tlaxcala with the Aztecs' enemies, Moctezuma urged him on to Cholula, a sacred city in his own empire only 60 miles from the capital city.

> *At dawn I came upon another large town containing, according to an inspection I made, more than twenty thousand houses. As I took them by surprise, they rushed out unarmed, and the women and children ran naked through the streets, and I began to do them some harm.*
>
> ■
>
> *Hernán Cortés (1986, 62)*

Cortés marched into Cholula with his new Tlaxcalan allies. He had the Cholulan lords and their retinue rounded up and locked in the major temple. He ordered his men to kill them all. According to an Aztec account, "Then the slaughter began: knife strokes, and sword strokes, and death" (León-Portilla 1962, 40).

Three thousand were dead in two hours, said Cortés; 5,000 to 10,000, say historians. Why Cortés committed this massacre remains unclear. He claimed Moctezuma had set a trap for him and his actions were in self-defense. Spanish eyewitnesses suggested Cortés wanted to make himself fearsome before marching into Tenochtitlán. He succeeded. The news traveled quickly to Tenochtitlán where, as the conquistador Bernal Díaz del Castillo said, "if we had a reputation for valour before, from now on they took us for sorcerers" (1928, 181). The people were terrified.

## Tenochtitlán

> ... we did not know what to say, or whether what appeared
> before us was real, for on one side, on the land, there were great
> cities, and in the lake ever so many more, and the lake itself was
> crowded with canoes, and in the Causeway were many bridges
> at intervals, and in front of us stood the great City of Mexico,
> and we—we did not even number four hundred soldiers!
>
> ■
>
> Bernal Díaz del Castillo (1928, 192)

The 400 Spaniards marched into Tenochtitlán with 6,000 Indian allies, but they were still overwhelmed by the numbers of Aztecs who crowded to see them, covering the pyramids and temples, filling the lake with their canoes, and squeezing next to the conquistadores in the plazas. Tenochtitlán was greater than any city the Spaniards had ever seen. It was not simply large, it was dazzling—the Venice of the New World with canals for streets. An island metropolis, its great causeways, 30 feet wide, stretched miles across Lake Texcoco and bridges, wide enough for "ten horses abreast" (Cortés 1986, 103), spanned city canals. Beautiful gardens and the royal zoo and aviary adorned the city. The palaces were so large that a single one could house all the Spaniards, their horses, and attack dogs. Unlike any European city, Tenochtitlán was glistening clean, thanks to its good drainage system and nightly garbage collection.

Cortés approached Tenochtitlán at the invitation of Moctezuma, an invitation proffered against the objections of his advisers, who wished to attack. But Moctezuma's word was final. His despotic power was apparent in the pearl-and-feather-covered litter that transported him to meet Cortés, and in the retinue ritually sweeping the street where he would stand on gold-soled sandals. Cortés was the divine ruler's guest, yet he was understandably wary. Once inside the city, he and his soldiers could easily be "obliterated from all memory." So he took Moctezuma hostage.

With Moctezuma as their protector, the conquistadores remained peacefully in Tenochtitlán for six months. To avoid an uprising, Moctezuma had told his people not that he was imprisoned, but rather that he preferred to live with the Spaniards. He continued to rule and was escorted from the palace to perform official functions. Not deceived, the Aztec nobility became increasingly angry with the foreigners. The Aztec treasury had been sacked by the soldiers-of-fortune who melted down cherished art works into gold ingot—and still demanded more gold. They also made outrageous requests regarding religious practices, condemning human sacrifice and demanding that an image of the Virgin Mary replace that of the tribal god, Huitzilopochtli. Moctezuma warned Cortés he should leave.

Peace ended during the annual celebration in honor of the patron war deity, Huitzilopochtli. Cortés was absent: in response to the landing of Governor Velázquez's troops, he was marching to Veracruz. Pedro de Alvarado was in charge of the remaining 140 troops in Tenochtitlán. Alvarado claimed he mistook the dances and festivities in honor of the god as a prelude to an uprising. To forestall the Aztecs, he led his own surprise attack on the sacred plaza, sealing off the dancers and unarmed celebrants and slaughtering them.

> *"Mexicanos, come running! ... The strangers have murdered our warriors!" This cry was answered with a roar of grief and anger; the people shouted and wailed and beat their palms against their mouths. The captains assembled at once ... Then the battle began.*
>
> ■
>
> An Aztec account (León-Portilla 1962, 77)

## The Noche Triste

Cortés returned to Tenochtitlán having quashed Velázquez's attempt to replace him in Mexico. His own forces and stables were more than doubled by Velázquez's men who were promised their share of the bounty. The numbers would do him little good. Permitted to enter the city, he walked into a trap. The palace had been under siege for a month. Attacks were frequent; food, scarce; retreat, a necessity.

In a bid for time, Cortés asked Moctezuma to calm his people. According to the Spaniards, the ruler went to the rooftop and was killed by rocks hurled by his own people who failed to notice him. According to the Aztecs, Cortés, no longer finding any use for the emperor, had him stabbed to death. With Moctezuma dead, so was the calming voice that had aided the conquistadores in the early months of the conquest. Cortés asked for a truce and was derisively hooted down. Reported Bernal Díaz del Castillo, "we were staring death in the face."

On June 30, 1520, under the cover of darkness and with their horses' hooves muffled by cloth, the Spaniards tried to escape. Known in the histories as the Noche Triste (sad night), or the night that "greed overcame wisdom," the retreat was a catastrophe for them. The Aztecs had pulled up the drawbridges in the causeways and built barricades throughout the city to block their enemies' escape. Cortés led the charge, throwing portable bridges over the gaps in the shortest causeway. He made it to the mainland, but the weight of those who followed collapsed the makeshift bridges. With the Aztecs descending on them in the thousands, the Spaniards jumped into the lake and attempted to swim ashore, but the gold hoarded in their pockets sunk them in the hundreds. More than half the Spaniards and 4,000 of their Indian allies died. Forty-six horses were killed. It is said that Hernán Cortés wept.

## The Final Conquest

Cortés survived because his Indian allies steadfastly stood by him. The Spaniards, reduced to a few hundred in number, were protected from the Aztecs by the Tlaxcalans. By May 1521 Cortés, strengthened by 50,000 Indian allies including the Texcocans, once part of the Aztec Triple Alliance, and buoyed by the arrival of new Spanish soldiers-of-fortune with their horses, cannons, and heavy guns, were ready to fight again. His strategy was to attack by ship as well as land, and his new fleet of brigantines, constructed in the intervening months, was carried through the mountains by 8,000 porters. Once at Texcoco by the lake, Cortés had the ships reassembled and was ready to lay siege on Tenochtitlán.

Cortés was aided by an unusual weapon: smallpox. "The illness was so dreadful that no one could walk or move...so they starved to death in their beds" (León-Portilla 1962, 93). Tens of thousands of Indians, including Moctezuma's successor, Cuitlahuac, had died from it by May.

The Aztecs under the leadership of Moctezuma's 18-year-old nephew Cuauhtémoc fought ferociously nonetheless. The city was deprived of freshwater; the only food was lizards, weeds, and dirt. People chewed leather to stay alive. Sickness was rampant, but the fighting continued for months.

Once inside the city, Cortés offered a truce to the starving survivors who replied they would rather die fighting. Cortés decided the only way to victory was to destroy Tenochtitlán. Cuauhtémoc was taken prisoner; years later he was executed by Cortés for allegedly conspiring against him. The city fell on August 13, 1521.

> These misfortunes befell us.
> We witnessed them in anguish.
> We lived through them with suffering.
> Broken spears and torn hair lie on the road.
> Houses are roofless, their walls now red with blood.

■

*Nahuatl poem, 1528 (Garibay 1953)*

*Ruins of the Aztec Great Temple complex surrounded by Spanish buildings in Mexico City. Only when some of the colonial buildings were destroyed in the 1980s did excavations reveal their Aztec foundations. Until then, it had been thought Tenochtitlán was totally destroyed.*

## How Did the Spanish Succeed?

The relative ease of the Spanish conquest of Moctezuma's empire has baffled many. The Spaniards themselves claimed they were mistaken for the god Quetzalcoatl (feathered serpent), a god who opposed human sacrifice and who had, in the myths, been banished by evil deities, but who promised to return some day from the east. This captivating story often is repeated in histories of Mexico, and the Aztecs themselves championed it during the later colonial period as a symbol of their eventual resurgence. Yet scholars have recently challenged this theory. There is no such return myth for Quetzalcoatl in the accounts of Aztec religion least tainted by contact with the Spaniards. And for the Aztecs, as for other Mesoamericans, all gods, good or bad, required human sacrifice to be nourished.

Why, then, was Moctezuma so indecisive when others, such as the Yucatec Maya and even subsequent Aztec emperors, fearlessly fought, and defeated, the conquistadores? Aztec accounts repeatedly quote the emperor as being worried about the harm that resistance would bring to the elderly and children "who still crawl on all fours" (León-Portilla 1962, 78). However, he clearly could not find a way to avoid war and

59

suffering in the heart of his empire. Perhaps he was defeated by circumstances, and as the Aztecs said: "He had lost his strength and spirit, and could do nothing" (León-Portilla 1962, 36).

Another nagging question is how could so few conquistadores defeat so many Aztecs? The more lethal weapons of the Spaniards are often cited as the cause. European swords were made of steel, not obsidian; moreover, the Indian obsidian blades were sharpened to wound (for gathering captives for sacrifice), rather than to kill. The Spaniards' guns and cannons, too, were deadly—when not misfired. Despite such advantages, however, the Spaniards found the Mesoamericans formidable adversaries once they adjusted to the European weapons. They were nearly overwhelmed by the Tlaxcalans and were lucky to make their alliance. The Maya sent the first conquistadores scrambling in defeat from Yucatán. Not until the pre-Columbians divided, adding tens of thousands of native soldiers to the ranks of the Spaniards, did the Aztec empire suffer defeat.

## Capital of New Spain

Two years after Cortés first marched on Tenochtitlán, the Aztec world was a smoldering ruin. The victorious Spaniards built their own capital over the ashes of Tenochtitlán. Aztec labor constructed it. Aztec-cut stones formed the foundation. The government palace replaced Moctezuma's. Construction began on a cathedral next to the Templo Mayor. The first hospital of the Americas was founded at the spot where Cortés and Moctezuma first met. The pre-Columbian land became New Spain. The new city was called Mexico, after Mexica, the Aztecs' name for themselves. In 1524 it counted only 30,000 inhabitants; not until the 20th century would its population once again equal that of Moctezuma's capital.

# 4

# THE FOUNDING OF AN EMPIRE: SIXTEENTH-CENTURY MEXICO

The country we have won is ours....

*Hernán Cortés, 1521 (Thomas, 543)*

While Cortés was conquering Tenochtitlán, no one in Spain paid the least attention; at the moment of victory over the Aztec capital, Cortés remained without official recognition from Charles V. Two years had already lapsed since the conquistador had sent his letter accompanied by Moctezuma's first gifts to Spain. But the Catholic king was too preoccupied with the Protestant Reformation and other European crises and too mired in local turbulence and petty politics to address the issues confronting him in the New World. The treasure from what was called "the new land of gold" did receive notice, however, as it traveled around Europe with the royal court.

With little preparation, Spain found itself ruler of a wealthy, civilized land many times larger than itself and far more densely populated. Spain might conquer such a kingdom as long as it had thousands of local allies. But how could it control and administer this empire? Indoctrinate it with Christianity and transform it into a European society? Yet all of this was accomplished in a matter of decades from a continent two months away by sea.

## Conquest beyond Tenochtitlán

While Spain dithered, Cortés was left to govern. Cortés normally would not have been the king's choice: conquistadores were just too independent

61

to be trusted representatives of the Spanish bureaucracy. Because his popularity made him irreplaceable, however, Cortés received his commission in 1522, nearly a year after the conquest and about the length of time it took Charles to learn of it. Finally, the "Emperor ... wrote him a letter, thanking him for the hardships he had undergone in the conquest, and for his service to God in casting down idols" (López de Gómara 1964, 329).

Cortés might easily have empathized with the Crown's distrust: he himself had trouble controlling his own soldiers-of-fortune. Their demands for more Aztec gold were nearly mutinous, though sometimes quite justifiable. After the royal fifth and Cortés's bounty (some said he stashed away three million pesos in gold), there was hardly any booty left over for everyone else. Soldiers received only one-fifth of the cost of their horses, and some were not paid enough to replace their ammunition. Rather than rolling in riches after the devastation of the conquest, the victors found that even food was in short supply. In an attempt to discover more treasure, including the gold lost in the Noche Triste, the conquistadores tortured and maimed Cuauhtémoc and other Indian rulers, but to no avail.

Cortés exploited the restlessness of his men to best advantage. Using the Aztec tribute lists as a guide, he sent them off to other parts of Moctezuma's empire to find food and supplies and, of course, gold.

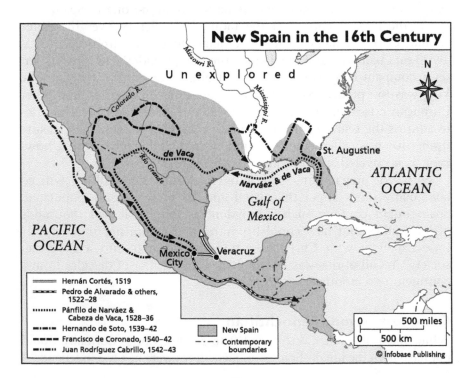

62

When resistance was encountered, as it was initially in Oaxaca, Tlaxcalan and Aztec allies helped to settle matters quickly. A port was built at Veracruz, and other ports were established on the Pacific coast at places like Acapulco, in order to search for the yet-to-be-discovered route to the Orient. And trusted captains were charged with the conquest of independent regions and the peoples like the Tarascans to the northwest in Michoacán and the Maya to the south in Yucatán where they often battled for years before succeeding. While following the trail of the Fountain of Youth and other fantastic places, the conquistadores and their successors made their way to farflung parts of the Americas, such as what is now the U.S. Southwest. They crossed the Pacific Ocean to the Philippines and, eventually, created a New Spain that was three and a half times larger than Mexico is today.

## The Mestizo Nation

*13 August 1521, Tlatelolco—heroically defended by Cuauhtémoc— fell under the power of Hernán Cortés. It was neither a triumph or defeat; it was the painful birth of the mestizo nation that is Mexico today.*

■

*Plaque on Aztec ruins in Mexico City*

The task of settlement required a different temperament from conquest, yet Cortés initially proved himself able to carry it out. To create European goods and commerce, he brought in the very first Spanish brood stocks—cows, sows, sheep, and goats—as well as seeds and mulberry trees for silk, vine cuttings, and sugar cane. He prevented his men from returning to Spain with their newfound wealth and, wanting families rather than just adventurers to settle, he advanced money to pay the travel costs of the conquistadores' wives. He encouraged others to marry indigenous women, and many conquistadores did just that, beginning the first legitimate mestizo, or mixed Spanish and Indian, families. Moctezuma's daughter Tecuichpo, baptized "Isabel," outlived her ruler-husband Cuauhtémoc as well as several Spanish captains; her daughter with Hernán Cortés, Lenor Cortés Moctezuma, more elevated by the powerful union of two worlds than tarnished by illegitimacy, was just one of her mestizo offspring. Most of the conquistadores' children, however, did not have such a romantic ancestry. Yet they all began what would become a most distinctive mark of Mexico: its mestizo majority.

## The *Encomienda*

> The natives of these parts ... possess such understanding as is
> sufficient for an ordinary citizen to conduct himself in a civilized
> country. It seemed to me, therefore, a serious matter at this
> time to compel them to serve the Spaniards ... [yet] I have
> been almost forced to deliver the chieftains and other natives of
> these parts to the Spaniards in recognition of the services they
> have rendered to Your Majesty ...
>
> ■
>
> *Hernán Cortés, 1522 (1986, 281)*

Settlement itself required economic incentives. In the New World,
the greatest inducement was gold, but the most reliable one was the
*encomienda* (land grants). The *encomienda* system, a thinly disguised
form of slavery, granted entire towns and their Indian populations to
an individual, the *encomendero*. Sometimes, depending on the grant,
the natives were forced to relocate onto the land. The Indians owed the
*encomenderos* tribute as well as free labor, and their labors usually supported the absentee Spaniards in grand style in faraway cities.

The *encomenderos* were supposed to Christianize and assimilate
the Indians into European culture; exploitation and abuse were more
common. With a few exceptions, the *encomiendas* reduced all Indians

# ALCOHOLISM

Mesoamericans fermented various juices to make mildly alcoholic
drinks. Who could imbibe alcohol (only male adults and elderly
women to warm their blood), how much (a few glasses), and when (in
ritual celebrations) were regulated in Aztec society by severe penalties.
A drunk's head was shaved in public, his house could be sacked and torn
down. *Pulque,* made from an agave plant, was popular with the Spaniards,
although Aztec nobles disdained it as plebeian, preferring their chocolate.
After the conquest, when Indians died in alarming numbers, many Aztecs
thought intemperate drinking of *pulque,* in the Spanish manner, might
be the cause. By the end of the colonial period, Mexico City residents
consumed enough *pulque* in a year to average 75 gallons each. *Pulque*
cantinas continue to attract the poor in modern Mexico.

to the same level of impoverishment and cultural deprivation. In central Mexico, where *encomiendas* were extensive, the price of this forced acculturation was tragic: Indian homicide rates increased, as did alcoholism. In the Caribbean Islands, as Cortés himself had complained to the Crown, *encomiendas* had resulted in the annihilation of the indigenous peoples.

Charles V, wanting to directly control his new vassals and, as vicar of the church, wanting to protect them, outlawed the *encomienda,* but not before Cortés had distributed the lands among the conquistadores. Cortés's professed concern over *encomienda* did little to restrain his use of it. Nearly all the Indians in central Mexico had been distributed among the conquistadores by 1522. Cortés was most generous with himself: in addition to vast tracts of land and many great cities, he "deposited" a million natives to his own care. It was said that nothing could stir up the conquerors more than the size of their grants. And nothing interfered more with Spain's control of its provinces since the *encomendero* had the right to all tribute and labor, not the Crown. The *encomienda* attracted settlers; it also created conflicts—and even Spanish rebellions—against both church and Crown when reforms were attempted during the 16th century.

## Cortés Sidelined

Cortés was presumed dead while on a daring expedition to Honduras through uncharted territory in 1524–26. He had abandoned Mexico City in order to regain control of Honduras from a renegade conquistador (much like he himself was in 1519). Attempting to fill the political vacuum with themselves, enemies of Cortés spread rumors that the governor had been disloyal to the Crown and had cheated the royal treasury.

Cortés returned from the dead after almost two years away. The upstarts were hanged, but the Crown remained suspicious. Charles V, having wanted to place his own viceroy in Mexico for some time, accused Cortés of misconduct. Hoping to clear his name, Cortés returned to Spain in 1528 with an entourage of Mesoamerican nobles, ballplayers, and dwarfs, with jaguars and armadillos, gold and silver. He dazzled all of Spain and was elevated to the nobility and made marquis. He was not reappointed governor of New Spain, however. One of the wealthiest men in his time, Cortés begrudgingly retired to the periphery of Mexican politics as Spain imposed its bureaucratic will over its New World empire.

# The Mendicant Friars Arrive

*Fray Marín de Valencia, the Pope's vicar, arrived in Mexico in the year '24, with twelve companions. Cortés received him with gifts, services, and honor. Whenever he spoke to them it was with cap in hand and one knee to the ground, while he kissed their robes as an example to the Indians who were to be converted.*

■

*Francisco López de Gómara (1964, 331)*

In keeping with the conquistadores' creed of gold and glory but above all God, Cortés had smashed many idols and his chaplain had baptized numerous converts. But as Friar Motolinia, one of the first missionaries, put it, the conquistadores "were content to build their houses and seemed satisfied as long as no human sacrifice occurred in public" (Thomas). Unlike the conquerors, the emperor could not perform his duties halfheartedly. Charles V was granted extraordinary privileges by the papacy to head the Catholic Church in all of Spain's domains because the conquest was seen as a sign of God's favor for the emperor: he alone was entrusted with all those souls. And Charles V proved himself a devout monarch.

Perhaps Cortés's most profound legacy was his recommendation to the Crown that the mendicant orders—the Franciscans, Dominicans, and Augustinians—be charged with the responsibility for the Indians' salvation. These missionaries, as opposed to the secular clergy, were educated individuals recognized for their devotion and respected for their vows of poverty. The religious orders and monastic life sustained them, not the charging of fees for services. Cortés believed their humble character would speed the conversion of the Mexican people. The emperor agreed.

The Franciscan volunteers arrived first in 1524. They quickly impressed the native population by walking barefoot from the Gulf coast port to Mexico City. Their simple dress and the self-inflicted suffering endured on their 50-day journey could not have contrasted more with the greed of the conquistadores. Nor could their thinking: rather than seeking fabled cities of unimaginable wealth, many of the friars saw the New World as an opportunity to create the monastic kingdom of pure charity—Thomas More's Utopia or Augustin's City of God. Their zeal was often fueled by the belief that Christianizing the Indians would create these ideal societies and thus pave the way for the second coming of Christ. The Crown, too, took its religious obligations seriously: when the first bishop, Juan de Zumárraga, arrived in 1527, he carried the title "Protector of the Indians."

## The Spiritual Conquest

With millions to convert, the friars counted only in the hundreds, yet they remained undaunted in the task of spiritual conquest. They fanned out across the country—eventually they, not soldiers, would be the first to venture into new territories in the north in order to pacify the native populations. (They were also the first Europeans to see the Grand Canyon.) In Mexico they built their chapels atop pagan pyramids and established simple living quarters amid the most ancient cities of the Americas. Nine million people were baptized in the central region by 1537: Friar Pedro de Gante said it was not unusual to baptize 4,000 people in a day; Father Motolinia thought he alone had baptized 300,000.

As the number of neophytes swelled, the friars needed churches, but the size required was well beyond any immediate building capabilities. So a uniquely New World architectural form was created: the open chapel,

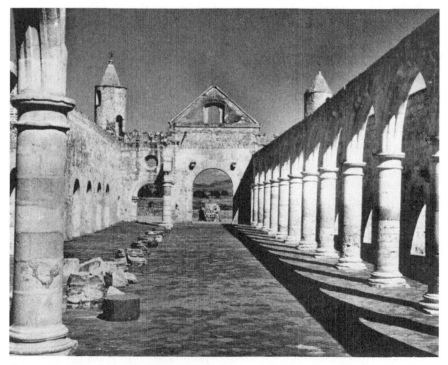

*Sixteenth-century Church of Cuilapán in Oaxaca*

a solution especially amenable to religious practices of Mesoamericans who had always gathered in large open-air plazas. Over time, open chapels were replaced by enclosed churches and vast monastery complexes such as the one at Cuilapán. Using Indian labor, the friars built 50 such establishments by 1540 and, eventually, a total of 400 dotted the land from Yucatán to Michoacán.

The rapidity of conversion was no less astonishing than the Spanish conquest itself. Given that Mesoamerican religion profoundly permeated the native view of the world, from the creation of the stars to the planting of corn, it is hard to understand how it could be so quickly eradicated. In fact, there is abundant evidence that it was not.

Similarities between the religions facilitated conversion. Both cultures believed in an afterlife and a world created by god(s). The cross was a symbol for both, being also the symbol for the Mesoamerican world tree that linked the supernatural and earthly realms; the Crucifixion of Christ was, for Mesoamericans, another example of their belief that sacrifice was needed for rebirth. Fasting, sexual abstinence, and even the ritual use of water, such as in Christian baptism, also resonated with indigenous practices. And both religions shared a ritual calendar that dominated the change of seasons and the march of the days. The Catholics honored their saints and the Mesoamericans their deities with religious processions, festively dressed idols, incense burning, music, and dance.

As the friars discovered, conversion often involved only the veneer of these similarities to Christianity: traditional beliefs and practices remained intact. It was one thing for the Indians to respect a new god so powerful as to have led the Europeans to conquer them. It was another to expect them to reject their own gods and not fear the consequences. Old ritual practices continued, most often in secret, although some were overlooked and even exploited by the priests—the dark-skinned Virgin of Guadalupe, for instance, conveniently made her miraculous appearance to Juan Diego, a Nahua peasant boy, near the shrine of Tonantzín, Aztec earth goddess and mother of humankind.

In other instances, the vestiges of paganism proved intolerable: Friar Diego de Landa, for example, was scandalized by the persistence in the Yucatán of sacrificial rituals among his most dedicated converts. He instituted an inquisition into native idolatry in 1562, torturing the heretics and burning the Maya hieroglyphic books. He was ordered back to Spain: the Crown realized the Indians simply did not yet understand the true faith. The Indians were subsequently exempt from the punitive powers of the Inquisition.

*Diego de Landa (1529–79). Although responsible for Indian torture and deaths during an inquisition, Diego de Landa also wrote the definitive work on Yucatec Maya customs, providing the key to decipherment of ancient Maya hieroglyphic texts that reveal the very Maya religion Landa hoped to repress.*

## Friars as Ethnographers

The priests understood that it was not just the Indians who required more thorough instruction. The friars needed a greater knowledge of native beliefs in order to eradicate them. From the beginning the fathers had been great linguists, learning the native languages and compiling dictionaries so that the catechism could be taught. Schools were opened for natives: one was a university for Indian nobles where they learned Latin so well they became the instructors for the Spanish settlers; others included the utopian communities established by Vasco de Quiroga in Michoacán where the Purépecha learned how to use their craftsmaking skills in order to be self-sustaining.

By the middle of the 16th century, the friars also became the first ethnographers, working in collaboration with the Indians and encouraging them to write about their own history and culture in their native languages. The most famous, Bernardino de Sahagún, working with a team of central Mexican nobles, compiled an encyclopedia of pre-Columbian Aztec life that described everything from sacred rituals to recipes for preparing hot chocolate. In the process, the nobles learned to write their own language, Nahuatl, in the Roman alphabet rather than in pictographs—a skill that greatly facilitated communication. On Sahagún's part, he left to posterity its greatest source of information on Mesoamerican life at the time of the conquest.

## Mesoamerican Catholicism

Such collaboration did much to profoundly Hispanicize and Christianize many Indians. Once the native leaders changed, many of the commoners followed suit. The daily relation of the Indians with their land, the sacred landscape of their ancestors, and with their traditional communities, however, often remained untouched—the church seemed to think such "household" practices meaningless superstitions. In many instances, conversion only created what many anthropologists now call "Mesoamerican Catholicism," a reworking of Christianity that incorporated, and partially modified, the Mesoamerican worldview, as can be seen in the distinctive imagery of this Nahua hymn:

> The roses, dark red ones, pale ones
> The red feather flowers, the golden flowers
> lie there waving like precious bracelets
> lie bending with quetzal feather dew.
>
> ■
>
> Indian hymn to St. Clare (Burkhart 1993, 210)

Today most native-speaking Mexicans are devout Christians and many make pilgrimages to the nation's patron saint, the Virgin of Guadalupe. But most anthropologists believe the Virgin represents a powerful synthesis of the Christian and Mesoamerican beliefs: she is still called Tonantzín by the Nahua. Many such instances of a syncretic religion have been identified, including the performance of Ch'a-Chak rituals to the Maya rain god, common in years of drought. Perhaps the survival of such beliefs would not have been possible if the vibrant intellectual exchange between native and European had not ended late in the 16th century when the friars lost much of their power to the secular clergy. Outside the cities, the Indians, who had often been officially separated from the colonists to keep them free of Spanish corruption, lost their only viable link to European ways. Without the friars and their investment in native education, the traditional communities themselves provided the daily context for religious observances.

## Mid-Century Reforms

The remarkable achievements of Sahagún and other friars, such as Vasco de Quiroga, occurred during the middle of the 16th century. In what has been called the "golden age of Christianity," this was a period of unusual collaboration between the native population and the foreigners, from the Aztecs advising the new government on how to control the flooding of Lake Texcoco to programs that taught Indians European skills, such as blacksmithing and carpentry. There never was similar harmony among the colonists, the royal functionaries and the religious, however. The clergy wanted to protect the native population, of course, and provide them with salvation; the conquistadores wanted to work them like beasts of burden. But even among these factions, relations improved after the disputes immediately following the conquest.

The cooperative spirit certainly was promoted by two enlightened individuals during the founding of New Spain: Mexico's first viceroy (1530–50), Antonio de Mendoza, and its first bishop and archbishop (1528–48), Juan de Zumárraga. These two could not have carried out the enormous task of institutionalizing the power of the Crown and church in the conquered land more competently. Mendoza, the count of Tendilla and related to the royal house, had been a diplomat in Rome; Zumárraga, a true Franciscan in his poverty vows, was the executor of many royal commissions and a militant champion of Christian values (he risked his life challenging the abuses of natives by early officials). Mendoza was followed by another superb viceroy, Luis de Velasco

# INDIAN RESISTANCE TO CONVERSION

**N**ot all Indians willingly participated in the new societal order. Armed rebellion did occur sporadically throughout the colonial period. The Mixtón Rebellion in 1541 near Guadalajara was one of the most threatening: 100,000 native rebels rose against 400 Spaniards. They were defeated by 30,000 Aztecs, for the first time armed with Spanish guns. Native resistance to the religious and political conquest more often took the form of escape into remote regions—especially toward the end of the 16th century. The Lacandón Maya did just that, remaining unconverted and unassimilated well into the 20th century when logging operations and population pressures destroyed the Chiapas rain forest that had so long sustained them. The contemporary Tarahumara Indians of the Copper Canyon in northern Mexico, known so well by tourists, and the Huichol of the Colima plateau, famous for their peyote cult, are other examples. Their cultural survival also is threatened by environmental devastation.

*A 20th-century Lacandón Maya Indian selling arrows at Palenque*

(1550–64), who became known as "Father of the Indians." These three shared many Renaissance humanist views and each was scrupulous in implementing the emperor's policies. They set the best example for the future administration of the colony.

Their humanism, as well as that of the religious community, resulted in the passage of reforms that protected the native population. Both a papal bull (1537) and a royal edict called the New Laws (1542) settled the matter once and for all that Indians were human, capable of salvation, and worthy vassals of the Crown—principles that Bartolomé de Las Casas, bishop of Chiapas, had been lobbying for since he had witnessed the genocide in the West Indies. Indian slavery finally was outlawed.

The period of relative cooperation that permitted such radical reforms may have resulted, in part, from the low numbers of Spanish colonists. By as late as 1560, the Spaniards in New Spain probably numbered barely more than 20,000. Initially there was plenty of land and, usually, more than enough Indians to labor on the *encomiendas* or, at least, provide tribute to sustain the colonists in an acceptable manner. But as the Indian population declined catastrophically, the settlers' demands for native labor increasingly clashed with the reforming goals of the church and government.

The truth was that Indian labor was too much in demand. The church required, and trained, artisans to build and decorate monasteries and chapels. The government expected its *tequio,* or public service, too, for building town halls or repairing streets. And then there was the *encomendero,* whose sugar cane and cattle ranches had to be maintained. Although the Indians had provided tribute and labor to Mesoamerican rulers, the Spaniards had tripled the levels of Aztec tribute despite the catastrophic declines in population.

The Crown attempted to protect the Indians from further loss, swayed by economic reasons as well as arguments from the religious that the exploitative colonists were at fault. (Friar Bartolomé de Las Casas claimed that the Spaniards' abuses made the natives refuse baptism for fear of having to spend eternity in their company.) In addition to banning Indian enslavement, Mendoza lowered the amount of free labor and tribute permitted. To boost the economy, more African slaves were brought to New Spain. (No ban on their enslavement was considered.) Although these slaves somewhat reduced the settlers' need for workers, they also cost money—unlike the Indians. Twenty thousand had arrived in the colony by 1553, and although their numbers equaled that of the European community, they hardly made up for the millions of Indians lost to infectious diseases and abuse.

# DEPOPULATION

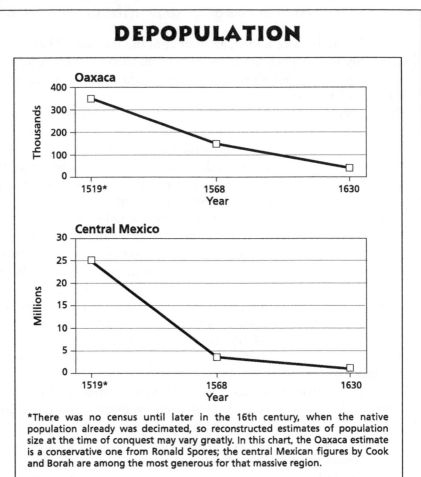

*There was no census until later in the 16th century, when the native population already was decimated, so reconstructed estimates of population size at the time of conquest may vary greatly. In this chart, the Oaxaca estimate is a conservative one from Ronald Spores; the central Mexican figures by Cook and Borah are among the most generous for that massive region.

© Infobase Publishing

Never having been exposed to European diseases, the Indians had no natural immunity to smallpox, measles, typhoid, chicken pox, yellow fever, or mumps. At least seven major waves of these diseases had washed through the native population by 1600. Famine often followed because so few individuals were able to work the land. These deaths added to those caused by abuse, homicide, and cultural dislocation resulted in what some have called "possibly the greatest demographic disaster in the history of the world" (Denevan). No one understood the nature of infectious disease at the time: Friar Bartolomé de Las Casas thought the encomienda system was the work of the devil to depopulate New Spain; the Mixtecs, too thought it was due to the supernatural and reverted to traditional curing rituals—called "witchcraft" by the church. By most estimates, the population decreased by 70 to 90 percent. Not until 1650 did the size of the native population begin to increase.

If restricted labor already was a cause for colonists to complain, the increased labor needs created by the first major mining strikes (1545–65) intensified the feeling. When, in 1564, the Crown tried to implement further reforms, it ignited treasonous ideas, especially since these reforms attacked the institution most sacred to the conquistadores' descendants: the *encomienda*. All *encomiendas*, it was ordered, would cease upon the death of the holder. No longer would the privileged status and wealth of *encomenderos* be inherited. Outraged, Alonso de Ávila, son of a conquistador, argued for independence from Spain. He suggested the new Marqués del Valle, Cortés's son Martín, should be made king of the independent nation. And he thought armed resistance was in order. The talk didn't get much further before Alonso de Ávila was arrested and beheaded along with his brother. The more fortunate Martín Cortés was exiled forever, and his stepbrother, the son of Cortés and Marina, was tortured. Others of the New World aristocracy were beheaded. But not only did all talk of rebellion end, so did any serious effort to eliminate the remaining *encomiendas*: eventually the practice would simply fade away.

## Utopian Experiments End

As the 16th century came to a close, the conflicts took a different shape. The Renaissance humanism that had so imbued the mid-century exchanges between Europeans and the native population with tolerance (and even a tinge of mutual respect) ended with the more dogmatic promulgations of the Council of Trent (1563). Following the Council of Trent, many books, such as those by Erasmus, were banned in Spain, although they circulated freely in Mexico and were part of the catechism.

Charles V was dead, as were Zumárraga and Mendoza; the native aristocrats who had been educated in Mesoamerican traditions were dying out. The official onset of the Inquisition in Mexico in 1571 marked the final demise of this most idealistic religious period. Not only did the friars no longer attempt to create utopian Indian communities, but such work bordered on the heretical. Treatises by former archbishop Zumárraga were banned; Sahagún's work languished in archives until the 19th century. The early humanists were too often replaced by more corrupt individuals who saw the Americas as an opportunity to make a quick fortune or to hide their vices from European view. Even the clergy occupied themselves in building ever more ornate churches, replacing religious zeal with their own material comforts, and advocacy with authoritarianism.

# MIXTEC CACIQUES THRIVE UNDER SPAIN

The *Codex Nuttall,* a pre-Columbian book, tells the story of the great Mixtec ruler, 8 Deer "Tiger Claw," in 1103 C.E. His descendants continued to rule in the Sierra Mixteca of Oaxaca well into the 19th century, whereas Moctezuma's dynastic line (more threatening to Spain) had lost the power to hold any office, however low, by 1565. In Oaxaca, the number of Europeans were fewer than in most parts of New Spain, never amounting to even 7 percent in contrast to 50 percent around Mexico City. The conquistadores could barely control Oaxaca City, which they founded; their influence was even less in the nearby rugged mountains, where they had sadly discovered during the conquest that "the terrain does not permit the use of horses." Cacique rights and territories were recognized in order to gain the Mixtecs' much-needed cooperation. The indigenous economy, not *encomiendas,* became indispensable to Spanish society; the traditional communities and native political order remained intact, including class distinctions.

In the mid-16th-century *Codex of Yanhuitlán,* Don Gabriel de Guzmán, cacique of the Mixtec principality of Yanhuitlán and descendant of the

*In this section of the pre-Columbian* Codex Nuttall, *the Mixtec ruler 8 Deer (on right) undergoes a nose-piercing ceremony.* (Drawing by Shannon Ernst)

pre-Columbian ruler 8 Deer "Tiger Claw," meets with a high-ranking Spaniard. Below him is his Mixtec name glyph of 9 House. The Mixtec caciques, such as Don Gabriel, oversaw vast territories and functioned as they had for many centuries, except tribute was paid to the Spaniards instead of to the Aztecs. In return, the caciques received Spanish privileges: Don Gabriel was granted the gentleman's title of *don,* a coat of arms, permits to raise livestock and the right to wear Spanish clothes, ride horseback, and bear arms.

*The Mixtec cacique Don Gabriel (on right) confers with a Spaniard, from the Codex of Yanhuitlán.* (Drawing by Shannon Ernst)

The new king Philip II reigned in these more severe times (from 1556 to 1598). Philip was more interested in the economy of New Spain than in the treatment of the native population. He was more sensitive to the jealousy of the settlers when Nahua nobles outdid them in schools than in attempts to enable the Indians to become fully realized vassals of Spain. The university was disbanded. Sympathetic to the colonists and their need for labor, Philip permitted the secular clergy, less educated and totally dependent on settlers' tithes, to take over from the meddlesome mendicant orders. The well-being of the native population became secondary to the need for a productive economy to sustain the Spanish empire.

## Spain Flourishes

As the first century of European involvement in the New World came to a close, the potential wealth of the colony had already become apparent to all. Silver bullion weighted down the Spanish galleons—enough to pay for the entire cost of administering all the American colonies, with plenty left over for Spain. The China trade was established in 1564: silks and spices and porcelains from the Philippines arrived across the Pacific to Acapulco, and then, after being carried across Mexico to Veracruz, accompanied the silver in its transatlantic voyage. The galleons carried much of Europe's wealth. And Spain owned it all.

Piracy occasionally helped England and France to get their share of American bounty. Sir Francis Drake, for example, looted Spanish ships from the Pacific to the Caribbean with the full sanction of England. European powers also tried to colonize other parts of the Americas: for example, French Huguenots tried, but failed, to settle Florida. Wishing to protect his very lucrative domains, Philip looked for a port in California, sent colonizers to New Mexico, and Juan Ponce de Léon to Florida. He strived not only to secure the passage of his galleons but to guarantee the continued flow of New World tribute and exports.

## New Spain Established

Before the end of the 16th century, a massive change had occurred: an indigenous civilization had been brought under the control of a European monarch. The wealth of a population of millions had been transferred to a few conquerors through *encomienda* and tribute; there was not a single aspect of the pre-Columbian culture that had not been transformed in the process: Indian writing had changed from pictographs to the Roman alphabet; ritual sacrifice had been eradicated, ribbons had replaced feathers in religious costumes, and once proud Mesoamericans who had believed their cities were the sacred centers of the universe, had been taught that the true center was far away in a foreign land. The very names of people and places had been changed: the sacred city of Teotihuacán was now San Juan Teotihuacán.

Until recently historians thought the viceregal and ecclesiastic control of native society obliterated preconquest institutions. Yet archival studies by historians such as Charles Gibson and James Lockhart have demonstrated that Spain's success lay in manipulating the native institutions to serve its own purposes. Replacing the imperial rulers of the Aztecs, the viceregal government achieved only an overlay of authority; under it and supporting it through trade and markets, farming and artisanship, tax collection and tribute, was a "Republic of Indians." Even the security of New Spain depended on the peacekeeping efforts and garrisons of native allies. In many regions, Spaniards relied on the old Mesoamerican political and social order, with Indian elites acting as intermediaries between their people and the foreign officials.

In less than 100 years after the conquest, viceregal government was fully developed, and the Catholic Church had sent its missionaries into most, if not all, recesses of the country. Spain's new government branch, the Council of the Indies, promulgated regulations to New Spain that affected everything from the location of a town church to the kind of crops that could be grown. But the forms of government and religion succeeded only because they took on a distinctly pre-Hispanic cast: Mexican in nature, the New World's institutions were as composite as its people were increasingly racially mixed.

The 16th century witnessed the formation of a new people and new institutions: a characteristic Mexican fusion. The bureaucracy of New Spain was in place and, as the century closed, Spain managed to remain the sole European power in this New World.

# 5

# THE COLONY OF NEW SPAIN

*Without the Indies or its trade, Spain would fall from its greatness, because there would be no silver for your majesty, for the ministers, for private individuals, for those holding ... inheritances, which all comes from the Indies ...*

■

*Marqués de Varina, 1687 (translated by Stein & Stein)*

There were two Spanish perspectives in regard to New Spain. Those living in Europe thought the colony should be exploited to enrich the home country; and those living in the colony viewed the land as an opportunity to make money, enough to either recreate a genteel Spanish lifestyle in the Americas or to return across the Atlantic rich enough to enjoy the real thing. People of either view saw Mexico as a pot of gold to be melted and molded into their own treasure.

During three centuries of Spanish domination, the land was transformed by new crops and technologies and trade, new cities and ports, European art forms and crafts. Policies changed according to the fashions in Spain, as did the arts and cities and continuously evolving population. But Spain remained firmly in control of Mexico's economic and religious institutions. Its legacy has endured beyond the colonial centuries, leaving a poorly developed economy, a class structure based primarily on racism, and a too-common belief among officials that the governance of Mexico is an opportunity to enhance personal wealth.

## The Capital

Spain's presence was concentrated in the colonial capital. Even before the pilgrims landed at Plymouth Rock, the avenues of Mexico City were broad, parks and plazas were graced by fountains, and stately mansions

*The heart of colonial Mexico City, with its cathedral, viceregal palace, and other administrative buildings, all constructed over the center of the Aztec capital* (Courtesy of the Bancroft Library)

were built of stone. Churches were numerous and imposing; the cathedral, magnificent. As one contemporary visitor said, "Besides these beautiful buildings, the inward riches belonging to the altars are infinite in price and value" (Gage 1981, 71). There were six hospitals (four for Europeans, one for Indians, and one for mestizos), even though surgeons were in fact no more than barbers and native curers were just as likely to be relied upon with no known disastrous effects. There were orphanage-schools for abandoned mestizos, Jesuit and Augustinian colleges, and the first university in the Americas, the University of Mexico, was founded in 1551—although centuries passed before a second one opened in Guadalajara. The city was abundantly provisioned, with foodstuffs from the surrounding countryside easily purchased at the huge outdoor market. Textiles and crafts came from New Spain; ivories and silks from the China trade, wine and olive oil as well as artists and paintings arrived from Spain.

Although the poor lived in squalor on the edges of the new city, it is no wonder that people of privilege found the city the only proper place to reside. The viceroy and his retinue resided here, creating an elegant

# ENVIRONMENTAL CHANGE

*The city floats in emerald circles,*
*Radiating splendor like quetzal plumes.*
*Around it chiefs are carried in canoes,*
*Veiled by a flowery mist.*

■

*Aztec poem (Garibay 1953)*

**M**exico City was not an island for long. The series of lakes surrounding Tenochtitlán were drained over the centuries. Roads replaced the dikes; wheeled carts and mule packs, the canoes. Gone were the waterbirds and fish that thrived in Lake Texcoco, gone the freshwater and *chinampa* agriculture that sustained the populace. Remaking Mexico City in the image of Spain, the Spaniards wreaked havoc on the environment. Initially, without the dikes, the city was repeatedly flooded in the 17th century. As the water levels fell, the central valley became increasingly infertile. Recently the northern traces of the lake wetlands, a wildlife refuge, were slated for airport construction.

court as the focus for European society. Here, too, resided the judges of the Audiencia who kept a watchful eye on the viceroy for the king. The seat of the other powerful authority in the Americas, the archbishop, was also in the capital along with an inordinate number of ordained priests. (Twenty-five percent, or 1,500, of the priests, both secular and mendicant, lived in Mexico City and another 1,400 lived in nearby Puebla, meaning that about half the priesthood of New Spain lived in central Mexico in 1650.) The capital and its environs were home to half the entire European population of the colony "who are so proud and rich that half the city was judged to keep coaches" (Gage 1981, 67). By the end of the colonial period, the city had as many racially mixed residents as Indians.

The capital reflected most of the wealth, power, and Spanish culture of New Spain. In 1800, with a population of 137,000—half that estimated for Tenochtitlán—it was the largest city in the Western Hemisphere and a symbol of European culture in the New World. The legendary city of Moctezuma had disappeared.

## Regional Diversity

> *Neither God nor his Majesty would have been served by the people of the provinces, as they are disorganized and have no head, and the land is sterile and has no products, nor has it silver or gold whereby his Majesty could be served.*

> ■

> *García López de Cárdenas, 1551*

Outside the capital, the impact of Spain and its settlers varied with the region. Viceregal control was as uneven as the distribution of settlements. Provincial administrators, called *corregidores*, existed in Spanish towns, such as Mérida in Yucatán; the *corregidores* were poorly paid and had limited authority, but they were notorious for finding ways to supplement their salaries. They oversaw and reported to the viceroy on the happenings in the municipality as well as in Indian settlements. These towns also had a local government separate from the royal *corregidor.* In the best of times local government officials were elected; when the Crown needed money, however, officials could buy their positions knowing that prestige and profiteering would amply reward their investment.

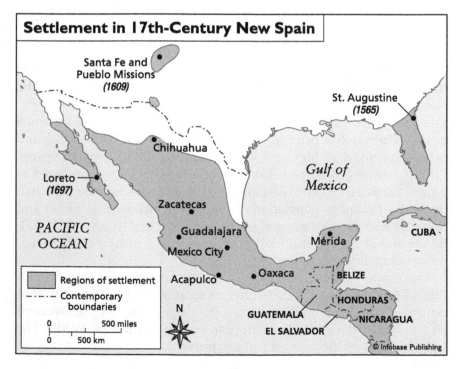

Settlement in 17th-Century New Spain

*Colonial building in the provincial town of Pátzcuaro, Michoacán* (Courtesy of the Mexico Ministry of Tourism)

Although such provincial towns were few and far between, all were organized according to royal decree: a main plaza dominated with the symbols of authority, the church and royal palace and town hall, and streets laid out perpendicular to the plaza in an orderly fashion. The 10 most important cities, such as Puebla, Oaxaca, and Guadalajara, were large enough to have cathedrals and grand palaces. Puebla eventually had a population of 100,000. The location of a town, the building of a church, and even the founding of a school were all regulated by the Crown through the Council of the Indies located in Seville, Spain. Although viceroys often ignored orders, claiming local conditions did not permit their implementation—"The law is respected but not obeyed" was the official response—the impact of royal edicts on the New World is unmistakable in the architecture of both provincial villages and regional capitals. More than 6,000 decrees governing life in the colonies were issued.

Hacendados often represented the only Spanish presence in many rural areas; and the mendicant fathers, though diminishing in number, continued to create missions in the hinterlands of the empire and to administer many of the 400 fortress monasteries they had built among their converts. Well into the 17th century, there were not enough parish priests to replace them, much less tend to the spiritual

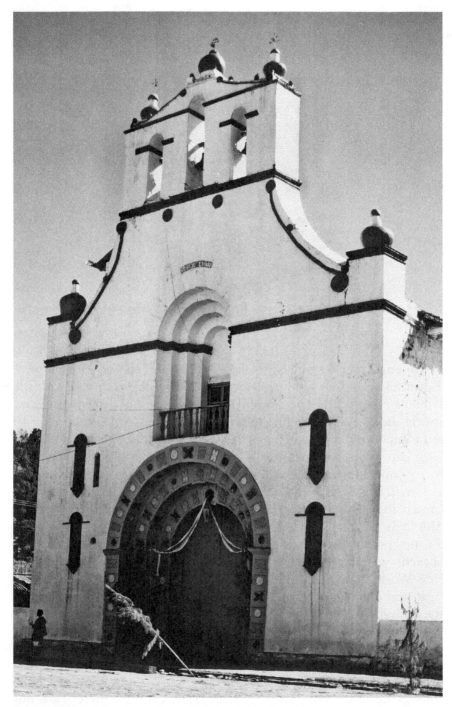

*Provincial church in the Maya village of San Juan Chamula, Chiapas*

needs of the expanding colony. Given the thin layer of Spanish and church officialdom, an administrative system of caciques (native governors) was, of necessity, created to oversee the indigenous peoples and fulfill Spanish tribute and tax levies. The cacique system paralleled the town organization and reinforced the existence of traditional Indian communities.

The intensity and quality of viceregal control in a given area depended, at the very least, on the ratio of the density of Spanish settlers to the native populace. The Spaniards preferred to settle near large populations of Indians who could support them. But they also preferred the regions that could most easily re-create life in Spain. The central highlands, with their temperate climate suitable for Old World crops and livestock, were ideal. Here Spaniards settled in the greatest numbers, and most intensely affected the lives of the indigenous peoples as well as the land.

The tropical lowlands were too hot for the Spaniards, however, the vegetation unfamiliar, and the malaria too threatening. Sugarcane haciendas were quite productive once Spain permitted the use of African slaves to work them. On the whole, the tropics were so unappealing that merchants didn't want to live in the ports of Veracruz or Acapulco; they simply set up tents on the beaches to await the arrival of the annual Spanish or Manila galleons. The Yucatán was hot, too, but unlike Veracruz, it had more than enough Maya Indians for labor. But it had no silver mines or good soil for growing wheat, so the Spaniards settled it only sparsely, leaving most of the land to traditional Indian cornfields. Here Mayas with the desire to live independently could find refuge. English pirates, too, found good hiding places along the isolated Caribbean coast.

The discovery of silver and gold could make any region attractive. The thinly populated northern regions would suddenly burst with activity when a strike was made. Not only did golddiggers race to the frontier, but hacendados created ranches to supply them. After its great silver strikes, Zacatecas became the third-largest city in New Spain early in the 17th century; only the capital and Puebla were larger. It would be joined by other silver cities, Guanajuato, Taxco, and San Luis Potosí among them, changing what had been considered by the Aztecs to be barbarian deserts into wealthy enclaves.

The viceroyalty of New Spain administered a vast territory that ranged from Panama to California and included some Caribbean islands as well as the Philippines. A few regions, such as the Philippines, were independently administered by *audiencias*. Some regions never were

| Comparative Chart of Spanish Populations* | | | |
| --- | --- | --- | --- |
| Region | Year | Total Population | Percentage of Spaniards |
| Mexico City | 1794 | 104,760 | 50.3 |
| Puebla | 1777 | 71,366 | 25.6 |
| Tlaxcala | 1794 | 59,158 | 13.7 |
| Oaxaca | 1794 | 411,336 | 6.5 |
| Yucatán | 1780 | 210,472 | 7.9 |
| New Spain | 1810 | 5,764,731 | 18.6 |

*-From Farriss (1984, 65)

settled, leaving great territories to be usurped by other European powers (SEE maps on pages 84 and 103). Although some ports in California, essential stops on the China trade route, were settled in the 18th century, Baja California had only a few impoverished Jesuit missions. The colony in Santa Fe wasn't supported by any settlement in southern New Mexico, however, nor did any chain of Spanish villages connect it with California. Even where there were settlements, communications among them could be difficult and resources nonexistent. These areas were barely integrated into New Spain, which administered them. As Friar Alonso de Benavides (1630) described life in the New Mexican pueblos, 1,800 very long miles from the capital, "five and six years were wont to pass without royal officials bethinking themselves about us ... and god only knows what it costs to remind them."

## Spain Regulates the Economy

The colony of New Spain was to be managed for the benefit of Spain. All traded items had to be approved by Spain and sent on Spanish ships—a severe burden given that the Spanish galleons sailed in protected convoy only once a year. Commerce with foreign governments was prohibited. Protectionism was unquestioned policy, preventing the free development of industries that competed with those in Spain. Usually items for domestic consumption were permitted—from wheat and mutton to handpainted majolica ceramics, while royal monopolies on gunpowder, silk, mercury for mining, tobacco, and cochineal guaranteed considerable income for the Crown and its merchants.

## The Hacienda

Initially the Spaniards had taken from the Indians whatever they could sell abroad and what they needed for their own comfort and sustenance, relying on the indigenous patterns of agriculture and industry to support them. Bishops were happy with mitres made by Aztec featherworkers; settlers found they could convert the native dye, cochineal, into Europe's most fashionable red tint—used also to dye the uniforms of the British redcoats worn against American independence fighters. Other native products made their way around the world: vanilla-flavored chocolate became the drink of Spanish royalty; maize found immediate popularity in Africa and the Middle East. The tomato and peanut, however, took longer to gain popularity. Tobacco took off more than any foodstuff: within a century, it was distributed and grown around the world.

The systems of tribute labor and *encomienda* that had at first sustained New Spain were inadequate once royal edicts had limited their scope and once the number of settlers grew. Also, as wealthy as the *encomienda* had made some Spaniards, it required great numbers of Indians to be productive, numbers that epidemics made nonexistent. Tribute had its limitations as well, if there were not enough Indians to contribute—and besides, the Crown wanted most of the tribute for itself. By the end of the 16th century, these early institutions no longer were adequate to supply the colony with foodstuffs, or support the more recent settlers.

The Spaniards were forced to become involved in shaping the economy of New Spain, and they shaped it to their Old World tastes. With Indian depopulation, there was less resistance to Spanish takeovers of land. Small estates were sometimes legitimately purchased and sometimes granted by the Crown; they also were seized from the Indians. In pursuit of the Spanish ideal of gentlemanly land ownership, many small plots were consolidated into huge estates called haciendas. Instead of indigenous maize and turkeys, wheat was planted and European livestock bred. Friars introduced the first olive groves and vineyards, but these eventually were prohibited by a monopolistic Spain that exploited the captive market for its own wines and oils.

At first, the cattle, sheep, and goats grazed primarily in the densely populated central areas, exhausting formerly rich agricultural lands.

The raising of livestock carried such prestige in the home country, however, that it was a preferred occupation in the New World: not only was there profit in exporting hides to Spain for leather but considerable status as well. Because cattle grazing didn't require a lot of workers, the hacienda owners with their silver spurs and wide-brimmed hats, and the chap-protected *vaqueros* (cowboys) soon found their more proper niche in the less populated grasslands near the mines of the north, where "Texas" longhorns thrived. Herds of 150,000 roamed the frontier regions. One family ranch extended over 11 million acres.

## Debt Peonage

Despite the introduction of plows and pack animals into New Spain, the agricultural haciendas flourished only where there was sufficient Indian labor. Under the New Laws, the hacendados had to appeal to Indians to work their land by paying them. Even under the continued *repartimiento* system, the "tribute" labor required for public works and the demonstrated needs of the colony, there was pay involved, if sometimes only a pittance. The natives could be forced into *repartimiento* for only a limited number of days each year, and each day was to begin at dawn and end before dusk so that the work didn't disrupt the Indians' own farming in support of their families. Such was the new, more humanitarian *repartimiento* system promulgated by Spain.

Practice, however, was another matter. The restraints on exploiting Indian labor were rarely observed—their lack of implementation provides, instead, a typical example of the discrepancy between royal word and colonial deed. The local *corregidores* made much of their income through their management of *repartimiento* labor in favor of the local hacendados. The abuses became so bad that agriculture was eliminated from the labor drafts under *repartimiento* in 1630. The hacendados learned that few Indians would voluntarily work for scandalously low wages. A solution was soon found, however, and along with it a new form of enslavement: debt peonage. Indians, promised generous sums of money paid in advance, were enticed to work on the estates. Many found it impossible to work off their debts, especially when they were forced to buy food and goods at inflated prices at the only nearby store: the one owned by the hacendado. And it wasn't unheard of to rig the accounts in the hacendado's favor. Not legally permitted to leave the hacienda with outstanding debts, the Indians were forced to work until their deaths. Their debts were inherited, unfortunately, bringing other family members into peonage.

# THE MIXTECA AND COCHINEAL

In the Sierra Mixteca change was drastic, but under native control. Thanks to powerful caciques such as Gabriel de Guzmán (see page 94), the Mixtec never gave up the right to their traditional lands, though they did use them in ways that were profitable to Spain and its settlers. Two Spanish enterprises were silk production and sheep grazing—the Sierra Mixteca was the only region where Indians owned more sheep than the Spaniards. And even when the silk industry died out at the end of the 16th century (due to competition from the Far East), the native red cochineal dye enabled the Mixtecs to flourish for centuries more.

Cochineal, tiny insects that live on prickly pear cactus, were cultivated, then dried and crushed to produce the dye. Cochineal had been traded by the Mixtecs in pre-Hispanic times and paid to the Aztecs in tribute. Under Spain, production increased dramatically for the burgeoning textile industry in Europe, and the dyestuff became the most valuable export after silver and gold. Some said the Mixtecs—at least the Mixtec caciques and cacicas (women chiefs, who were among the wealthiest individuals in all of Oaxaca)—were wealthier under Spain than their preconquest ancestors had ever been. By controlling their own lands and the production of major commodities, the Mixtecs were unusual among indigenous communities in that they never labored directly for the Spaniards, who were too few to take control beyond tribute and tax demands. Through the Mixtecs' participation in the colonial economy, Oaxaca became one of the most important regions in New Spain, and by 1797 its capital was the third-largest city.

## Mining

*I went to a mine called the Trinity ... Respecting its wealth, persons worthy of belief who know the region [of Pachuca] told me that in ten years this mine has produced forty million pesos, with nine hundred to a thousand men working daily.*

■

Gemilli Carreri, 1697 (reported in Charles Cumberland 1968, 84)

Agriculture was New Spain's primary economic endeavor: maize production alone often exceeded silver in total value. Yet it was the mines, not the corn, which preoccupied the Crown. Gold, and especially silver, were produced in extraordinary quantities. During the colonial period, the equivalent of $2.25 million worth of silver and gold were extracted. In the 18th century, Mexico produced as much silver as the rest of the world combined. Spain gained so much wealth from the mines—it received approximately 20 percent of the value of all precious metal production in taxes, fees, the royal *quinto* (or fifth), etc.—that it foresook its own moral principles in regard to them. Even after *repartimiento* officially ended for farm labor, it was condoned for the mines despite the high death rates. For 12 hours a day, workers descended into the damp and dangerous mine shafts—the one called "the mouth of hell" in Guanajuato was 2,000 feet deeper than any mine in the world—returning with 200, even 300, pounds of ore on their backs. Working conditions led to labor unrest and rebellions, and the mines had difficulty meeting production schedules. Eventually market forces, not the Crown, eliminated *repartimiento* labor in the mines: rising prices for silver encouraged the mining companies to pay adequately for much needed skilled labor. Once properly paid, workers were in plentiful supply.

## The Social Classes

A social caste system based primarily on race existed in New Spain and was reinforced by law. At the pinnacle was the white ruling class, comprising 1 million of the entire population of 7 million by the end of the colonial period. Distinctions were made among the whites, however. Preferences were given to those born on the Iberian peninsula of Spain *(peninsulares)*, even though the vast majority returned to Spain after serving their terms of office. In fact, their lack of engagement in New Spain was the reason for their royal preference. To preserve their absolute loyalty to the Crown, viceroys and other royal officials usually served limited terms, often no more than five years, and they were banned from owning property (though some managed to make a considerable fortune during their terms) or marrying in the colony without special permission (though fewer than 10 percent were women).

These *peninsulares* ranked higher than Mexican-born Spaniards called criollos (Creoles): the pale-skinned children of conquistadores and permanent settlers found a guaranteed high position in society regardless of how lowly their ancestors' status had been in Spain. However, Creoles could not hold royal office, because the Crown suspected that their place of birth tarnished their loyalty.

Only whites were permitted to wear European silk finery, ride horses, and be called *damas* (ladies) and *caballeros* (gentlemen). So important

| Racial Composition of New Spain, 1810 | | |
|---|---|---|
| | Number | Percentage |
| Indians | 3,676,281 | 60 |
| Whites | | |
| *Peninsulares* | 15,000 | 0.3 |
| Creoles | 1,092,367 | 18 |
| Mestizos | 704,245 | 11 |
| Mulattoes and *zambos* | 624,461 | 10 |
| Black | 10,000 | 0.2 |
| Total Population | 6,122,354 | |
| Based on Meyer & Sherman (1983, 218) | | |

was it to pretend to be pure white, and so unlikely was that to be the case in New Spain, that the Crown would certify all Indian or African blood "extinguished" in a family—for a fee.

Beneath the Spanish upper stratum were the peoples of color. Spain developed an elaborate terminology for what it perceived as 16 relevant permutations of European, African, and American peoples—mulattoes (African and white), and *zambos* and *coyotes* (Indian and African), among them. The African slaves often labored under the worst conditions in the tropics and the mines, but as personal property they seldom were concentrated together in sufficient numbers to maintain a separate group identity. One runaway slave, Yanga, established a stronghold of 80 individuals near Veracruz; after defeating royal troops, he forced the viceroy to recognize their freedom, permitting them to establish the town of San Lorenzo de los Negros. On the whole, the numbers of African slaves diminished over the years to 6,000 by 1800, as they either escaped to remote Indian regions or bought their freedom (permissible under Spanish law). The number of individuals with some African heritage, that is mulatto or *zambo*, was over 600,000.

And, of course, there were the more numerous mestizos, a group that would continue to grow throughout the country's history. Immediately after the conquest, both church and Crown encouraged intermarriage; under the more rigid colonial society, they simply looked the other way in regard to concubinage—mestizos often were the illegitimate children of Spanish men and Indian women. The mestizos predominated where the Spaniards did: in central Mexico. Although legally lower than the whites, they were subject to the same taxes and military duties even if they were not granted the same privileges. Their treatment varied. Some, born to the famous, such as Cortés's illegitimate son, were treated as aristocracy. Others were ranchers and soldiers on the frontier; and still others, in a social intermediary role, supervised native laborers for Spanish overlords. Many were simply poor and considered inferior. Some found their greatest opportunities as vagabonds and thieves who prowled the countryside.

Below the mestizo but above the slaves and with protections not granted to the Africans were the Indians, the largest class of all. Although considered wards of the Crown and church, Indians suffered abominably whether because of debt peonage or mine labor. At least one half of Indian children died in their first year; 75 percent died in early infancy. Excluded from formal education, their lot became that of illiterate and abjectly poor laborers and peasants. Of course, there were interesting exceptions, and the harshness of their fate varied according to region and position in native society. In fact, the pre-Columbian class structure, divided between a ruling native aristocracy and commoners, survived the centuries in many traditional villages and was inadvertently reinforced by viceregal recognition of local caciques.

## CACIQUE AND COMMONER IN THE SIERRA MIXTECA

Caciques, chosen from the Indian nobility, inherited their position. In the flourishing Oaxaca region of the Sierra Mixteca, they also inherited wealth. Cacique Guzmán of Yanhuitlán, descendant of the pre-Columbian leader 8 Deer, had 980 acres of farm and grazing land, and many houses and animals—more than owned by any Spaniard—and a salary of 400 pesos plus the tribute due him from his people for the administrative services he rendered. By contrast, most commoners left only a shack, a small piece of land, and a few animals to their descendants. Some among the Mixtecs accumulated a bit more: the 1710 will of Domingo Ramos left farmlands, an adobe house, a storage chest with key, a bed, a skirt, a quilt, 21 mares, cloth, some silver, and what appears to be a pre-Columbian preference for green feathers—nearly 1,200 of them (Spores 1984, 116).

## The Church and Culture

In Spain, the religious orders were primarily charged with education, just as they were in the conversion of the peoples of Mexico. Their responsibilities also included the first generation of Creoles, whose conquistador fathers were mostly uneducated. The high status of Creoles in New Spain required that they be educated, and the religious community taught them in seminaries and colleges; in Spanish communities of any size, the Jesuits and Augustinians provided primary school education. During the colonial period, the University of Mexico granted 4,000 undergraduate degrees and 1,000 postgraduate ones, training the doctors, scientists, priests, and lawyers of New Spain.

Creole education (and primarily that of the males) became the only educational preoccupation of the established colony. By 1800 there were only 10 primary schools in New Spain. Indian schools, even the famous Franciscan college of Santa Cruz de Tlatelolco where Aztec nobles were taught theology and rhetoric, did not last beyond the 16th century. Mestizos and Indians were banned from most professions including the law, although like much else in colonial life, there were always exceptions.

Even in the trades, there was considerable discrimination. Initially the friars had taught Indians how to paint Renaissance murals from copy books and had trained them in European trades: blacksmithing, tailoring, carpentry. And they had engaged them in constructing the first church with a true vault. As time went on, the whites took control of the trades and often permitted only themselves to rise to the rank of master craftsman.

The skill of the artisans in New Spain, even when they were not granted master status, can best be judged by the quality of the approximately 12,000 churches built during the colonial period—most of them finely frescoed or carved, all adorned with elaborate altarpieces and silver chalices, and fitted with lavishly embroidered vestments. Their style varied according to the fashions in Spain, beginning with the Renaissance and Spanish plateresque style of the 16th century and evolving into 17th-century baroque. Although European artists provided inspiration for the colony—such as the Spanish painting tradition of Francisco de Zubarán and Bartolomé Murillo—the peninsular styles were often interpreted according to the colony's own needs and preferences. The open chapels of the 16th century (SEE page 67), for example, and the exuberant ultrabaroque style, called Churrigueresque (SEE page 105), is another local development that resulted in some of the finest buildings in 18th-century Mexico. Such artistic bounty, sustained over several centuries, was the work of thousands of anonymous artists, both Indian and mixed race.

The church was not only the educator of New Spain, but also the great patron of colonial art. And it had the money to sustain such creative and lavish outpourings, having been the beneficiary of royal land grants and

*The old Basilica of the Virgin of Guadalupe (ca. 1700). Patron saint of Mexico and the favorite of the poor, the Virgin's shrine attracts an estimated 14 million pilgrims annually, more than either the Vatican or Lourdes.* (Courtesy of the Mexican Ministry of Tourism)

church tithes as well as bequests from everyone from Mixtec caciques to wealthy Creoles. It would eventually own half the land in Mexico.

> There are no more devout people in the world toward the Church and clergy. In their lifetime they strive to exceed one another in their gifts to the cloisters of nuns and friars. Some erect altars ... worth many thousand ducats ... others at their death leave to them two or three thousands ducats for an annual stipend.
>
> ■
>
> Thomas Gage, 1648 (1981, 70)

Because of the church, Mexico was left the legacy of two of its greatest colonial painters. Miguel Cabrera (1695–1768), a mestizo born in Oaxaca and abandoned to an orphanage, became the most popular baroque painter in Mexico (see portrait on page 98) and a favorite of the archbishop. His contemporary, Juan Correa (c. 1645–1716), son of a freed African slave and a mulatto physician from Spain, was one of the most prolific painters of his age, contributing many works to the Mexico City cathedral. Given Mexico's artistic heritage, it was appropriate that when the Academy of San Carlos was established in 1785, it granted admission to artists of all races.

The introduction of the printing press in 1537 enriched the cultural life of the colony. Even though there was no newspaper until 1805, weekly gazettes and literary reviews were published. Fifteen thousand books (all passing the Inquisition's censorial review) were printed in Mexico during the colonial period. The first book published was a bilingual one in Nahuatl and Spanish by Bishop Zumárraga; others were written in a total of nine different native languages, and most books were devoted to religious topics. Books were imported as well, and Juan de Palafox y Mendoza (1600–59), who served both as bishop of Puebla and viceroy, collected a personal library of 43,000 volumes, the largest in the Americas.

The cultural life of Mexico City created two outstanding literary figures: Sor Juana Inés de la Cruz (1651–95), the great Mexican poet, and her friend Carlos de Sigüenza y Góngora (1645–1700), a historian, scientist, mathematician, and poet. The latter wrote an ode to the Virgin of Guadalupe and a history of pre-Columbian civilization, yet, like most of his class, held the native peoples in contempt.

The friars introduced sacred music into the colony from the earliest days, by training the Indians for the church choirs (and exempting them from tribute when they participated) and teaching them to make European instruments. The Indians not only made the instruments and performed, they also composed church music and recorded it on choir-

## SOR JUANA INÉS DE LA CRUZ

**B**orn in Mexico and of illegitimate birth, Sor Juana was the first great poet of the postconquest Americas and one of the most esteemed baroque poets in the world, as well as an early champion of women's rights. Her beauty and genius for learning made her a favorite of the viceregal court, but instead of marrying she joined a nunnery—the only institution in that era in which women could devote themselves to intellectual pursuits: "for it seemed to me no cause for a head to be adorned with hair and naked of learning," wrote Sor Juana in "La Respuesta" (translated by Margaret Sayera Peden, 30).

In an age when most girls were taught needlepoint and ladylike deportment, Sor Juana composed all kinds of poetry (including some in Nahuatl and others in the language of nearby African slaves), wrote plays (one based on Greek and Aztec mythologies), and essays (in one, "La Respuesta," she defended the right of women to education and culture). Today she is an icon of Mexican culture and an inspiration to contemporary writers.

Portrait of Sor Juana Inés de la Cruz painted by Miguel Cabrera in 1750

sheets. Later in the colonial period, Creoles composed chamber music and operas (Manuel Zumaya's *La Partenope,* performed in 1711, was the first). Every element of society enjoyed more popular music, from the African marimba and Spanish-introduced fandangos and guitar ballads to Indian festival dances and flute-and-drum music. Wrote Thomas Gage in 1648, "I dare be bold enough to say the people are drawn to their churches more for the delight of the music than for any delight in the service of God."

## The Spanish Legacy

By 1700 New Spain had been transformed from the land of the Aztec and Maya to that of an exotic European colony. Cochineal dye was produced near fields of grazing sheep, wheat spread through the central highlands, and cornfields were everywhere. The people, too, were increasingly mixed: Africans with Indians and Europeans along the coasts; Europeans and Indians in every town. Indian myths and language infused the poetry of even the highest classes. The wheeled cart slowly replaced human carriers and canoes; the burro took the burden off native carriers. The Catholic domain was, nonetheless, a cultural patchwork: at its most rural recesses, indigenous traditions remained unassimilated, contrasting with the Spanish cattle ranches and European cities. The Spanish caste system spread illiteracy, racism, and official corruption through the land, setting one group against the others.

Although most indigenous peoples were reduced to illiteracy, the Yucatec Maya scribes continued their pre-Columbian tradition of recording the events of their people in books of the katuns. The books, written in Yucatec but no longer in hieroglyphs, were kept secret from the Spanish world throughout the colonial period. Sometimes the words are unforgettable reminders of the changed world of the indigenous peoples of Mexico:

> Then the Indians had no sickness; they had no aching bones; they had no burning chest. They had no abdominal pain; they had no consumption; they had no headache. At that time, the course of humanity was orderly. The foreigners made it otherwise.
>
> ■
>
> Book of the Chilam Balam of Chumayel, 17th century
> (translated by Ralph Roys)

# 6

# THE BOURBON REFORMS
# AND INDEPENDENCE
# (1700–1821)

*The condition as conquerors of a conquered land, makes them
[the Spaniards] the first inhabitants, the preferred and the
privileged of all America; and woe to us, woe to the peninsula,
and woe to the Indies the day we lose our ascendancy, source
and sole shield of obedience and subordination.*

■

*Merchants Guild of Mexico to the Spanish Cortes, 1811*
*(translated by Stein & Stein)*

The Enlightenment brought changes to New Spain in the last century of colonial rule. A new faith in science and reason led the
Bourbon monarchy to modernize the administration of the colonies
and to squeeze out yet more profits for Spain. As the century progressed
to embrace both the American and French revolutions, increasingly
radical ideas filtered into New Spain—ideas about social equality and
self-governance. After a long and destructive battle for independence,
the Spanish colony would become the free country of Mexico.

## The Last of the Spanish Hapsburgs

In 1700, the Hapsburg control of Spain's monarchy ended. Given the
devastated condition of the empire, the end should have come sooner.
Too many battles—and too many defeats—had bankrupted the country
and resulted in the loss of considerable European territory. The former
war machine had become so pitiful that soldiers ran from battle. The
nation chosen by God to rule the New World, suffered English, French,
and Dutch colonies on American soil.

# CAN EK, 1697

A Maya dynasty, said to descend from the ruler of the great Yucatec city of Chichén Itzá, ended around the same time as the Spanish Hapsburgs. The Itzá, having fled to the remote Petén jungle, reestablished themselves on the islands of Lake Petén Itzá, now in Guatemala. Their numbers swelled to 25,000 with Maya refugees from Spanish rule. These Maya painted their bodies red and black and tattooed their faces—all forbidden by the early friars. They built stone temples and colonnaded palaces, they worshiped the old gods, followed rituals dictated by their hieroglyphic books, and lived under the rule of the Can Ek dynasty that demanded, and received, tribute from Maya in Spanish-controlled areas of the Yucatán peninsula. After 200 years in the New World, the Spaniards finally forged a trade route through the region. They captured the last Can Ek and destroyed the Itzá kingdom of Tayasal—their guns being as effective against feather-decorated spears as they were under Cortés. The last Mesoamerican ruler became a symbol of resistance, his name taken by future Maya rebels.

For all its monopolies and protectionism, Spain was broke. Its preference for precious metals had led the empire to ignore its industrial development—a plentiful silver supply had made it too easy to purchase manufactured products from the rest of Europe. War, not investment in the nation's economic infrastructure, drained the treasury and forced Spain to borrow. In the end, two-thirds of its silver bullion went to pay off debts in foreign European banks. Spain had become a third-rate economic power.

In an enlightened age, Spain was intellectually stifled by the Holy Office of the Inquisition. In time of tolerance and scientific understanding, it was ruled by feeble-minded Charles II (1665–1700), called "The Bewitched." With his death in 1700, the Spanish Hapsburgs, too, came to their grueling end.

## Bourbon Reforms

Although most courts in Europe could make some claim as to their right to rule Spain, it was the French dynasty of the Bourbons that maneuvered Philip V (1701–46) onto the throne and successfully kept him there through the War of the Spanish Succession (1701–13).

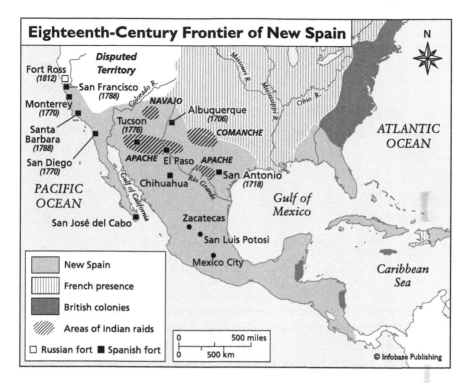

**Eighteenth-Century Frontier of New Spain**

N

Disputed Territory

Fort Ross (1812)
San Francisco (1788)
Monterrey (1770)
Santa Barbara (1788)
San Diego (1770)

NAVAJO
Albuquerque (1706)
Tucson (1776)
COMANCHE
APACHE  El Paso  APACHE
Chihuahua
San Antonio (1718)

ATLANTIC OCEAN

PACIFIC OCEAN

San José del Cabo
Zacatecas
San Luis Potosi
Mexico City

Gulf of Mexico

Caribbean Sea

New Spain
French presence
British colonies
Areas of Indian raids
☐ Russian fort  ■ Spanish fort

0      500 miles
0    500 km

© Infobase Publishing

To make their trading empire more efficient, the Bourbons streamlined the viceregal administration of New Spain, replacing 200 provincial *corregidores* and local mayors with 12 regional *intendentes*. The *intendentes* were well paid and experienced administrators—quite able to collect the taxes and tribute owed to the Crown. In an effort to preserve the frontier areas of New Spain against additional foreign encroachment—the Russians had ships in California waters; the French were in Louisiana—the Crown developed the first professional army of New Spain and established a colony in San Francisco and missions in Texas. To increase the volume of trade, it broke up old monopolies, permitting more ports to compete with Veracruz and Acapulco (such as Campeche and Progreso in Yucatán) and allowing direct trade among the various New World Spanish ports. The number of Manila galleons increased by two annually. Also some taxes were lowered to encourage silver mining.

Such modernization had its greatest impact under Charles III (1759–88). Silver production, assisted by new technology as well as royal incentives, rose from 3.2 million pesos in 1700 to 27 million pesos in 1804. Gold production tripled. Cochineal production also increased, becoming the second most valuable export and employing 30,000 Mixtecs. Agricultural products, especially sugarcane, increased

| Revenues from New Spain, 1786–1789 | |
| --- | --- |
| | Peso Value |
| Tobacco | 16,000,000 |
| Sales tax (includes silver) | 15,500,000 |
| Royal grant: silver and gold | 9,000,000 |
| Coinage | 6,000,000 |
| *Pulque* | 3,500,000 |
| Indian tribute | 3,500,000 |
| Customs duty | 3,000,000 |

Source: José Miranda, et al., *Historia de México* (1971, 263) as presented in Meyer & Sherman (1983)

in export value. And royal monopolies on domestic production of tobacco and *pulque,* the native alcoholic drink, further increased revenues. Tobacco revenues alone were greater than those from mining; those from *pulque* equaled all Indian tribute. At Veracruz, the more liberal trading policies attracted up to 500 ships in one year.

The reforms worked for Spain because the Bourbons sent able viceroys to Mexico. The rule of Antonio María de Bucareli (1771–79) was marked by peace and exceptional prosperity. Another great viceroy, the count of Revillagigedo (1789–94), created the first public transportation system and lowered the crime rate in the capital by lighting the streets.

## The Impact on New Spain

*Spain's concern was always Spain. . . .*

■

*Charles C. Cumberland (1968, 95)*

*The world's trade flourishes at the expense of the peoples of America and their immense labors, but the riches they draw from the bosom of the fertile earth are not retained.*

■

*Memoir to viceroy of Mexico, 1723
(translated by Stein & Stein)*

The reforms made Mexico the most prosperous of all Spain's colonies. And they made Spain wealthy. But they also had adverse repercussions in the colony. Many of the reforms benefited *peninsulares* and, indeed, increased emigration from Spain. This class of aristocrats expanded, at the expense of the Creoles. The regional administrators were all from Spain, save one, and, worse, they replaced creole local officials. The *pulque* and tobacco monopolies increased prices on locally consumed products and displaced those who had haciendas producing

# CHURRIGUERE/QUE ARCHITECTURE

*Churrigueresque church facade in Tepotzotlán*

The Mexican baroque style of the 18th century is the great cultural legacy of rich Creoles. The silver barons could afford to fund the construction of entire churches, and one, José de la Borda of Taxco, offered to pave the road from Veracruz to the capital in silver coins if the pope would agree to visit. The cities they graced with their mansions, gold altarpieces, and churches are part of-Mexico's artistic heritage. Historically preserved and protected, the cities— among them Guanajuato, Querétaro, Puebla, and Zacatecas —today attract considerable tourism.

them. The demand for productivity created more hardships for those who labored, and Indian tribute to the Crown was more vigorously collected.

In 1810 New Spain produced 75 percent of the profits from all of Spain's colonies. Yet Spain reinvested little of the monies, the bulk of which went to Europe or toward the administrative costs of other colonies. The end result was an economy as undeveloped as that of backward Spain. There were few manufactured goods. The roads that existed were better for pack animals than coaches—and there were too few of them. Many whites, living like the landed gentry of Europe, owned vast tracts of land, but too often worked very few acres. The land of vanilla and chocolate and cotton had to import these items because their production was so neglected. The country was regulated to an extreme: a ranchero needed a permit to slaughter his cattle for his own dinner table. Cattle and sheep roamed everywhere, in countless numbers, yet there was not enough wool or fresh beef.

Not only did waste and overregulation and corruption still exist after the Bourbon reforms, the racist class system remained undisturbed despite the egalitarianism of the Enlightenment. While the economy prospered in the Bourbon years, the wealth remained concentrated among the white population. Yet more than 80 percent of New Spain was nonwhite by the end of the century, and the squalor that most were destined to suffer couldn't have contrasted more sharply with the opulence of the ruling class: In 1784 300,000 Mexicans died from either famine or diseases related to malnourishment.

## The Creoles

Despite problems with the economy, the Creoles were not rebellious. They were conservative and supported the monarchy. And no wonder—as dependent as the economy was on Spain, it made most Creoles fabulously wealthy. Only the galling inequities in their treatment by the Spanish festered.

Given their number in the colony, the *peninsulares* were disproportionately wealthy. Yet the Creoles did very well. Count Regla, a mining baron and Creole, was the wealthiest man in 18th-century New Spain; over 30 years, the net profit from his silver mine in Pachuca alone was 15 million dollars. Count Bassoco, like 50 other fabulously rich Creoles, received his noble title after a generous contribution to the Crown—in his case, a gift of 200,000 pesos. Count Valenciana, although not the richest of the rich, earned 1 million pesos each year just from his famous silver mine in Guanajuato. Merchants and ranchers made their fortunes, too. In the north, hacendados had immense landholdings for their herds. The Sánchez Navarro family estate—the largest in the New World—was about the size of Portugal. The Creoles traveled and studied in Europe and took on the high styles of that continent. They built ornate palaces for themselves at home and contributed to the building of entire Churrigueresque churches.

Wealth didn't entirely satisfy the New World aristocracy: resentment of the privileges of the *peninsulares* intensified. Phenomenally rich, many Creoles were like royalty themselves with their own mining and ranching kingdoms. They increasingly took pride in their Mexican heritage: their Spanish was peppered with Indian words, their chicken with chile. And they called themselves *"americanos."* The condescension of the Spanish-born toward these provincials rankled—especially when a *peninsular* originally came from the lower classes, as many did.

By mid-century, the Holy Office of the Inquisition could no longer keep out the pervasive ideas of the European Enlightenment—ideas about human rights versus the divine rights of kings, about liberty and social equality. Yet here the Creoles were treated like second-class citizens in their own country; the highest church and government positions were not open to them. A Creole village priest, for example, could make as little as 100 pesos, in contrast to a *peninsular* bishop's 100,000. The Bourbon reforms brought no new social and political opportunities—even at a time in which the United States gained its independence from Britain (1776) and the French Revolution (1789) overthrew the Bourbons.

## Political Ferment

The Creoles wanted more control over the future of New Spain, but few had any interest in upsetting the society that had so amply rewarded them. There were critiques of Spain—of the brutality of the conquest and centuries of colonial enslavement; there were satires on the more absurd aspects of Spanish rule. There were even foreign agitators, from newly independent France and the United States, who tried to bestir the Mexicans.

Only a few conspired for independence. Military officers, kept out of the highest ranks, and small merchants and bureaucrats gathered in "literary" societies that were fronts for their plots. Among the most radical were some parish priests who, finding themselves in the poorest regions, tended their Indian parishioners with the care of the most humanistic 16th-century friars.

Most Creoles, however, realized that their privilege and prestige resulted from the imperial system. They were satisfied to tinker with the colonial system, maintaining their loyalty to the Spanish monarchy but demanding equality with the *peninsulares* or, better yet, their replacement by the Creoles themselves.

The nonprivileged classes heard little or nothing about the Enlightenment. Their own lot was itself enough to foment rebellions—and they did occur, but usually were not organized well enough to spread beyond a local community. By the 18th century the Indian population was once again on the increase, intensifying frictions over land use. On the whole, the native peoples were so downtrodden that some Spaniards deluded themselves into thinking they were naturally servile. Economic growth encouraged some Indians to leave their traditional communities in order to participate in the broader society and some managed to do well, taking on Spanish customs and language. Even the caciques took on more Spanish customs and were expected to be, at the very least, bilingual. Frequently employed as mediators or merchants within the traditional communities because of their bilingualism, these Indians were often the worst oppressors of their own people.

Many *castas*, or mixed-race individuals, were able to find more remunerative work and responsibility in the expanding Bourbon economy.

---

# CAN EK REBORN

One Indian rebellion was led by the shaman Jacinto Canek, who took the name of the legendary Maya leader. He was crowned king, he said, in order to lead his people out of their servitude through armed revolt against the Spaniards. His message appealed to many in the Yucatán and terrified the white population until royal forces entered Canek's village in 1761 and killed half of the 1,200 armed Maya assembled there. Canek escaped, but was later captured, tortured to death, and cremated. Some rebels were drawn and quartered; others, after being flogged, had one ear cut off to mark them. Canek's village was razed in the hope that, like the leader himself, no trace of the event would be left.

The caste system prevented them from being truly assimilated into the society, however. At times light-skinned mestizos and mulattoes "passed" as whites; others successfully bribed priests to register their children as Creoles; still others maneuvered into the trades, the clergy, and the burgeoning militia. For most, their color meant a lifetime of resentment and exploitation.

The increasing numbers of nonwhites living free, out of debt peonage and slavery, would have made natural allies for the more liberal Creoles—if they had so wished. For most Creoles, the entire class system could be endangered by such alliances, and so there was little interest in organizing broader protests.

Despite the lack of fervor for independence, political events in Europe made radical change a necessity. Charles IV (1788–1808), far from the wise monarch his father had been, permitted the plunder of the colonies. In 1804 the charitable funds of New Spain, belonging to the church and used not only to help the poor of Mexico but also to give credit to Creoles, were taken for the royal treasury to pay off European war debts. The church had to call in all mortgages, destroying some Creoles financially; clergy no longer were able to respond to even the most disastrous circumstances of needy parishioners. The church was already festering, because Charles III had expelled the Jesuits in 1767 and confiscated all their property, closing schools and frontier missions.

Charles IV was destructive of Spain, too, where uprisings led him in 1808 to abdicate in favor of his son, Ferdinand VII. The turmoil continued when Napoléon I forced both Spanish Bourbons, Charles and Ferdinand, into exile and placed his brother Joseph Bonaparte on the throne in 1808. Various rival governments, or juntas, in support of the Spanish monarchy took charge in areas outside Napoléon's control. Without the monarchy, the Mexican Creoles thought they should rule themselves; the *peninsulares* believed otherwise. The tug of war in both Spain and Mexico created instability: Mexico had four viceroys in just two years. Worse, the policies of the Spanish juntas were despotically conservative in regard to the colonies: they ordered the arrest in the Americas of anyone agitating for reform; the Holy Office of the Inquisition became a spying arm of the government, rather than an enforcer of religious standards; and important individuals were arrested and deported. The Creoles no longer hoped that their political fortunes would improve through peaceful means. By mid-1810, Creoles in every major city had formed secret societies in opposition to the government.

# Miguel Hidalgo

*My children ... will you free yourselves?*

■

*Father Miguel Hidalgo y Costilla, 1810*

In 1810 when Miguel Hidalgo gave his famous Grito de Dolores, the cry to action that is reenacted every September 16 in modern Mexico, he gave Creole leadership to the disorganized stirrings of the mestizos and other *castas*, the Indians, and other disenfranchised masses of Mexico.

Considered the father of the Mexican nation, Miguel Hidalgo y Costilla (1753–1811) was born to a Creole family on an hacienda in the province of Guanajuato where his father was manager. He was sent to a Jesuit College in what is now Morelia, but his education was soon interrupted by the expulsion of the Jesuits. Having learned a lesson in imperial whimsy, Hidalgo enrolled in another college and received his degree from the University of Mexico in 1774. He was ordained as a priest in 1778. Eventually he became rector of the prestigious college of San Nicolás in Morelia, founded by the 16th-century utopian Vasco de Quiroga. Like Quiroga, he studied Indian languages, but unlike Quiroga he soon was investigated by the Inquisition (1800), and although nothing against him could be proved, he lost his position: he was too much a child of the Enlightenment, reading banned literature, questioning church dogma—and keeping a mistress. He ended up in the village of Dolores, where he tried to improve the economic well-being of his parishioners. It was in Dolores that he met others who would become the martyrs of independence.

Hidalgo belonged to a secret society in Querétaro that included Ignacio Allende and Juan de Aldama, both officers in the army; a former *corregidor* of Querétaro and his wife, the Mexican patriot Josefa Ortiz de Domínguez; a postal clerk; and others. Until his famous proclamation catapulted him into the position of leadership, Hidalgo was a minor figure in the central Mexican Committee of Correspondence conspiring for independence. His particular group gathered arms for an insurrection set for December. But when, on September 13, 1810, Josefa Ortiz de Domínguez let out the news that royal officials were arresting those involved, the uprising was prematurely launched.

Receiving the news, Allende, Aldama, and Hidalgo managed to meet at the small town of Dolores. They decided to go forward with the insurrection. In the predawn hours of September 16, Hidalgo tolled the

*Father Hidalgo with torch of independence in* Carnaval de Ideologías *(1937–39), a mural in the Guadalajara Government Palace painted by José Clemente Orozco*

bells to call his Indian and mestizo parishioners to church. His cry for independence went well beyond narrow Creole interests; he attacked the conquistadores' confiscation of Indian land and declared an end to tribute. Later, Hidalgo would also declare an end to slavery. He gave the rallying cry in the name of the dark-skinned Virgin of Guadalupe. In response to his "Viva Guadalupe!," his parishioners are said to have shouted "Death to the *peninsulares!*"

The ferocity of the rebellion unleashed in Dolores caught everyone by surprise—even Hidalgo, who suddenly was swept to the forefront of the movement. He had naively thought the mere threat of insurrection would lead everyone to the reasonable position of agreeing to independence. Marching under the banner of the Mexican Virgin of Guadalupe, his forces swelled with the oppressed, armed only with the peasant's machete, the miner's pick, the bow and arrow, and, occasionally, a gun. By the time he captured what is now Morelia, his forces numbered 60,000—and thousands more were fighting with Allende farther north. More poor joined Hidalgo at Morelia, until their numbers swelled to 80,000. Instead of well-disciplined soldiers led by army professionals, the insurrection was fought by a barely controllable mob and an overwhelmed priest. Said Lucas Alamán, an eyewitness, "The pillage was more merciless than if done by a foreign army" (1943: vol 1, 403).

The insurrectionists swept through the countryside, confiscating land and livestock—some ate the first beef of their lives. Wherever resistance was met, they attacked viciously. In Guanajuato the hundreds of frightened *peninsular* families who had gathered together in the granary were slaughtered. And even though 2,000 rebels were killed by royalist guns and grenades, they kept fighting. After their victories, towns were sacked, markets stripped of food, baroque mansions looted of silver. The capital remained untouched, because Hidalgo, fearing the worst bloodbath imaginable, didn't invade despite Allende's urging; historians believe such an invasion could have achieved independence early in the fighting. Yet in just over a month the rebels controlled much of central Mexico, from Guadalajara and Zacatecas to the Pacific and Gulf coasts.

Despite their stunning victories, the insurgents soon suffered major setbacks. The royalists, under General Félix Calleja, regrouped and regained Guanajuato and other cities. Calleja fought mercilessly and executed innocents as gruesomely as the revolutionaries did. In March 1811, Hidalgo and Allende were captured in Texas and returned to Calleja. Both were executed, and their decapitated heads were hung from the granary walls in Guanajuato for 10 years as a macabre warning to the public.

## José María Morelos

The popularity of the independence movement diminished. Some poor were content to work the land they had "liberated." Creole support plummeted: fearful of the attacks on personal property and of slogans promising social change, the privileged shifted their allegiance. They realized only too well that for the masses, there was little difference in appearance between the *peninsulares* and themselves—and little difference in their exploitation of workers.

Not surprisingly, the movement that continued was under the leadership of a mestizo, the priest José María Morelos y Pavón, who had been recruited to the cause by Hidalgo. A military genius with clear political objectives, Morelos brought together a fighter force that included students and peasants, military officers, and Indian caciques. Each wore the badge of the Virgin of Guadalupe who, in addition to being the protector of the poor, had become the symbol of a free Mexico. Morelos organized his soldiers into small bands well trained in guerrilla warfare. Gradually, they won enough territory, from Oaxaca to Tampico, to encircle and isolate the capital.

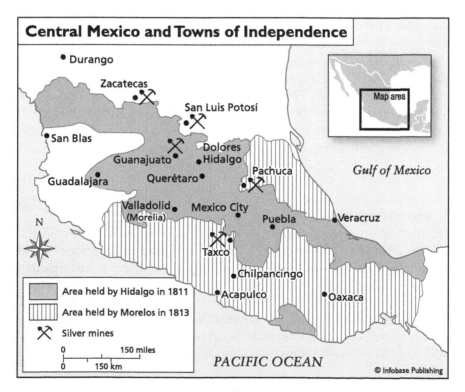

Central Mexico and Towns of Independence

In 1813, Morelos convened a constitutional convention to govern the liberated territories and alarmed the Creoles and clergy alike with his politics. He advocated the end of the caste system as well as equal rights for all regardless of race; he even recommended that church lands be redistributed among the poor. In independent Mexico, he said, "the only thing that will distinguish one American from another is vice and virtue" (Herrejón 1985, 133–134). Spain itself would champion such liberal ideas in a decade, but the conservative Creoles found them thoroughly objectionable. Moreover, Morelos extolled not European culture but rather the preconquest past, laying the foundation for a unified, and uniquely Mexican, nation.

> Spirits of Moctezuma, Cacamitzin, Cuauhtémoc Xicotencatl, Calzontzin! Take pride in this august assembly and celebrate this happy moment in which your sons have congregated to avenge your insults!
>
> ■
>
> José María Morelos, 1813 (translated by Charles Cumberland)

The royalist forces under the ruthless General Calleja once again succeeded in winning back cities. To guarantee a firm hand during the war, a revived Spanish monarchy made Calleja viceroy. Morelos was captured and executed in 1815, nearly ending the struggle for independence. Only a few continued the fight: Guadalupe Victoria (the nom de guerre of Félix Fernández), hiding out in the mountains above Veracruz, and Vicente Guerrero on the Pacific slopes. Most defected; others were pardoned. By 1816 the fighting was so sporadic that Spain felt safe enough to replace Calleja with a more moderate viceroy, and by 1819 offered amnesty to the insurgents.

## Independence

By 1820 Spain again controlled all the Mexican cities and most of the territory. Yet in a short time, with barely any bloodshed, Mexico would be independent. Under threat of a military coup, the restored Spanish monarchy was forced to function under a liberal constitution, which recognized the sovereignty of the people. The constitution permitted free speech and open trade and clipped the powers of the church and its vast properties—a common anticlerical position of the Enlightenment. Although Morelos was long dead, his specter seemed to haunt Mexican conservatives.

Finding Spain too liberal, the Creoles, even the most conservative, opted for independence. They were supported, and partially funded, by the church. Their modus operandi was a military coup, and their chosen leader was Agustín de Iturbide, a greedy and vain individual who had resigned from the royal army when accused of corruption. The Creoles' goal was to institute a constitutional monarchy with a member of Europe's royalty who would preserve their privileged position in Mexican society.

The Creoles convinced the viceroy to reinstate Iturbide in order to defeat Vicente Guerrero once and for all. Iturbide took his army to the state of what is now Guerrero and, instead of going to war with him, negotiated with the rightly suspicious Vicente Guerrero to join forces to fight for independence. On February 24, 1821, they signed the Plan of Iguala, a platform permitting all of Mexico's factions to agree. Above all, it declared independence for all people, whether of Indian, European, or African descent. In addition, it stated that the nation would be governed by a constitutional monarchy, headed by either King Ferdinand of Spain or some European prince. It also declared that the state religion would be Catholic, and no other, and guaranteed the properties of the church. Lastly, it stated that all citizens could be employed in any position without distinction other than merit. Iturbide came away with the necessary document for independence; he also managed to confiscate a silver shipment for Manila into his own safekeeping.

The plan appealed to conservatives and liberals alike. The viceroy, realizing that the army and most municipal officials supported the Plan of Iguala, resigned. Spain, forever hopeful, sent as a replacement Juan O'Donoju, a liberal Spaniard of Irish descent. He quickly realized that independence was to be a reality and met with Iturbide to ratify the plan. Iturbide negotiated one modification in what then became the Plan of Córdoba: in the event that a European prince could not be found to rule, an appropriate Mexican could be monarch.

On September 27, 1821, Iturbide marched into the capital with Vicente Guerrero and Guadalupe Victoria at his side. After too many years of wars and atrocities, Mexico was independent from Spain.

# 7

# YEARS OF CHAOS
# (1823–1876)

*Somber events engulf us. Although the revolution is over, its consequences keep us exposed to grave perils; various parties, some swollen by triumph, others bitter over defeat, divide our reborn society . . .*

■

El águila mexicana, 1823 (quoted in Stein & Stein 1970, 130)

**M**exican hopes that independence would bring a modernized economy and more egalitarian society were not realized in the next century. Instead, the legacy of the battle for independence was the increased importance of an unscrupulous military and a bankrupt treasury.

Feuds and class differences that had been matters of life and death during the fighting—between aristocratic Creoles and mestizos, between liberal anticlerics and the church, between monarchists and republicans, and rich and poor—remained unresolved. Worse, none of the social reforms hoped for by the masses fighting the war were instituted.

In its first 40 years, Mexico had more than 50 governments. Sometimes two or three different factions claimed the office simultaneously. One year there were as many as five changes in the presidency. The newly independent nation was ruled by military coups d'état, not a constitution; graft, not government. Taking advantage of the unsettled political situation, foreign governments intervened.

These disturbing times have left the Mexican consciousness with one of its greatest heroes, the first Indian president, Benito Juárez, as well as a fully developed distrust of its northern neighbor, the United States, to whom half of Mexican territory was lost. It also defined, though did not fully end, the power struggles between the church and the modern secular state.

## Emperor Iturbide

A significant misfortune for the new nation of Mexico was to have the disreputable Iturbide as its first leader. Joel Poinsett, a minister from the United States, described him as "distinguished for his immorality" in a society riddled with corruption. After staging an unruly demonstration in support of himself in the streets of the capital, Iturbide was able to bully the Creole-dominated congress into making him the emperor of Mexico.

Iturbide was to govern a fledgling but enormous nation, covering 1.73 million square miles from California through Central America to Panama (SEE map on page 103). Its borders with the United States to the north and Belize to the south were not clearly demarcated, however. And not all its territories had participated in the War of Independence: Some Central American governments had to be encouraged with the threat of invading troops to remain part of Mexico. Ferdinand VII of Spain had not completely accepted his expulsion and managed to keep troops on a fortress island in the Veracruz harbor. The United States was territory hungry, and both Great Britain and France were seeking special trade concessions.

As his first concern for leading such a vast nation plagued by so many foreign policy issues, the pompous ruler devoted himself to making elaborate plans for his coronation a few months later on July 21, 1822. A French baroness, former couturier to Napoléon, was hired to design costumes for the new emperor. A court etiquette was issued, outraging republican factions who deemed it inappropriate to be forced to kiss Iturbide's hand. A bankrupt nation issued new coins engraved with the emperor's portrait.

## Economic Legacy

Iturbide and his Creole supporters had thought that replacing the *peninsulares* in government would automatically rectify the ills of the Mexican economy. The profits would remain in Mexico, in Creole pockets, and the taxes would support the new government. They had overlooked the 75 million peso debt the country had incurred during the War of Independence. They hadn't factored in the loss of gold and silver currency the *peninsulares* would take with them as they fled the country. The mines themselves, near the primary battlegrounds for independence, were flooded and the machinery damaged, requiring considerable capital to return them to working order. Textile mills were closed because banditry and bad roads prevented the transport of cotton. Haciendas had been burned and sacked. Returning soldiers could not find jobs: as many as 20 percent of adult males were without work.

The colonial economy was destroyed. The first Mexican empire none-theless lavished money on Iturbide, granting him a million-peso bonus. Congress appropriated 80 percent of its revenues—more than the vice-royalty had spent during the independence wars—for the emperor's cronies, the military. Nothing was invested in restarting the economy: not even the bloated military made an effort to open the roads for com-merce. The country was at an economic impasse. When short of funds, the government attempted to borrow them, incurring more debt. When even those funds were insufficient, loans were decreed from the church or money confiscated from citizens.

It didn't take long for Iturbide to lose support. The devastated country-side could not properly provision the cities. The congress was outraged by Iturbide's arrest of enemies and censorship of the press—so the emperor dissolved it. Some Creoles, embarrassed by Iturbide's excesses, wanted a European prince installed as monarch, but many a confirmed monarchist joined the republican side. When a military coup forced the emperor to abdicate his majestic office only eight months after coronation, Mexico's debt was as remarkable as the disarray of its government.

## General Santa Anna

Mexico learned from the Iturbide interlude to distrust monarchies. A republic, governed by an elected congress and president, was established under the Constitution of 1824—a document that would be repealed and fought over, but returned to over time. Much to the chagrin of the mon-archists and centralists, this federalist constitution divided the Republic of Mexico into 19 states and four territories (excluding the provinces of Central America, which declared their own independence in 1823). Catholicism was the state religion and the only permitted religion. There were free press and free speech. Indian tribute was abolished, in law if not always in deed. By 1829 slavery was officially ended, too. In reality, the new political order had minimal impact on the majority of Mexicans who lived in rural isolation and for whom voting rights mattered little because they were illiterate and, often, did not speak Spanish.

Even under the republican regimes, military heroes of the Wars of Independence with no administrative experience, were elected to—or grabbed—the presidency. The first president, for example, was the rebel leader, Guadalupe Victoria. Uneducated, uncontrollably jealous of rivals, and unable to inspire the republic, he nonetheless did manage

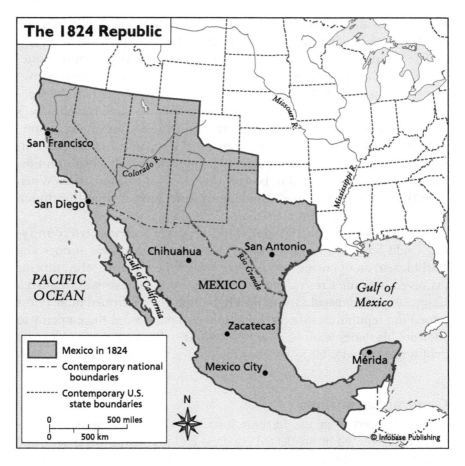

**The 1824 Republic**

San Francisco

Colorado R.

San Diego

*Missouri R.*

*Mississippi R.*

PACIFIC
OCEAN

*Gulf of California*

Chihuahua

San Antonio

*Rio Grande*

MEXICO

*Gulf of
Mexico*

Zacatecas

Mérida

Mexico City

Mexico in 1824
—·—·— Contemporary national
boundaries
-------- Contemporary U.S.
state boundaries

0          500 miles
0      500 km

N

© Infobase Publishing

to continue the bad economic policies of the empire by spending more money on the military than revenues could sustain. Many of these military bosses, called caudillos, kept their politics more local, ruling the countryside with their band of armed adherents and ready to make trouble when their interests were not served. They would usurp the power of all but a few presidents.

The most remarkable figure in this turbulent period was General Antonio López de Santa Anna (1794–1876). Repeatedly president of Mexico, yet disgraced almost as often, exiled, and, in the end, executed for treason, Santa Anna's political life spanned the first critical decades of Mexican Independence. His opportunistic vacillation between liberal and conservative causes, his constant engagement in military coups and foreign confrontations (he called himself the liberator of Mexico), his fine-tuning of political corruption, personified this era of anarchy.

Santa Anna first walked onto this historical stage under Iturbide. He was commander of Veracruz, charged with eliminating the sole remaining Spanish troops on an island fortress in Veracruz harbor. Instead, he declared against the unpopular Iturbide and formed an alliance with

*Antonio López de Santa Anna, a Creole born in the state of Veracruz, quickly found his niche in the military. Both as president and from behind the scenes, he controlled and disrupted Mexican politics from 1824 to 1855 and in the process made himself a millionaire. (Courtesy of the Bancroft Library)*

the old independence rebels, Guadalupe Victoria and Vicente Guerrero. After seeing the emperor depart Mexico, he returned to Veracruz to expel the Spaniards from their fortress in 1825.

Again and again Santa Anna issued pronouncements against various regimes. In 1829 he defeated 3,000 Spanish soldiers who had landed in Tampico on the Gulf coast in order to reconquer Mexico for Ferdinand VII. Finally he himself was elected president in 1833—he would hold office a total of 11 times—but instead of governing, he retreated to the sanctuary of his Veracruz hacienda and let his vice president, Valentín Gómez Farías, take care of the boring day-to-day details.

## Church Power Confronted

Gómez Farías typified the more liberal element of the Creoles. An anticleric, he subordinated the church and seized its properties for the greater welfare—an action that would repeatedly bring conservative reaction throughout the century. Like Morelos before him, Gómez Farías considered the wealth of the Catholic Church wasteful: indeed, its wealth was estimated at 180 million pesos when the total annual Mexican budget was only 13 million. The church was powerful, its clergy numerous, yet most priests resided in the cities, leaving themselves open to charges that they inadequately administered to the faithful in smaller towns and rural areas. Since the church was responsible for educating the populace, their absence from the countryside also contributed to illiteracy, legitimizing the call of liberals like Gómez Farías for secular education.

Gómez Farías also tried to bring the military under greater state control. He attempted to reduce its size and to eliminate its exemption from civil trials. In doing so he took on at least one too many powerful groups. President and General Santa Anna bestirred himself from his hacienda and once again proclaimed. This time he marched against his own vice president, dismissed the congress, suspended the federalist constitution, and assumed dictatorial powers in 1834.

A charismatic figure, Santa Anna was able to contemptuously disregard the constitution and desperate needs of his country. While the conservatives and liberals feuded over matters of substance, the president assumed the pomp and excessive show of a sultan. Having lost his leg in battle, he had it ceremoniously interred and enshrined in the presence of the entire cabinet and diplomatic corps. His greed and graft knew no limits during his last presidency when, assuming the title "His Most Serene Highness," he raided the treasury to finance lavish balls and build

# MEXICO CITY DURING A COUNTERREVOLT

anny Calderón de la Barca, the English wife of a Spanish diplomat, visited Mexico during the Santa Anna years and recorded her lively impressions in a diary. Here is her description of the capital during Santa Anna's military coup of 1840:

> . . . The chief danger to those who are not actually engaged in this affair, is from these bullets and shells, which come rattling into all the houses. We have messages from various people whom we invited to come here for safety, that they would gladly accept our offer, but are unwilling to leave their houses exposed to pillage, and do not dare to pass through the streets. . . . We were astonished this morning at the general tranquillity, and concluded that, instead of having attacked . . . the government was holding a parley . . . Innumerable carriages, drawn by mules, are passing along, packed inside and out, full of families hurrying to the country with their children and moveables. Those who are poorer, are making their way on foot—men and women carrying mattresses, and little children following with baskets and bird-cages (234–236).

an opera theater as ornate as any in Europe. His blatant disregard for the well-being of the nation culminated in the act that would bring about his final downfall: he sold the Mesilla Valley, 30,000 square miles in southern Arizona and New Mexico, to the United States (where it was called the Gadsden Purchase) in 1853 to pay for his extravagances.

## The Alamo

Santa Anna's legacy to his nation was more than corrupt government. His role in the battle for Texas resulted in great territorial losses to the United States. Not only did the president command the troops at the decisive battle of the Alamo, his policies precipitated the crisis. As a dictator, Santa Anna's sympathies were most naturally with the centralists. After the suspension of the federalist constitution in 1834, Mexico was reorganized into larger territories more directly under the control of the president. Various parts of the country, including Texas, agitated against these centralists shifts and had to be pacified by the army.

In the hope of limiting U.S. expansion into its colonies, Bourbon Spain had encouraged the settlement of Texas by favorable land-grant policies. The primary beneficiaries were Anglo-Americans from the United States who brought their slaves to till the fertile land and cultivate cotton. In exchange for nearly free land and initial tax exemptions, these settlers agreed to become Catholics and assume Mexican citizenship.

The land-grant system did at least part of what Spain expected: it settled Texas. Eventually, the immigrants outnumbered the Mexicans by more than 20,000 to 4,000. However, assimilation into Hispanic culture did not occur, and Anglos continued to speak English and practice the Protestant faith; cultural conflict between the groups were not uncommon. Centralism, however, incorporated Texas into a much larger, purely Mexican province, so that Anglo culture and economic interests were made subservient.

Before the outbreak of open rebellion, Mexico had seen the problems brewing in Texas. Mexico hoped that a by-product of outlawing slavery in 1829 would be to make Texas less attractive to U.S. citizens—it did allow Anglo-Texans a temporary exemption, however. In 1830, Mexico closed its borders to new immigrants but like today, the frontier between Mexico and the United States was extremely porous. Mexico also increased its customs duties on exports, greatly affecting Texan trade with the United States. There was also the threat of U.S. annexation: some private armies had already attempted to invade Texas. To protect its borders and territorial integrity, Mexico assigned more military units to the region.

Stephen Austin, son of the founder of the Anglo colony, protested both centralist policies and new customs regulations. Both liberal Mexicans and U.S. politicians encouraged him to throw off the dictatorship of Santa Anna. When the Mexican government learned Austin was advocating separation under the name of the Lone Star Republic and encouraging Texans to arm themselves, President Santa Anna sent army reinforcements. When Austin forced their surrender and departure from Texas, the president himself led 6,000 troops to Texas.

> ... *zealous in the fulfillment of my duties to my country, [I] declared that I would maintain the territorial integrity whatever the cost ... Stimulated by ... courageous feelings I took command of the campaign myself, preferring the uncertainties of war to the easy and much coveted life of the palace.*
>
> ■
>
> President Santa Anna, 1835 (1969, 49–50)

The rebel Texans, including Davy Crockett and Jim Bowie, barricaded themselves into the old Franciscan mission of the Alamo in San Antonio. General Santa Anna laid siege for several days. On March 6, 1835, his soldiers attacked the seemingly impassable walls and faced the heavy artillery of the Texans. Hundreds died while others broke through the walls. Government forces greatly outnumbered the Texans, and the government won, leaving not a single survivor.

A few weeks later another Mexican general surrounded the town of Goliad, forcing the Texan forces of Colonel James Fannin to surrender. Both sides understood that the Texans' rights as prisoners of war would be respected. But upon learning of the incident, Santa Anna ordered their execution as pirates.

More than the slaughter at the Alamo, the death of 365 prisoners galvanized public opinion in the United States. Supplies were sent. Volunteers joined the Texans. Within weeks, Sam Houston was in a position to strike back. The Mexican army was defeated, and Santa Anna was taken prisoner.

The peace treaty Santa Anna signed promised that all hostilities would cease and the Mexican army would withdraw south of the Río Bravo (as the Rio Grande is known in Mexico). Santa Anna, not at the moment stimulated to "courageous feelings," also signed a secret treaty that promised to arrange recognition of Texas as an independent republic in exchange for his personal freedom. An outraged Mexico refused to recognize either treaty.

## Mexican-American War

From 1836 to 1845, Texas remained independent. Turbulent domestic politics and military revolts as well as a French invasion and the bubonic plague made any intervention too difficult. Yucatán, too, declared its independence, and Mexico concentrated its armies there from 1839 to 1842. But when President John Tyler introduced a joint resolution to the U.S. Congress for the annexation of Texas, Mexico could ignore its northern frontier no longer and was brought to the brink of war.

More than Texas was at stake. The Lone Star Republic, now the 28th state, falsely claimed its western border to be the Rio Grande, which doubled its size. The additional territory included the heart of the old colony of New Mexico around Santa Fe and half of what is now Colorado. The United States, under President James K. Polk, not only claimed the disputed territory, but also wished to add California and the remainder of

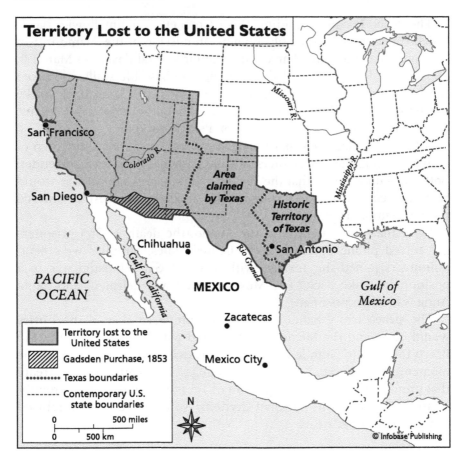

**Territory Lost to the United States**

San Francisco

San Diego

*Colorado R.*

Area claimed by Texas

Historic Territory of Texas

Chihuahua

San Antonio

*Missouri R.*

*Mississippi R.*

*Rio Grande*

PACIFIC OCEAN

*Gulf of California*

**MEXICO**

*Gulf of Mexico*

Zacatecas

Territory lost to the United States

Gadsden Purchase, 1853

Texas boundaries

Contemporary U.S. state boundaries

Mexico City

0        500 miles

0      500 km

N

© Infobase Publishing

New Mexico to the package; these he was willing to purchase, however: $5 million for New Mexico, a minimum of $25 million for California. A total of 1 million square miles of territory was at stake.

When Mexicans learned that Polk's representative, George Slidell, was coming to Mexico to negotiate such an offer, they were indignant. Their national identity was at issue. Vast territories would be lost. Newspapers threatened rebellion if the government accepted the terms. While the Mexicans fulminated, Polk considered a declaration of war over the disputed territory. He decided to wait for an incident to justify such an act, and it came on May 9, 1846. General Zachary Taylor, leading his forces into the Mexican territory disputed by Texas, encountered resistance from the Mexican army. Sixteen of Taylor's soldiers were wounded or killed. Just enough for Polk to go to Congress for a declaration of war, disingenuously claiming that Mexico had invaded U.S. territory.

Instead of devoting itself to the awesome responsibility it confronted in the north, the Mexican army engaged in presidential politics. Finally, after a coup, General Santa Anna was installed again in office. By then, U.S. forces were already well organized. General Stephen Kearny marched on Santa Fe where he met no resistance. Leaving forces to occupy New Mexico, others went south to Chihuahua while Kearny headed for California. By the time Kearny arrived, California had already been taken by the navy under John Sloat and John Fremont. There had been little resistance. In Chihuahua, the Mexicans resisted but were poorly armed.

At Monterrey, however, General Taylor met the forces of General Pedro de Ampudia who was able to stall Taylor's advance by several days. Then Santa Anna arrived with a hastily assembled army of 20,000. The initial battle of Buena Vista was a stalemate: the next morning, fighting should have resumed. Instead, Santa Anna inexplicably began his return to Mexico City. Mexico's northern territories were lost.

## Invasion of Mexico City

Mexico's losses were too great for its leaders to simply end the struggle. While they debated what to do, the United States under General Winfield Scott led the battle to the capital. Landing at Veracruz, Scott cleverly cut off the well-armed troops in the old island fortress by landing above the city and surrounding it from the rear. He then bombarded the helpless residents and ignored all appeals to let innocent women and children leave. A total of 6,700 shells bombarded the city. Civilian casualties were double that of the military. Veracruz finally surrendered.

Scott marched toward Mexico City. Santa Anna tried to cut him off but was either outmaneuvered or rejected by the citizenry who didn't want their cities devastated like Veracruz had been. The capital tried to prepare itself, but the old conflicts rendered a unified effort impossible. Some thought the city was impossible to defend and that peace should be negotiated. Provincial leaders refused to contribute to the corrupt central government, and congress was reluctant to give the general the support he requested given his recent failures in battle.

The U.S. forces were well drilled and well supplied, and they outnumbered the Mexican troops. But on August 20, 1847, during the Battle of Churubusco on the outskirts of the capital, the Mexicans fought hard. Even after intense hand-to-hand combat exhausted them, they refused to give up. Scott, believing the Mexicans defeated, asked for their surrender. Santa Anna used the negotiations to buy time and reinforce his position.

Resuming the battle at Molina del Rey, 4,000 Mexicans were killed and wounded, 1,000 Americans. Scott marched on.

There was only one fortification of the city left: Chapultepec Castle. The castle, surrounded with land mines, was occupied by a military academy and defended by 1,000 soldiers and young cadets. Scott ordered the castle stormed on September 13. The land mines didn't explode, and the invaders were able to scale the walls. The cadets joined in the struggle, choosing death over surrender. It was the last battle. Santa Anna retreated and went into exile. Under the resultant treaty of Guadalupe Hidalgo (February 2, 1848), Mexico lost its vast northern territories (SEE map on page 126). As something of a compensation, the loss included less than 2 percent of the population and no known natural resources (until the San Francisco gold rush only months later corrected this misimpression). In exchange for its territory, Mexico received $18 million, less than half its annual budget.

For Mexicans, the U.S. invasion of the "Halls of Montezuma" is symbolized by the young cadets called the Niños Héroes (heroic children), who died fighting at Chapultepec Castle on September 13, 1847. The cadets are immortalized in the street names of nearly every town. Statues depict their martyrdom throughout the republic, but none is more monumental than the one at the foot of Chapultepec Castle where it is said one cadet hurled himself wrapped in the Mexican flag. These battles would become a part of the new national consciousness, inevitably tinged with Yankeephobia.

## Neocolonialism: Mexico at Mid-Century

By the mid-19th century, Mexico was exhausted and humiliated. More than half of its territory had been lost to the United States, a country the liberals had admired and aspired to emulate. Apaches attacked northern, and rebel Mayas almost took control of the entire Yucatán peninsula in the Caste Wars (1847–49). In central Mexico, revolts and counterrevolts had created thousands of army deserters for whom banditry was the only means of support. The continuous upheaval had destroyed a considerable amount of property, some belonging to foreigners whose governments then demanded compensation. This situation created its own ludicrous results in 1838 when war with France followed Louis Philippe's demand for $600,000 in payment to a French chef for the pastries devoured by hungry Mexican soldiers in the city of Puebla. Mexico couldn't pay, so France sent its warships. (And Santa Anna came to the rescue once again, defeating the French troops in Veracruz.) The chaos made Mexican soil fair game for every adventurer: a Frenchman tried to create paradise lost in Sonora; an English pirate claimed Baja California.

With no peace, Mexico had made little progress since gaining independence. Foreign investment—British, French, and U.S.—had revived the mining industry, however; production had increased to the levels of the late 18th century by 1855. Here and there, especially in the increasing number of foreign-owned mines, more modern technology was introduced. For the future of Mexico, the problem would be that the Creoles did not invest their wealth in commerce and industry, leaving later Mexicans to struggle with the problem of foreign ownership of national resources.

But mining, the one bright spot in the economy, functioned despite the obstacles. All commerce was impeded by the lack of transport. Apart from mule paths, there were only three roads, each in deplorable condition; in 1860 there were only 15 miles of railroad tracks whereas the United States had 30,000, and bandits added to the expense of any commerce. A thriving national economy and unified people could hardly result from such circumstances. Marketing domestic products beyond the local level was next to impossible, although the textile mills in cities rapidly developed. On the international market Mexico continued to export raw products (92 percent of which were silver and gold)

# THE SIERRA MIXTECA AND COCHINEAL

With independence, the Spanish elite who had exported cochineal left Oaxaca. During the decades of political turmoil, Oaxaca's economy became isolated from the rest of Mexico. By mid-century chemical dyes had destroyed the European market for cochineal. The Mixtec in the highlands of Oaxaca, so long favored by circumstances, fell on more difficult times. The number of aristocratic Mixtec caciques fell from 45 in 1700 to only eight. Then, noble titles were outlawed after independence, so that Mixtec caciques officially lost theirs along with the Creole counts. A few continued to inherit their wealth, but they no longer were politically powerful. Even the family of the aristocratic cacique Gabriel Villagómez, descendant of the great 8 Deer "Tiger Claw," sold some of their estates.

# THE MAYA CASTE WARS, 1847–1849

In the Yucatán, near the ancient city of Chichén Itzá, the Maya found the time had come, as foreseen by their prophets, to reclaim their land from the *dzul* (whites). They had been armed by Yucatecan Creoles in a war for independence from Mexico, and they had been promised better conditions, which were not forthcoming. At the very moment Mexico was preoccupied in Texas, numerous villages joined together under the divine direction of the Maya-Christian cult of the Speaking Cross. They succeeded in battling the *dzul* practically into the sea. Those whites who remained were packing to leave Mérida, their last stronghold, when the Maya suddenly abandoned the fight in 1849. Sighting clouds of winged ants, the traditional sign of the first rain, the Maya had returned to plant their corn fields so as not to offend the gods of the *milpa*. The *dzul* fought back and by 1855 had regained their lands and control of central Yucatán. The rebel Maya retreated to the undeveloped Caribbean section on the peninsula where they maintained an independent state under the cult of the Speaking Cross until the beginning of the 20th century.

for foreign manufactured goods, remaining as industrially undeveloped as under Spanish rule but even poorer.

In principle, free trade with many nations—the United States, Britain, France—was an improvement over colonial times. It also provided the government with one of its few sources of taxable revenues, but custom duties became so high that smuggling often replaced sanctioned trade. There are no measures of the trade and production in this period; the chaos extended to official record keeping. Taxes proliferated—on windows, dogs, *pulque* cantinas—and still Mexico defaulted on its loans. There was a tax on every adult male, but even that tax was undermined by the wars, poverty, and social decay: population levels stagnated.

Despite the language of social equality found in the constitution, some historians argue that conditions for the poor actually worsened. At the very least they did not improve. The aristocratic Creoles took on greater airs in replacing the *peninsulares:* most Mexicans they considered worthless rabble. Access to the best positions and to wealth remained open to very few. Indian lands were increasingly gobbled up by hacienda owners. Miners had to work four days in order to earn enough to buy a sack of corn. Entire families, children included, needed work to survive, yet work was too frequently unavailable. Sometimes the poor were not properly buried because they could not pay the church fee. Educational opportunities were as scarce as any route to improvement; at best, one in 10 Mexicans was literate. The society remained so unchanged—despite years of war and devastation in the name of human rights—that many called the first century of independence the "neocolonial" period.

## Cultural Life at Mid-Century

*The barbaric European overlooks nothing.*
*He breaks, fells, and annihilates*
*With an army of fury.*
*It's his pleasure to convert*
*Cities into desert wastes.*
*(What honorable deeds!)*

■

*Ignacio Rodríguez Galván "Profecía de Guatimoc," 1839*
*(Read 1939, 59)*

The Creole failure to modify the social order was not for want of ideas. The intelligentsia agitated for change, arguing for the elimination of debt peonage and for improved schools. In this postindependence period, romantic poets and writers searched for a uniquely national identity; they attacked some of the most central tenets of the European-focused Creoles. Mexican civilization began with its pre-Columbian heritage, they argued, not with the barbarity of the Spanish conquest: Mexicans were Americans, not Europeans. Even the spelling of *Méjico*, they argued, should be changed to the more Indian *México*. A literary society, the Academia de San Juan de Letrán, included the best playwright of the time, Fernando Calderón (1809–49), whose works satirized Santa Anna, and the foremost poet of the day, Ignacio Rodríguez Galván (1816–42). Rodríguez's most famous poem, "Profecía de Guatimoc," is dedicated to the Aztec emperor Cuauhtémoc.

In art, sculptors like Pedro Patiño Ixtolinque found patriotic subjects in pre-Columbian rulers and heroes of independence. These historical themes were echoed in paintings and woodblock prints, and in the search for a national identity, the native landscape of volcanoes and tropical exuberance, Indian ruins, and Catholic churches.

131

These beginnings of a national art lost their impetus, temporarily, when Santa Anna hired all European teachers for the Academy of San Carlos. Outside the academy, however, provincial artists such as José María Estrada (active 1830–60), Agustín Arrieta (1802–74), and Hermeneguildo Bustos (1832–1907) left an enchanting legacy of local life in their portraits and still lifes.

## The Liberals and Benito Juárez

*Adversity discourages none but the contemptible.*

■

*Benito Juárez, 1867 (Smart 1964, 276)*

In 1855, the Liberal Party chased Santa Anna and the Conservatives out of government. The country, fed up and desiring a government that might unify the nation, gave an unusually broad base of support to the Liberals in the armed struggle known as the Revolution of Ayutla. Based on the principles promulgated in the Constitutional Convention of Ayutla (March 1, 1854), they were committed to free and honest elections, free public education, the separation of church and state, and a federalist republic as delineated in the Constitution of 1824.

The Liberals were members of the younger intelligentsia. Some were poets, such as Guillermo Prieto. Some were Renaissance men, such as Melchor Ocampo who was a naturalist as well as the translator of French political works and a student of Indian languages. All had been active in politics: Prieto had been jailed by Santa Anna; Ocampo had been governor of Michoacán. Many were exiled by Santa Anna to Louisiana, where they formed a revolutionary group. Numerous liberals were mestizos and other peoples of color who had worked their way through the ranks of the army or had managed to obtain an education.

The most famous leader, and certainly the individual most indicative of a new social order, was Benito Juárez (1806–72). A Zapotec Indian who is often described as the Abraham Lincoln of Mexico, Juárez was born in a hamlet in the highlands of Oaxaca. Orphaned at the age of three, he had the good fortune, when going to the city of Oaxaca at 12 years of age, to work for a Franciscan friar who paid for his education. Upon graduating from law school, Juárez entered politics and eventually became governor of Oaxaca where he was recognized for his honest management of the state. Like other Liberals, he was later exiled by Santa Anna.

## The Reform Laws

The new Liberal government, with Juárez as secretary of justice, targeted the church and military for its most controversial reforms. The Ley Juárez eliminated the special exemption the clergy and military received from standing trial in civil courts—even for crimes such as

*Portrait of Benito Juárez (1871), by José Escudero y Espronada in the National Museum of History, Mexico City*

133

rape and murder. As they had in reaction to previous attempts at change, Conservative Creoles, clergy, and militia rallied themselves into a frenzy. Although forced to install a new president, the Liberals remained in power.

But the new president also antagonized the Conservatives by promulgating the Ley Lerdo (1856). This law, acceptable to the moderates for the revenues it would generate, required all institutions, both religious and secular, to divest themselves of property not used in their normal operations. States would keep the governor's mansion and office buildings, for example, but all other properties would be sold at public auction. For the church, with its vast holdings beyond its churches and monasteries, the losses would be particularly painful.

The next reform sensibly gave the state the power of registering births, marriages, deaths, and the like, instead of the church. In the Ley Iglesias it also deprived the church of the right to set its own fees: no longer could the poor be forced to pay for receiving the sacraments. All these reforms were incorporated into the new Constitution of 1857, along with freedom of speech and press, freedom of education and, for the first time in Mexico, freedom of religion. Only this last article was defeated by the Catholic Church.

There were disastrous consequences of the Reform Laws. One was the effect of the Ley Lerdo on traditional Indian villages. Although the independence hero Morelos had argued for something akin to the Ley Lerdo, he had wanted to redistribute church properties to benefit the poor. Nothing of the sort occurred under the liberal Reform Laws, because only the wealthy could afford to buy the properties. And included in the auctioned properties were *ejido* lands, the communal farms belonging to the Indian villages. Under the republic, the separately functioning Indian communities had been outlawed—after all, free and equal Indians could vote along with non-Indians for the municipal government. The Indians, however, rarely gained office even when they constituted the majority. Communal Indian lands were absorbed by the larger municipality and, under Ley Lerdo, were sold to pay off state debts. The aristocratic caciques were thereby deprived of the last vestiges of their political power and Indian communities lost their voice in Mexican affairs. Ley Lerdo not only created larger estates for the rich, it severely undermined the autonomy so long enjoyed by indigenous peoples in more remote areas, such as Oaxaca and Yucatán. For this reason, the Liberal reforms have been called "the second conquest."

Another result of the reforms was war. Anticlericalism had been resisted by the church since the struggle for independence, and the church reacted once again. The wealthy were threatened with excommunication for purchasing church property. Those who swore allegiance to the constitution also would be excommunicated. Pope Pius IX entered the fray, declaring the Mexican constitution "null and void" in regard to the "Most Holy Religion." The state required an oath of support from its civic officials, and those who worried about the consequences with the church lost their jobs. In this devoutly Catholic nation, the church and Mexican state polarized the entire society.

## The Reform War: 1858–1861

Once again Mexico found itself incurably divided into two camps: This time the issue was the proper function of the church in Mexico. The army declared the Conservative General Félix Zuloaga, president. Many Liberals escaped north to Querétaro where Benito Juárez was declared president. A war ensued. The clergy and military supported Zuloaga. But some Indians did, too, such as the Yaqui in the north, because the Liberal government's Ley Lerdo had deprived them of their *ejido* lands. Others were convinced that the Zapotec Juárez would have their best interests at heart.

Mexico was again at war, this time for three years. Many noncombatants were treated brutally. The Conservatives shot doctors who treated

## THE SIERRA MIXTECA

Although the glory days of the Mixtec aristocracy passed with cochineal, geography continued to protect the Mixtec villages from the ravages experienced by other traditional communities of Mexico. Despite the Ley Lerdo, the region retained most of its communal lands. Sugarcane had replaced cochineal in Oaxaca as the profitable cash crop, but hacendados had little interest in growing it in the mountainous Sierra Mixteca. As one Mixtec village appealed to the government in its effort to be exempted from the law:

> we lack lands that are called "plough lands" since the places where it is not steep hillsides are rocky and cut by ravines.

■

*Eusebio López, mayor of Nuyoo, 1856 (Monaghan 1995, 264)*

Liberal soldiers; the Liberals abused priests who wouldn't administer to them. Thousands of innocents were wounded. Haciendas were burned, and churches were used as stables. The war continued until the Liberals defeated the Conservatives, marching into Mexico City on January 1, 1861.

## French Intervention: Cinco de Mayo

Juárez was elected president. The treasury was empty. Juárez declared a two-year moratorium on payment of foreign debt—some of it outstanding since Iturbide's time. The Europeans, who had had their citizens wounded or killed and their silver shipments stolen, were driven to action. France, England, and Spain, with the pope's blessing, agreed to a joint occupation of the customs house at Veracruz. Without interfering with Mexico's right to govern itself, they intended to garnishee the receipts to pay off their loans.

Close to 9,000 foreign troops landed in Veracruz in 1862. It soon became clear that the French had designs on Mexico that extended beyond the repayment of loans. In fact, Mexican Conservatives in exile had been agitating in Europe for the installation of a monarch. France, under Napoléon III, had agreed. Spain and Britain withdrew their troops in protest. And 6,500 French soldiers marched toward Puebla with the intention of occupying Mexico. On May 5 (the famous date Cinco de Mayo, in Spanish), the Mexicans routed the French in Puebla under the leadership of General Ignacio Zaragoza and Brigadier General Porfirio Díaz. It would be a year before the French could resume their march.

## More Anticlerical Reforms

Such a long-awaited victory against at least one of Mexico's many foreign invaders became a rallying cry for the nation, except for the Conservatives, who thought that only through the reinstitution of a European monarchy could authority—and peace—be achieved. Aristocratic Creoles aided the French troops. Conservative guerrillas assassinated Liberals in the countryside, including such luminaries as Melchor Ocampo. Priests used their Sunday pulpits to support the French and advocated the overthrow of the Juárez government.

The Reform Laws had most affected the clergy, and they had been sharpened during the Reform War, when new laws were issued that clearly made the church subservient to the state. All church properties had been confiscated. Monasteries were closed. Public religious displays were curtailed. Now, in an attempt to end what he perceived as the traitorous influence of the church, Juárez decreed that the religious were forbidden to wear their vestments in public and threatened imprisonment to any priest fostering disrespect for the government and its laws.

Juárez's efforts, however, didn't stop the French government from creating the second empire in his country. With the United States embroiled in its own civil war, Napoléon III realized he could proceed unchallenged. Thirty thousand additional troops were sent to Mexico. Puebla was taken after a two-month siege that reduced its populace to eating rats. The Mexican army was decimated. Juárez, realizing he did not have the troops to defend Mexico City, evacuated the capital and withdrew the government to the north, establishing it near the U.S. border in what is now El Paso.

## Maximilian and Carlota

In consultation with Napoléon III, arch-conservative Mexicans selected the Austrian archduke, Ferdinand Maximilian of Hapsburg, as the vehicle for restoring themselves and the church to power in Mexico. Maximilian stipulated that he must have the support of the Mexican people before he took the throne of Mexico, yet the eager conservatives failed to perceive his liberalism. And the ill-fated Maximilian believed their cynical assertions that a plebiscite of the Mexican people had resoundingly approved him as emperor.

Maximilian and his beautiful wife, Carlota, the Belgian princess born as Marie-Charlotte-Amélie-Léopoldine, were both romantics and youthful in their innocence—he was 32 and she only 24. Embracing Mexico and all things Mexican, they disappointed the Europeanized conservatives. Endorsing the Reform Laws, they scandalized them. As foreign interlopers, not even their liberalism and idealism could prevent them from being enemies of Juárez; as monarchs, the republican government in exile could only plot to overthrow them.

The second Mexican empire endured for only a few years. Arriving in Veracruz on May 28, 1864, Maximilian was forced to surrender three years later. On June 19, 1867, he was executed by the Juaristas. In those years, the French constantly were fending off the guerrilla attacks of the Liberals. They managed to pacify only parts of central Mexico, and in 1865 they captured Oaxaca from Porfirio Díaz. But the struggle was unceasing. At one point the army deceived Maximilian by claiming Juárez had given up and had withdrawn to the United States. Arguing for summary execution of all remaining republican agitators, they were granted permission by the emperor—who thereby sealed his own fate.

In the capital, the royal couple established their court at Chapultepec Castle but did not isolate themselves. They received the people weekly to learn about their concerns and toured the countryside to acquaint themselves with their realm, which they found quite beautiful. When it was suggested that a marble arch should be dedicated to Carlota, Maximilian thought one commemorating Mexican independence would be better. He outlawed debt peonage, and he granted communal lands to Indian villages that had lost them under the reforms. Yet none of these sympathetic acts could redeem the foreigner in the eyes of most Mexicans.

No sooner did the U.S. Civil War end, than President Abraham Lincoln threw his support behind Juárez. Having fought its own war of independence, the United States had declared in the Monroe Doctrine that the Americas were off limits to European colonization. Juárez was permitted to purchase arms, and 3,000 Union soldiers joined his army. The United States advised the French to leave, and Napoléon, also under pressure in Europe, recalled his troops in late 1866.

With the French army gradually withdrawing, Maximilian found he had few choices left. The Conservatives no longer approved of him; the Liberals never had and never would. He considered abdicating the throne. Carlota convinced him to remain while she traveled to France and then to Rome to secure support. But neither Napoléon nor Pope Pius IX, who was disgruntled that church lands had not been restored, was willing to help. Carlota went insane and was institutionalized in Europe.

By the end of 1867, the Juaristas had recaptured much of northern Mexico and Oaxaca. Most of the French had withdrawn. Maximilian still considered abdication. Instead, as a gesture of his Hapsburg pride, he joined the last French troops in the city of Querétaro. The Juaristas surrounded them. Maximilian resisted for 100 days. His entourage arranged for his safe escape; he refused, finding it more dignified to stand his ground and surrender.

Juárez ordered that Maximilian be tried for violation of Mexico's sovereignty and, when found guilty, executed. Mexicans, both men and women, implored him not to kill the well-meaning emperor. Presidents and monarchs from around the world appealed to him for clemency. Juárez, however, could not forget the executions of his own men ordered by Maximilian nor the 50,000 Mexicans who had died fighting the French. He followed the letter of the law. Maximilian faced the firing squad.

## The Restored Republic, 1867

While the story of Carlota and Maximilian has captured the imagination of filmmakers and romance writers, the reality for Mexico of this quixotic interlude was not so inspirational. The nation was saddled with Maximilian's war debt, which Juárez refused to pay. The economy was even more deeply disrupted and local caudillos, or political bosses, had more power than ever. The foreign debt in 1867 was 375 million pesos in contrast to 56 million in 1850. There was not a peso in the treasury.

Although the war against the French defined a new sense of nationalism, the anarchy had intensified regional autonomy at the expense of federal control. Thirteen years of war had destroyed the Conservative army that always had been ready to stage a counterrevolt; yet many ambitious caudillos were included in the Liberal army. And the underclasses—Indians, shop keepers, laborers—had been asked to fight the French, empowering them in a way that they had not experienced since Hidalgo.

Having temporarily quieted their Conservative opponents and having moved the church out of politics and education, the Liberal Party had to control its own internal divisions. The middle class thought the large landowners (also members of the party because of the windfall property obtainable through the reforms) should take their fair burden of the taxes. Instead, many hacendados paid no more than landless workers. The poor thought there should be a major redistribution of the hacendados' land. The rifts were there, but while Benito Juárez was alive, the party united behind him.

## The Juárez Presidencies, 1867–1876

*Until Juárez took control, Mexico never was governed.*

■

*Justo Sierra, 1867*

Under Benito Juárez, Mexico finally experienced a period of extended political stability and peace. As a civilian president, he stood in marked contrast to the military heroes who had dominated politics since independence. In 1867 he was elected to his third term as president: the first one that would not be interrupted by war.

Juárez's popularity in no small part helped prevent the usual military coups, but he also had to juggle many competing interests in the Liberal Party. To keep the hacendados behind him, Juárez granted them absolute privileges over their domains—no small matter when some, such as the Terrazas family, owned properties in the north the size of a state and when the injustices of debt peonage had yet to be eliminated. The middle class was pleased with the increasing number of positions in the government bureaucracy and the growing number of public schools in the cities, from fewer than 2,500 in 1857 to more than 8,000 in 1874.

The Liberals were basically satisfied with Juárez's public policies as well. Although the federalist state had become more centralist, the elections were more open than they had ever been, if not totally free of state tampering. The press was free, and indeed, intellectuals such as Ignacio Altamirano (1834–95), an Indian historical novelist, did not hesitate to criticize the president. The anticlerical reforms remained intact, though no one contested the church's quiet procurement of new urban properties. And the legislature was strengthened as a branch of government.

There were serious problems, however. To control the military and to save the treasury money, Juárez dismissed 40,000 of the 60,000 soldiers who had fought the French. Many caudillos were furious, expecting more spoils from the war; some plotted against Juárez—including the hero of Cinco de Mayo, Porfirio Díaz. The unemployed soldiers added their numbers to the bandits already plaguing the countryside, making all travel unsafe and attacking rural towns and haciendas.

The land problem, exacerbated by the Reform Laws and Juárez's favorable policies for hacendados, was an explosive issue for the Indians—one that would divide the country just as the church had done. Juárez was sympathetic to certain checks on debt peonage, but congress overruled him. Indian revolts were increasing, squatters frequently took over hacienda land until federal soldiers arrived. Famine, such as that in 1869, further inflamed the situation. Some estimate that one-fifth of the population was dispossessed, scavenging for food in the countryside or begging in the city streets.

Peace, however, and a conscientious government, enabled some improvements in the economy, especially in the area of transportation. A railroad was built between Veracruz and the capital; roads were upgraded for stagecoach travel. A police force, called the *rurales,* provided increased security on the roads, which facilitated commerce. Commerce did improve. Although cochineal had become inconsequential, hide exports were 20 times greater than during the viceroyalty, and Yucatán profitably exported sisal, or *henequén,* for making rope and cordage. Lumber and coffee became major exports, too. Yet gold and silver retained their number one position, especially with the opening of new mines in northern regions such as Chihuahua.

Mexico attempted to attract both foreign settlers and foreign investment. Given its recent history, however, Mexico was considered a poor risk. Some capital found its way to the mining and textile industries. European immigration was encouraged in the hopes of gaining skilled labor and increasing the population. With so many deaths due to war and high infant mortality, Mexico's population remained under 9 million in 1874—only 2 million more than at the end of the colonial period. Yet by 1876 a mere 25,000 Mexican residents were foreign born.

## Stable Juárez Period Ends

In 1871, Juárez decided to seek a fourth term—against sound Liberal principle. He appeared an absolutist rather than the constitutional president he had been. It was a hotly contested election with three candidates: Juárez, General Porfirio Díaz, and Sebastián Lerdo de Tejada, chief justice of the Supreme Court. No one won a majority, so the legislature decided the matter in favor of Juárez. Lerdo came in second. Díaz, like so many military caudillos before him, proclaimed himself in revolt. Few joined him and Díaz was defeated—temporarily.

On July 19, 1872, Benito Juárez died of a heart attack. As chief justice, Lerdo succeeded him as dictated by the Constitution of 1857. In the next election Lerdo was chosen for president over Díaz by a massive majority and continued the progressive policies of his party. In a few years he had further increased the number of primary schools and had contracted for more railroads. He also connected all the provincial capitals by telegraph wires. Less popular was his diligent implementation of the Reform Laws, closing convents and confiscating church properties.

## Foundations of the Modern State

Until the French invasion, it would have been hard to discern more than factionalism and wars and their disruptive effects on the population in 19th-century Mexico. After the French intervention, Mexico became a more unified nation, and when Juárez died in 1872 the country had at least experienced a constitutional and democratic government. Progress had been made in separating religious and civil authority, and Lerdo had continued upholding the laws of the constitutional republic. General Porfirio Díaz, however, would reverse the course that had been so painfully set.

# 8

# THE PORFIRIATO
# DICTATORSHIP
# (1876–1910)

*Don Porfirio's slogan was "Bread and the Club": bread for the army, bread for the bureaucrats, bread for the foreigners, and even bread for the Church—and the club for the common people of Mexico and those who differed with him.*

■

*Lesley Byrd Simpson (1962, 258)*

For 34 years Mexico was ruled by a man who fought his way into power on the slogan of "no reelection": Porfirio Díaz. This dictator left an extraordinary legacy. He attracted foreign capital and modernized the economy. Cities were beautified and the countryside rid of banditry. His most exceptional legacy, however, was the Revolution of 1910. Because all he achieved was at the expense of the Mexican people, he is considered the villain in 20th-century Mexican history. It is not his statue that graces village squares, but rather that of Francisco Madero, who stood against him for democracy; it is not Díaz who rides the white horse in Mexican muralist art, but rather Emiliano Zapata who fought for the return of peasant lands. These events, the Porfiriato dictatorship and the Revolution, created a Mexican national identity that survives to this day.

## No Reelection

Since independence, the uncompromising factionalism of Mexico had benefited the military. First, it created Emperor Iturbide. Then His Most Serene Highness Santa Anna. With Juárez the country took a breather from generals, if not from war. And finally the political process of pronouncements and revolt favored yet another caudillo, General Porfirio

Díaz (1830–1915). Díaz, a mestizo born of a Mixtec Indian mother, was from Juárez's state of Oaxaca. He went through a similar educational process as Juárez but never finished law school. After joining the army, he became a national hero of the Liberal cause during the battle of Cinco de Mayo. Later he liberated the capital, as well as Puebla and Oaxaca, from the French and took up a position in Congress under Juárez.

Initially Díaz tried to get himself elected president legitimately, arguing that Juárez and Lerdo, by seeking reelection, were despots not democrats. After losing, in good caudillo fashion, he proclaimed against the government and led an armed revolt on the principle of "no reelection." The idea was quite popular with the middle class, because—when extended to municipal and state elections—it meant that a lot more people would have a chance at office. Against Lerdo, Díaz succeeded in toppling the government. And during his first term (1876–80) he unified the country behind him when the United States, under President Hayes, encroached on Mexican territorial sovereignty by permitting its soldiers, who were in pursuit of Apaches, to cross into Mexico. Díaz held firm, despite threats of war by the United States, and gained considerable popularity by standing on principle.

But Díaz would soon be found to hold few principles so strongly as to defeat his own interests. The Constitution of 1857 stood. Why bother to create the controversy that would be aroused by repealing it when it could simply be ignored? So compelling was the principle of no reelection, however, that Díaz arranged for a stand-in candidate his second term. After his third, no one dared complain, but to maintain a facade of legality, the law was changed to permit unlimited terms at every level. All other officials, local and federal, were handpicked by Díaz and held their positions as long as they were in favor. And when they were not in favor, they more often than not were assassinated by Díaz's personal police called the Bravi. Elections continued throughout the Porfiriato, but because the outcomes were always known in advance, few bothered to vote.

## Pax Porfiriana

*There are no drunken riots ... little thieving ... The least disorderly action, even loud talking in the streets, causes prompt arrest ...*

■

*J. Hendrickson McCarty, 1888*

Given the decades of Mexican anarchy, Díaz's ability to forge a strong centralized Mexican state is a testament to his political toughness as much as it is to Mexico's exhaustion. Díaz faced the usual disruptions in the countryside during his first term. There were peasant uprisings, Apache raids, and more than one revolt by a regional chief. By expanding the rural police force, the *rurales,* Díaz quickly put any such trouble down. And he did so ruthlessly. Under Díaz, the *rurales* included notorious bandits who were permitted to murder anyone and justify their acts by the Ley Fugo: "Shot while trying to escape." Operating outside the constraints of any due process, the *rurales* were known for their fearlessness against presumed enemies of the regime. Well paid by Díaz, their loyalty was unquestioned. Order was achieved.

Díaz used more than repression in consolidating his power. He was a political wizard capable of conciliating and co-opting the various factions of the middle and upper classes. The army, for example, was appeased by a larger budget and new weapons at the same time it was decentralized and depoliticized by the simple expedient of assigning soldiers in smaller battalions to different regions on a constant rotation. In a classic Díaz maneuver of balancing one group against another, he created several militia groups, such as the *rurales,* to compete with the army. The church was satisfied that Díaz did not actively enforce the Reform Laws, permitting them to build up their properties and wealth and to reopen their schools. Although the anticlerical constitution was technically still in effect, Mexico under Díaz encouraged the clergy to expand in number from the 500 under Juárez to 5,000.

The middle class, the intelligentsia, the petty caudillos, and the haughty Creoles supported Díaz because he brought them increased prosperity. He did so by doing all the right things to attract foreign capital and know-how. First, his Pax Porfiriana enabled commerce to resume unimpeded. Second, he stabilized the government by buying off the various factions. And third, but no less astonishing, he gradually put the government on a sound financial footing. Continuing Juárez's policy of streamlining the government, Díaz brought in professional financiers such as José Yves Limantour to manage the budget. By 1894 the budget was balanced; by 1910 there was a comfortable surplus.

## Modernization

In 1876 Mexico was basically the same feudal society as during the viceroyalty, and while rigid social stratification had yielded to permit more people of color into the ranks of power, most of the population was unskilled and living in peonage. Three-quarters of the society was rural. Only in the cities was there any sophistication. Modernization was practically nonexistent: oxen, not tractors, plowed the fields, and most silver was extracted with 16th-century technology. Mexico City, which was regularly flooded during the rainy season, was less capable of building dikes and ditches than Aztec Tenochtitlán. The ports, even Veracruz, were in need of dredging. Instead of trains, burros and human carriers (used since pre-Columbian times) transported goods.

Díaz believed modernization would come only with foreign capital and the immigration of skilled Europeans. Government policies, such as special tax and legal exemptions, were implemented. Laws were passed not only permitting investors to profit from the products they extracted, but granting them subsoil rights that had previously been reserved for the government: a boondoggle for investors in the case of metals and petroleum.

With domestic peace and a sensible budget, Mexico was deemed one of the most creditworthy nations in the world. Foreign loans were readily available and were repaid in a timely fashion. Investors liked the welcoming attitude and privileges offered to them. Hydroelectric plants were built. Steam and water power became available for modern machinery—5,500 textile mills and cement factories, sugar and flour refineries, and breweries were the result by 1902. Telephones and tele-

Citlaltépetl (1879), a painting by José María Velasco in the National Museum of Art, Mexico City

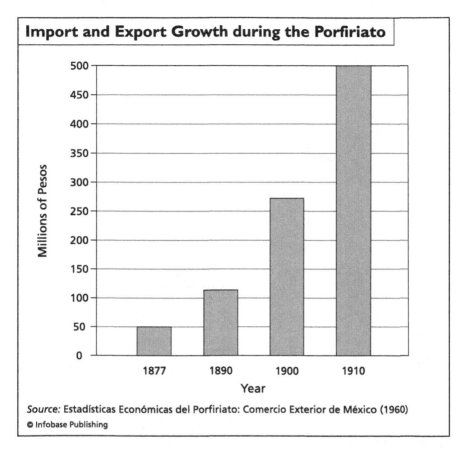

**Import and Export Growth during the Porfiriato**

Source: Estadísticas Económicas del Porfiriato: Comercio Exterior de México (1960)
© Infobase Publishing

graphs linked the nation. The first steel mill in Latin America produced 60,000 tons annually from Monterrey, which was fast becoming the industrial capital of Mexico. The British built a six-mile tunnel through the mountains that protected the capital from flooding. Foreign monies and technology dredged the harbor of Veracruz and improved ports such as Tampico, Manzanillo, and Mazatlán: foreign trade increased nearly tenfold during the Porfiriato. Silver and other metals were more easily extracted with new technology: Silver production quadrupled, gold increased from 1.5 million pesos in 1877 to 40 million 11 years later; copper became a major export.

The greatest impact on Mexico was the completion of a rail network of more than 15,000 miles by 1910. Subsidized by the Mexican government, the railroads were constructed by foreign companies and owned by foreign banks. Around 1908, Mexico took a controlling interest in most of them to form the National Railways of Mexico—many claimed it overpaid to appease foreign interests. The tracks radiated from the capital to major cities such as Guadalajara, Puebla, Monterrey, and Oaxaca; they connected the coasts from the Pacific to the Gulf and linked the major ports with production centers and Mexico City with its Guatemalan frontier. Initially, the lines extending to the Texan border at El Paso and Laredo and from Guaymas on the Pacific to Nogales, Arizona created considerable concern. Mexicans feared, after the losses in the Texas wars, that the railways would simply facilitate a U.S. takeover of the rest of Mexico.

The railroad network had its gaps—for example Yucatán was not connected at all. Yet it unified much of Mexico and helped Díaz control the various regions with a stronger arm: troops could arrive quickly to any problem area. But above all, the railroads enabled the Mexican economy to develop more rapidly than ever before. For the first time, cotton arrived expeditiously and affordably to the textile mills and silver to the smelters and ports. Shipping costs were lowered so much by rail transit that what had cost $67 to ship in 1877 cost only $3 in

1910. The trains created a profitable domestic and export market for agricultural surpluses: farm exports, sisal, and goat hides, for example, generated more than 100 million pesos, up from 7 million.

## The Gilded Age

The impact of a strengthened economy and a modernized infrastructure on Mexico cannot be underestimated. Those who benefited from the economy—most of the middle and upper classes—gained a new sense of pride in their country. European governments gave honors to Díaz. Visitors from abroad extolled the nation's progress. With peace, the population grew to more than 15 million, and the population of Mexico City finally exceeded the population of Aztec Tenochtitlán at 470,000.

Most of the population growth was in the cities, especially Monterrey, Chihuahua, and Durango in the more industrialized north. But smaller towns such as Salina Cruz, now reachable by train, also blossomed. The commerce brought a construction boom and an expanding middle class that resided mostly in the cities. Government workers and school teachers, skilled artisans and professionals, clergy and petty army officers increased in number and income; initially from the lower classes, they now could afford indoor plumbing, some fashionable clothes, and meat a few times a week.

Mexico was more confident, but not so much so that it didn't borrow European culture and fashion. The literati studied the classics. Cities such as Guanajuato and Mérida built magnificent Belle Epoque opera houses, importing Italian marble and artisans to create them even though Mexico had marble and skilled artisans of its own. The upper classes sent their children to French universities, joined French cultural societies, and assumed the latest French fashions (SEE page 152). The bishop of Mérida was transported in a jewel-encrusted carriage purchased in Paris. An opera by Gustavo Campo on Nahuatl poet and king Nezahuacóyotl was entitled in French, not Spanish.

For all its pretense at progress, the Porfiriato did little to improve educational opportunities. The middle classes in the cities and women found schooling more accessible, but higher education remained almost exclusively the preserve of the elite. Rural areas, predominated by poor peons and Indians, were even less well served. The number of schools did double; the number of teachers almost did too, although they were paid no more than a housemaid. Yet the population doubled as well. The national illiteracy rate was 80 percent.

In the mid-19th century, Fanny Calderón de la Barca despaired that "the women of the landed class were condemned to a life, the vapidity of which makes us yawn at the very thought." Their education was neglected; most were as illiterate as they were gracious and kind. During the Porfiriato an increasing number of women were educated for the professions. The first woman graduated from the medical school in Mexico City in 1887 and a commercial school for women was opened to great demand in 1903. A feminist group, the Admiradoras de Juárez, was founded in 1904.

Intellectuals and artists were able to pursue their interests as long as they did not criticize the dictatorship. Some journalists and newspaper publishers found this difficult: Filomena Mata was jailed 34 times for the independence of his publication. The period did produce sophisticated literature in the modernist tradition, which eschewed politics for a purer art-for-art's-sake aesthetic. Amado Nervo (1870–1919) was the most talented and prolific writer, best known for his first novel, *El bachiller* (1895). Typical of the age, he resided in Paris. Historians produced scholarly studies of the long-past (hence politically safe) colonial period, such as Joaquín García Icazbalceta's (1824–94) biography of

Porfirio Díaz and the Científicos *(1957–60), a mural by David Alfaro Siqueiros in the National Museum of History, Mexico City*

Bishop Zumárraga. Justo Sierra (1848–1912), Díaz's minister of education, wrote *México: su evolución social,* an interpretive history of the nation.

Positivism was the dominant intellectual movement and the one that rationalized Díaz's dictatorship. This philosophy, also borrowed from France, originated with the emphasis on scientific thinking in the philosophy of Auguste Comte. Positivists, called *científicos* in Mexico, controlled the highest governmental positions. They argued that the country's problems could be solved by the application of statistics and sound thinking. Rational policies and social order would bring the nation to the level of Europe and the United States. This thinking was never more effective than in Minister Limantour's handling of national finances. However, the policies were less "scientific" when a dash of Social Darwinism was added to preserve the privileges of Creoles and the ruling class, who argued that only they were fit to govern. Mexico wasn't ready for democracy, Justo Sierra said from the Ministry of Education. And the indigenous masses, inferior according to these *científicos,* would never be ready.

European tastes predominated in art, setting back the national themes that had prevailed after independence, especially during Maximilian's reign. The capital's most elegant avenue, the Paseo de la Reforma, had been designed by Maximilian but was not sufficiently European for aristocrats of the Porfiriato. It was redesigned to look more like Paris's Champs-Élysées and lined with statues, many commissioned from abroad. Don Porfirio also found little in national art appealing. The Mexican entry at the Paris World Fair of 1889 was neo-Greek in style and flanked by sphinxes. The dictator appointed a director of the Academy of San Carlos who agreed with his preferences and who brought in many other European instructors to "civilize" local tastes.

Fortunately, fashion didn't dictate all art of the period. Many artists continued to seek a Mexican style. José María Velasco (1840–1912) and José Guadalupe Posada (1852–1913) created works that are among the finest examples of art. The soft grandeur of Velasco's Mexican landscapes (see page 146) derive from the academic tradition. In fact, Velasco was an instructor at the academy and one of Diego Rivera's early teachers. By contrast, Posada was trained as a printer's apprentice. He created his expressive and often fantastic engravings for street gazettes; his illustrations of folk ballads and his political satires and amusing *calaveras* (skulls) for Day of the Dead editions were meant for popular audiences. The Daumier of Mexico, Posada created what is considered the earliest example of the modern Mexican art style that predominated after the Revolution.

## Foreign Dependency

*The North American, the foreigner, had prospered in Mexico, but not its native sons.*

■

*Regis Planchet, 1906 (quoted by Charles C. Cumberland)*

Just about everything in Mexico was foreign owned. There were more than 1,000 mining companies: 85 percent were North American and a few of them, such as Daniel Guggenheim's American Smelting and Refining Company and Anaconda Copper Company, operated many different mines in most of the states in northern Mexico with a total value of some $12 million. Petroleum was first drilled successfully in 1901 by Edward Doheny, a Californian who owned 600,000 acres along the oil-rich Gulf coast; when he sold his wells to Standard Oil Company, they were producing $1 million worth of oil a week. A second

*La catrina (1913), metal cut by José Guadalupe Posada in the National Museum of Prints, Mexico City, satirizes the French fashions of the Porfiriato.*

dominant producer of Mexican oil was the Briton Sir Weetman Pearson, later Lord Cowdray. Many banks were in foreign hands, too, as well as most industries.

The foreign firms gave job preference to their own nationals and even in Mexican-owned firms, the manager was often a foreigner. So prevalent was this practice that Mexicans rarely made their income from management, but rather as intermediaries for foreign investors with the government. Although European companies included Mexicans on their boards and in other capacities, U.S. firms rarely did. And in a practice that would lead to conflict, foreign workers doing the same job as a Mexican usually earned much more.

The economy was fueled by foreign trade. Although Mexico was becoming somewhat industrialized, especially in the north, it exported primarily raw, not manufactured materials—just as it had in colonial times. The economy depended on the strength of European and U.S. demands for these products. For most of the Porfiriato, Mexico benefited from an expanding U.S. economy. The potential profits from foreign trade had transformed the agricultural sector into producing cash crops. Yucatecan hacendados found that sisal alone brought such incredible profits on the world market that they planted nothing else.

# THE ANTIQUARIANS— A DIFFERENT KIND OF INVESTMENT

Not all foreigners came to Mexico for aristocratic balls or to make a fortune. Many Europeans and Americans wished to know more about the ancient ruined cities. Edward Thompson, U.S. consul in Mérida, used his spare time to investigate the Maya ruins of Yucatán state for the Peabody Museum of Harvard University. In 1894, permissive Mexican land policies enabled Thompson to buy the Hacienda Chichén, 100 square miles of land that happened to include the ruins of Chichén Itzá, a pre-Columbian city of 50,000 inhabitants in A.D. 880. Thompson devoted himself to the study of the ruins and befriended his Maya workers, who permitted him to observe rituals and dances that they said were preserved from ancient times and could be seen carved in the walls of Chichén.

The states of Chiapas and Tabasco, too, had little diversification, gambling on the world market for their coffee and rubber exports to keep the wealthy wealthier. In the north, where the economy was more diversified with mining and industry, cash crops such as chickpeas and profitable animal grazing dominated agriculture.

## The Land Grab

> *[One of Mexican agriculture's] greatest drawbacks is that the whole country is divided into immense haciendas or landed estates, small farms being rarely known ... Some of these estates comprise square leagues instead of square acres in extent and are said to have irrigating ditches from 40 to 50 miles in length.*
>
> ■
>
> *D. A. Wells, 1887*

By 1910 only 2 percent of the population held title to land and 3 percent of the properties covered 58 percent of Mexico. Nearly 70 percent of those titles had been acquired since the reforms of Ley Lerdo in 1867. Yet seven out of 10 Mexicans were farmers; most were forced into debt peonage in order to survive.

Under Díaz, two policies concentrated land in the hands of the privileged. The first, the Ley Lerdo, had not been extensively implemented in regard to Indian community lands under Juárez. Now it was ruthlessly implemented. The second was the vacant lands survey in which allegedly untitled or "public" lands were surveyed and put up for sale; in total, surveyed land constituted the size of California and was sold to Díaz favorites and the surveyors themselves for a pittance. Worse, it was often confiscated from the legitimate owners.

Under either policy, when an Indian had been deprived of land, there was little hope of rectifying the injustice. Yet some did try. If Indians could find the money and wherewithal to file a complaint in court, they not only rarely won but sometimes were fined by judges for daring to besmirch the name of the hacendado or gentlemanly surveyor. When land wasn't taken under the guise of the Ley Lerdo or survey, it could be taken by cutting off the water supply. Or by force. The Yaqui Indians of Sonora, for example, after holding off the army in bloody battles for years, finally were routed and sold as laborers to *henequén* plantation owners in the Yucatán where they were forced to work in chains. Their fertile lands went to the American Richardson Company.

## Hunger

In 1910 only 10 percent of Indian communities held land. The land-owners held vast territories. When the arable lands weren't devoted to cash crops for export, they often lay fallow. When hungry Indians asked to rent such land in order to grow their subsistence corn and beans, they too often were refused. Despite a 50 percent increase in population, Mexico produced less maize in 1910 than in 1877. Mexico failed to be self-sustaining in wheat, too, even though this grain was favored by the upper classes. Economists estimate that there were on average two pounds of maize available daily to each Mexican at independence; a century later, in 1910, there was less than a pound—including imported grains. The price

# CASH CROPS IN TWO REGIONS

Called "green gold," the Yucatán's *henequén* crop represented the most extreme consequences of commercial agriculture. It was so lucrative to grow the fibrous sisal for international cordage that cattle were killed in order to use the pasture to grow more *henequén*. In fact, so many animals were killed that serious meat shortages were created, even for the wealthy. And hacendados encroached on traditional Mayan *milpas*, too, with near impunity, so they could plant yet more sisal.

Finding themselves dispossessed, the Maya repeatedly rebelled against the hacendados, creating serious labor shortages. When the military arrived, they fled toward the less developed Caribbean where other rebel Maya congregated in what is now the state of Quintana Roo. Those who did not escape were forced to work the sisal fields, slaves in all but name. When synthetic cordage was developed after World War I, the *henequén* market collapsed along with the Yucatán's economy.

In contrast to the Yucatán and the rest of Mexico, the Sierra Mixteca—and indeed all of Oaxaca—managed to retain most of its communal lands not just during the Reform Period but throughout the Porfiriato. Historians are uncertain of the reason, but some believe the continued absence of a large wealthy hacendado class meant few were in a position to buy up the lands. Also, with the loss of cochineal and with erosion caused by overgrazing, there was no cash crop that especially attracted foreign monies to the area.

of the little maize that was available cost twice as much, and beans, now an export crop, cost six times more. Wages, however, remained the same throughout the 19th century. Mexicans were starving.

## Survival of the Fittest

*The white is proprietor; the Indian, proletariat. The white is rich; the Indian, poor, wretched . . . The white lives in a magnificent town house; the Indian is isolated in the countryside and lives in a miserable shack . . . two different people in one land; what is worse, two people to a certain degree enemies.*

■

*Francisco Pimental, 1865 (translated by Stein & Stein)*

The circumstances of the poor masses were dreadful during the Porfiriato. The shameful state in which most Mexicans were forced to live is reflected in equally dismaying statistics. Sixteen percent of Mexicans were homeless. Of those with shelter, half lived in hovels that the government census deemed unfit for human habitation. Sanitation was nonexistent: public baths were rare, and a bar of soap cost 25 percent of the basic wage. Hungry, the poor were beaten to work under onerous conditions—regardless of the provisos against forced labor in the 1857 constitution. In both factory and hacienda the masses labored seven days a week, 11 to 12 hours a day. Not surprisingly, the national life expectancy in 1910 was 30—in contrast to 50 in the United States. In some rural, predominantly Indian areas 800 out of every 1,000 people died before reaching their first year; the national average was bad enough, at nearly 450 per 1,000.

Peasant uprisings became common. All were put down mercilessly with the support of those profiting from the Porfiriato. When confronted with the embarrassing reality of the mortality statistics, the privileged had a ready answer: the Indians were to blame. It was their innate laziness, not the lack of food and wages (most were paid in chits at the company store, not cash), that made them poor workers. It was their stupidity, not their lack of education, that made them illiterate. Alcoholism, they said, not hunger and poor sanitation, caused their early deaths.

Indians, the *científicos* claimed, held back the progress of Mexico. In the age of social Darwinism, pseudoscience glossed over blatant racism: the Indians were inferior, and there was no way to improve their lot; no education or training would enable them to farm better; no wage increases would improve their work; and no improved housing, nutrition, or sanitation would improve their health. So said the *cientíicos*.

## European Immigration

Most of the population increases were in cities. In many regions there were severe labor shortages. But European laborers and small farmers were preferred, not Indians. Díaz embarked on a program to encourage immigration. The *cientíicos* believed increasing the number of Europeans would add intelligence and energy to the labor force. Citizenship was made easy, and "vacant" lands were available at low prices so that the Indian presence could be "diluted." Although Europeans were preferred (to diffuse the influence of the North Americans as well), Mexico failed to attract them. Mexican wages and working conditions could not compete with the appeal of the United States, where an average of 3,500 Europeans arrived daily in 1907. Most who did take advantage of the welcome were from the United States, half of whom were illiterate drifters looking for a handout. In perhaps the worst racist policy since the colonial caste system, Díaz and his *cientíicos* managed to insult most Mexicans in order to attract just over 100,000 foreigners.

## Growing Nationalism

After 1900, the results of Porfiriato policies culminated in increasing dissatisfaction and rising opposition. In a surge of nationalism Mexicans, from northern hacendados to factory workers, were resentful of privileges granted to foreigners but not to them. The wealthy Madero family of Coahuila opposed a U.S. company's attempt to monopolize water rights. Young professionals saw only foreigners in the management positions they wanted and only 60-year-olds in the government of the aging Díaz. Small businesses couldn't get bank loans. Workers saw North Americans gain the best jobs in factories.

In this atmosphere of growing resentment, an increasing number of liberal publications found their voice. One, *Regeneración*, published by the Flores Magón brothers attracted enough attention to land the brothers in prison and eventually to self-exile in the United States. But from there they continued to publish—despite an assassination attempt ordered by Díaz—and received support from young Mexican intellectuals in their call for freedom of the press and better conditions for the poor. They wanted an end to child labor, an eight-hour work day, and the redistribution of uncultivated land.

A more serious challenge to the regime came from industrial workers who went on strike for equal pay with foreigners, thus disrupting the Pax Porfiriana. Some of the strikes, involving thousands of laborers, received national attention—and brutal repression. In 1906 striking textile workers in Veracruz, who had the audacity to request that Díaz arbitrate, were massacred.

To aggravate matters, the U.S. press called for the annexation of Mexico, and the U.S. government realized Mexico's worst fears when it militarily intervened on behalf of its business interests in Guatemala and the Caribbean. Mexicans wanted Díaz to reverse his favoritism of the United States. He tried, but not openly, and thereby gained no political advantage at home. Meanwhile he offered to Great Britain government oil contracts that formerly went to the United States, thereby gaining the enmity of his northern neighbor.

## Economic Depression: 1907–1908

Material progress had secured support for the dictatorship among the middle and upper classes. In the last decade of the Porfiriato, however, the economy faltered. First, inflation became a serious problem when foreign investment tripled and when Díaz adopted the gold standard for currency. Real wages fell. And a depression (1907–08), triggered by a slowing U.S. economy, caused layoffs and further reductions in wages. A bad harvest caused food prices to increase. In Chihuahua, for example, wages decreased 20 percent as basic living expenses increased 80 percent.

In the midst of its first economic crisis, the laissez-faire policies of the Porfiriato did little to provide relief. In fact, the government made matters worse by increasing taxes on the middle class in an effort to keep its treasury full. The foreign banks made credit tighter: many of the upper class defaulted on their loans. Everyone was affected by the catastrophe. For the first time, national (not just local) opposition groups formed advocating the violent overthrow of the dictator.

## "No Reelection" Revisited

In 1910 Díaz was 80 years of age and running for reelection. Foreign investors and supporters had been uneasy about his successor for some time. To guarantee a peaceful transition after his death, the *científicos* had urged him to run with a vice-presidential candidate as early as 1904. This time there was discontent among so many sectors of society that opposition grew to his running for office at all. Three national opposition groups formed; two of them advocated a violent overthrow of the regime.

Díaz made the mistake of telling a U.S. reporter that Mexico was ready for democracy and that he would not stand for reelection in 1910. In fact, he had no intention of retiring and was surprised when the article, "Thrilling Story of President Díaz, the Greatest Man on the Continent," reached Mexico. His opponents took Díaz's remarks to mean they could support other parties and candidates without fear of reprisals from the dictator, even if he himself ran.

Díaz maneuvered the most serious contender into a position abroad. He left the diminutive Francisco Madero from Coahuila alone, however, thinking that the northerner was a harmless idealist. Madero was disenchanted with Díaz's dependence on foreign capital and, like most wealthy individuals from the border states, he especially disliked the growing influence of the United States. Nationally known for a book he had written on presidential succession (which basically flattered Díaz), Madero argued that Mexico should return to the Constitution of 1857 with free elections, a free press, and an independent judiciary. He formed the Anti-Reelectionist Party, but social reforms in land and working conditions were not part of his platform.

Much to Díaz's surprise, Madero was enthusiastically received as he campaigned throughout the country with his call for "No Reelection." Even some hacendados in the north, angry that Díaz had supported calling in their defaulted mortgages during the depression, threw their support behind Madero. Increasingly concerned by his opponent's visible popularity, Díaz trumped up charges against Madero and had him temporarily imprisoned. The dictator and his vice president were reelected, of course, and Madero, escaping to Texas, claimed that the results of the 1910 election were fraudulent.

## Centennial Celebration: 1910

*I consider general revolution to be out of the question as does public opinion and the press.*

■

*Karl Bunz, German envoy, 1910 (translated by Frederick Katz)*

On September 16, 1910, Mexico celebrated the centennial of its independence. Emissaries from around the world arrived in Mexico City to honor the success of the young nation and to pay homage to the dictator on his 80th birthday. Amid the glitter of the month-long celebrations, Díaz seemed at the apogee of his power. The city was festively hung with lights, too bright for most to notice what all the poor saw as an omen in the dark night sky: Halley's Comet. With the poor rounded-up so as not to offend visitors' sensibilities, few could imagine that in seven months don Porfirio would be forced into exile.

The government spent 20 million pesos, more than the entire education budget, on lavish celebrations to impress the world with its prosperity and cultural sophistication. Operas were performed under a glass curtain designed by Tiffany. Plays in French were attended by all. At one ball alone, 20 carloads of imported French champagne were consumed. With only European waiters (or European look-alikes), no one would be reminded that Mexico was the land of Moctezuma rather than Cortés. In what has been called surreal illogic, Díaz arranged for a costly exhibit of Spanish art in a building especially constructed for the purpose as part of the independence celebrations. Mexican artists, led by the painter known as Dr. Atl (1875–1964), scraped together several hundred pesos to stage their own protest exhibit in the corridors of the Academy of San Carlos.

A hundred years after independence, Mexico was right to celebrate its modernization. The railroads and telegraphs, the international commerce, did much to unify a nation that had previously been fragmented. The political peace did permit the nation several decades in which to grow more confident in itself.

But there were other Díaz legacies: racism, xenophobia, starvation. The repressive and exploitative manner in which Díaz achieved modernization was about to exact its toll on Mexico with 20 years of war and even more of political turmoil. Peace and progress belonged only to the upper classes and had been achieved at the expense of the masses. The Porfiriato only too naturally led to revolution. A hundred years after the call for independence, Mexico was again at war with itself.

# 9

# THE REVOLUTION OF 1910 (1910–1940)

*The Revolution ... was an explosion of reality.*

*Octavio Paz, 1961*

The most devastating civil war in Mexican history produced modern Mexico. In the 10 years of its military phase, between 1910 and 1920, as many as 2 million people may have been killed, or one out of every eight Mexicans. Trains were blown up, haciendas were burned, and corruption prevailed. Yet the Mexican Revolution created new political structures and produced the Constitution of 1917. It destroyed the privilege of the Creole and gave birth to the mestizo nation. It ended feudalism and peonage and created labor unions and redistributed land. It gave birth to such Mexican heroes as Emiliano Zapata and Lázaro Cárdenas and such Mexican artists as Diego Rivera. The revolution gave Mexicans a sense of national pride and a deeply held appreciation for their own culture, called *mexicanidad.*

## The Beginning
A century after Hidalgo's declaration of independence, Francisco Madero (1873–1913) declared himself provisional president of Mexico from the safety of San Antonio, Texas. A member of the upper class, Madero typified his era by having been educated in both Paris and the United States. His family owned large estates as well as a smelting factory and mines. Liberal in his thinking and actions, Madero provided schooling and medical care for his workers and peons. Much like Hidalgo, he seemed to have little understanding of the forces he was about to unleash. Like Hidalgo, he thought political, not social, change

would rectify the nation's problems. He had previously opposed unseating Díaz by violence, but now realized that honest elections were impossible under the dictatorship.

In October, Madero issued his Plan de San Luis Potosí calling for Mexicans to rise against tyranny on November 20, 1910, after 6 P.M. His call to arms was vague enough to appeal to everyone with a complaint against the Porfiriato. On the appointed day small guerrilla forces sprung into action throughout much of Mexico. Like the caudillo revolts of the Santa Anna epoch, these poorly armed groups were inspired by local leaders and, except for local members of Madero's Anti-Reelectionist Party, were not coordinated with each other. The fighters were teachers, mechanics, merchants, and miners; and they were the unemployed, the soldiers of fortune, and bandits. They were Creoles who received too few favors from Díaz and the *científicos*. They were hacendados like Madero, who were concerned with electoral reform and foreign influence. Living off the countryside, the revolutionaries found plenty of support among the peasants, who quickly swelled their ranks. The radical and liberal, wealthy and poor, no matter their differences, united against Díaz.

Díaz tried to defeat them. He sent the army; he sent the *rurales*. He did quash the rebellions in most regions. But in the state of Chihuahua, he had no success. Chihuahua had long been simmering under the despotic hand of Luis Terrazas and his family. Terrazas was the richest man in Mexico, made more rich and powerful by Porfirio Díaz. He personally owned 50 haciendas and ranches that covered 7 million acres; his son-in-law, Enrique Creel, owned nearly another 2 million by himself. They owned mines, banks, telephone companies, textile mills, and meatpacking plants. Family members were governors, state legislators, and senators. Nothing happened in Chihuahua without their permission.

The revolutionary movement in Chihuahua grew under the leadership of a former mule skinner, Pascual Orozco, Jr. Joining him was the cattle rustler Pancho Villa. Orozco had lost his business because Terrazas did not favor him. Pancho Villa had escaped from debt peonage. Both understood what was at stake in changing the established order. And there were many others on the outs with the Terrazas clan. The Chihuahua rebels successfully routed a large contingent of the federal army and took control of most of the state.

In February 1911 Madero crossed the border into Mexico to join forces with Orozco and Villa: he would be the political symbol; they would be his army. It turned out to be a fragile alliance between civilian and military authority, one easily broken by strong personalities and military might. Unfortunately, it would typify the problems of governance in Mexico for the next decade.

Victories in Chihuahua reignited the rebellion in other states—Coahuila, Puebla, and Morelos—and soon revolutionaries such as Emiliano Zapata controlled most of the Mexican countryside. On May 8, Orozco and Villa captured the first large city, Ciudad Juárez. The rebels, against Madero's orders, defeated the army and occupied the city as their provisional capital. Other cities in the north and central Mexico were soon in rebel hands.

Federal troops began deserting. Madero's supporters demonstrated in the capital. Newspapers attacked Díaz. Businesses faltered. President Taft stationed U.S. warships off Veracruz to express displeasure at the continuing civil war. Díaz finally realized his situation was hopeless: an armistice was negotiated and signed on May 21.

The news spread though the streets of Mexico City. Mobs of people gathered in front of the National Palace shouting for Díaz to resign. The dictator responded as he always had—with force. Two hundred demonstrators were gunned down. He did resign on May 25, 1911, and surreptitiously slipped away to Paris. An interim president was appointed until an election could be arranged.

## President Madero

*Madero has unleashed a tiger; let's see if he can control him.*

■

*Porfirio Díaz, 1911 (quoted in Meyer & Sherman)*

Madero marched into Mexico City to the joyful cheers of mobs of Mexicans. In a matter of months, he had swept away the Porfiriato, and yet he would find it difficult to satisfy the aspirations of most of those who greeted him in the capital that day.

The most agile and charismatic leader would have stumbled, and Madero was neither. He appointed family members, some quite conservative, to important posts and left them to undermine the reforms he advocated. He invited charges of corruption against his government by giving out contracts to his family businesses. Most important, he did not fully understand the injustices requiring redress: early in his presidential campaign he had said that Mexico needed liberty, not bread. He thought the battle was over with a free and open election. He naively agreed to disband the revolutionary army.

Meanwhile Porfiriato conservatives were still active. Foreign businesses required profit. Workers demanded better conditions. And Emiliano Zapata, recognizing that Madero's victory did nothing for his cause, never stopped fighting for the return of peasant lands in the south. Workers struck for better conditions, but despite good intentions, Madero did little more than disperse the strikers. There were many factions Madero needed to appease, but he satisfied few. When he announced his support of a tax on idle land, those fighting for land redistribution were as disappointed as any foreign investor.

Many caudillos declared against him. Unfortunately for Mexico, they would continue declaring for the next decade, sometimes for their political principles but just as often out of envy and personal pique. The factions fought not only the Porfiristas, they fought each other. Against Madero, the first to proclaim was his former commander Orozco. Another was President Díaz's nephew. And there were others. He put them down with the assistance of Victoriano Huerta, who would later turn out to be traitorous.

Events overtook Madero and the fledgling democracy he instituted. Too kind to execute conservatives who had risen in arms against him, Madero imprisoned most of them in Mexico City where they proceeded to join forces. On the morning of February 9, 1913, they mysteriously gained release from prison and led their troops to the National Palace. Indifferent to the plight of the capital's residents, they brought their battle to the heart of the city. Madero responded with General Huerta in charge. For 10 days, called the Decena Trágica, the city suffered machine-gun fire and shelling, looting, and panic and hunger. Civilian casualties were in the thousands.

Madero demanded to know from his general when the fighting would stop. The next day it did, because Huerta had switched sides. The U.S. ambassador appointed by President Taft, Henry Lane Wilson, in the interest of protecting American business investments, had negotiated the resolution of the battle. Throughout Madero's term, Wilson had meddled and even called for Madero's resignation—especially when the president decided to tax oil production. In a shameless instance of dollar diplomacy, Madero was arrested, forced to resign, and murdered. General Huerta became president.

## The Social Revolution

The Mexican Revolution did not truly begin until the Madero regime ended. Until that point, most political changes had fulfilled the democratic values of the liberal middle class. Fighting had not been so drastic as to disrupt the economy. *Científicos* and foreign interests had influential allies in the Madero government.

With Madero's death the revolution intensified and swirled through the country like a tornado touching down to wreak havoc on the people and the economy while destroying enemies. Then feeding on its destructiveness, the violent winds would find new enemies—over and over again. For seven years, the factions would realign themselves, splinter, and gust ahead. When the dust settled in 1920, Mexico's institutional and intellectual underpinnings would be drastically changed from the preceding centuries. And the people who occupied the positions of power would be those who had been held in silence so long.

The breakdown of the racist class system that had presided in Mexico since the conquest can be seen in the personal histories of the revolutionary leaders, many of whom became presidents of the republic. Unlike previous Mexican power brokers, most were either mestizos or Indians from rural areas, and many were poor. Pancho Villa (1877–1923), the most colorful of the revolutionaries, was uneducated and was 25 years old before he could sign his name, yet he taught himself to read during a stint in prison. A bandit by trade, he was called Mexico's Robin Hood by the U.S. press. He fought the revolution, he said, for land reform and "so that every Mexican child could go to school" (Guzmán 1965, 393). Yet his impetuosity and cruelty—he gave free rein to Rodolfo Fierro, "the Butcher"—were as legendary as his daring and brilliance as a cavalry leader.

Emiliano Zapata (1879–1919) was a small landowner and horse trainer who had battled in court against the injustices of Díaz's land reforms to no avail. He was a trusted leader of his Morelos village and spoke the Nahuatl of his mostly Indian followers as well as the Spanish of politicians. In his Plan de Ayala, which called for the return of land illegally seized under Díaz and for the expropriation of lands, woods, and water from monopolists for the "majority of Mexicans who own nothing more than the land they walk on" (Meyer & Sherman 1983, 515), he articulated the agrarian issues that would be central to the revolution, issues that he would die fighting for under the banner Tierra y Libertad (land and liberty).

Although Zapata and Villa forced the basic issues of social reform, neither would assume political power. Others would, from similar backgrounds of poverty and political oppression. Victoriano Huerta's mother was a Huichol Indian, his father a mestizo. Although he made his way up through the army ranks by keeping the peace for Díaz

*Emiliano Zapata, detail of a mural (1929) by Diego Rivera (Cortés Palace, Cuernavaca)*

against the Yaqui in the north and the Maya in Yucatán, he was never truly accepted by the elite society of the Porfiriato. Álvaro Obregón was a mechanic and small rancher who had witnessed the awful confiscation of Yaqui lands in his home state of Sonora. Plutarco Elías Calles was an impoverished schoolteacher who did not own a pair of shoes before he was 16 years old. Lázaro Cárdenas had only three years of schooling and, at the age of 12, was the sole supporter of his family. He joined the revolution when he was a teenager.

## The Defeat of Huerta

The array of personalities and shifts of power in Mexico is dizzyingly intricate. Yet the individuals and their causes—or lack of them—are well known to every Mexican schoolchild. Madero is the symbol of democracy; Zapata the symbol of peasants' land rights. Pancho Villa is the fearless leader of the cavalry charge. Movie stars clamor to play these war heroes; novelists describe the dehumanization of the long struggle; artists paint U.S. capitalists meddling in Mexican affairs; war songs have become Mexican folk songs. The events are integral to contemporary Mexican nationalism.

The first political setback of the revolution began with the opportunist Huerta. He defied the constitutional rights the Madero revolution had fought for and created a dictatorship (1913–14) with Porfirista support. With surprising shrewdness for a man who was not often known to be sober, he held on to the presidency for 17 long months—repeatedly using political assassination against those who criticized him. Huerta could not assassinate, however, the new president of the United States, Woodrow Wilson, who refused to recognize his government of "usurpers" and who recalled Huerta's ally, Ambassador Henry Lane Wilson. But Huerta could use renewed European support to threaten U.S. business interests.

What would destroy Huerta were the revolutionary armies that sprang up against him and the support they received from Woodrow Wilson. Outraged by the murder of a compatriot, Venustiano Carranza, a conservative governor of Madero's home state, pronounced against Huerta on a platform similar to Madero's and formed the Constitutional Army of the North, declaring himself the "first chief." Other chiefs in the north, including Pancho Villa, Álvaro Obregón, and Plutarco Calles, signed on for the fight even if they were disgruntled by Carranza's presumptuousness in naming himself their leader. President Wilson permitted arms to be shipped across the border to them; payment was made with cattle stolen from the Terrazas clan. Emiliano Zapata had never stopped fighting and although he remained independent of the Constitutional Army, he forced Huerta to fight in the south as well as the north.

The revolutionary struggle resulted in the total militarization of Mexico. Huerta closed all businesses on Sundays so civilians could receive military training. The trains were preempted for military personnel, and the federal army grew from 50,000 to a quarter of a million troops. When the number of volunteers was inadequate, the poor were rounded up—outside a cantina, inside a jail—and tied up in a wagon for transport to the field. Huerta's programs supplied fresh recruits when they were most needed and were continued by others throughout the revolution. One-third of the budget went to Huerta's army.

Initially, Huerta was successful against the revolutionaries. In the south the Zapatistas were driven into the mountains, and their village

# WOMEN IN THE ARMY: SOLDADERAS

The army of the north, whether riding hard on the prairies or commandeering the trains, was like a massive migration of people. Women joined their husbands, often foraging for food and nursing the wounded, but also as *soldaderas* (women soldiers), slinging a rifle over one shoulder, a child on the other. When the federal government tried to banish women from its army, the troops threatened revolt.

*Popular among the troops was*
 *Adelita*
*The woman the sergeant adored*
*Because she was as brave as she*
 *was pretty*
*So even the colonel respected her.*

■

"Adelita," a revolutionary folk song

Yaqui Indian soldier of the Mexican Revolution (Courtesy of the Bancroft Library)

supporters were placed in concentration camps. In the north Carranza and Villa were pushed back. By 1914, Huerta controlled two-thirds of Mexico, the ports, and the vast majority of its population. The war effort was paid for by forced loans on businesses and taxes on oil—and church support that revived the old anticlericalism of the Juárez reform war. Debts were permitted by banks thanks to the financial backing of Great Britain and Lord Cowdray's Mexican oil interests.

Huerta's successes were reversed by the infusion of U.S. military aid in 1914. The competition over oil between Britain and the United States combined with the anti-Americanism of Huerta, moved Woodrow Wilson to openly support Carranza and his Constitutionalists. These armies of the north began taking cities from Huerta at the same time Zapata and his bands of guerrillas took over more areas in the south. The United States then intervened with its warships along the Gulf coast, attempting to force Huerta to resign.

The U.S. effort backfired when marines landed at Veracruz and thereby almost united all of Mexico behind Huerta. This insult to Mexico's sovereignty forced even Carranza and Zapata to denounce the invasion. Wilson agreed to permit some South American countries to mediate while he imposed an arms embargo at the port of Veracruz. The Constitutionalists, still supplied from the northern border, gained considerable ground in the fighting. In negotiations, Britain and the United States resolved their own disputes. The Huerta government was bankrupted and isolated. Huerta sailed into exile on July 20, 1914. On August 15, Obregón led the first troops of the Constitutional Army into the capital and Carranza, as first chief, proclaimed victory for the revolutionaries. The Porfiristas had been defeated once again.

## Anarchy

*With Carranza's whiskers*
*I'm going to weave a hat band*
*To put on the sombrero*
*Of his better Pancho Villa*

■

*"La Cucaracha," a revolutionary folk song*

Having successfully united against Huerta, the revolutionaries rediscovered their differences. Villa and Zapata had been confiscating and redistributing haciendas during the fighting. Carranza, a political reformer but not a social activist, disapproved. Too autocratic to listen to the other side, Carranza could not understand that elections, especially when they usually were rigged, were not the overwhelming concern of most of those who had been fighting—a change in the social order was.

There were personality clashes, but also class differences in the divide. Mostly Indian peasants had fought with Zapata under the symbol of the Virgin of Guadalupe, soldiers wearing sombreros and white peasant clothing who had been deprived of both land and water. Villa's army, the largest and most professional in the Mexican Revolution, was more diverse but included many who had gone hungry—peons, cowboys, and miners. Although these revolutionaries attracted their share of intellectual supporters, most of the middle class had supported Carranza. As Villa said to Zapata in their historic meeting in Mexico City, the Carrancistas "are men who have always slept on soft pillows. How could they ever be friends of the people, who have spent their whole lives in nothing but suffering" (Quirk 1963, 135).

In October 1914 the various military factions gathered at the Convention of Aguascalientes to select a provisional president. Villa controlled the outcome, which meant that a puppet president, rather than Carranza, was selected. The result was five more years of war.

> *Villa? Obregón? Carranza? What's the difference? I love the revolution like a volcano in eruption; I love the volcano, because it's a volcano; I love the revolution, because it's a revolution.*
>
> ■
>
> The Underdogs, *Mariano Azuelo, 1916*

Each faction claimed its own capital, provisional president, and issued its own currency. But Carranza, based in the port of Veracruz and near the foreign-owned oil fields, was able to get an infusion of munitions and mount the strongest army. Obregón, siding with Carranza, defeated Villa in 1915 in the famous battle of Celaya with only half the number of Villa's 20,000 troops. Of the Villistas 4,000 died, 5,000 more were wounded, and 6,000 were taken prisoner. Obregón claimed fewer than 200 dead among his soldiers. By 1916 Villa was forced to retreat to the Chihuahua hills where he had begun as a cattle rustler. But he remained a dangerous threat to Carranza, raiding towns and attacking the army.

As a bizarre aside to the upheaval, Pancho Villa provoked an intervention by the United States in 1916. Having failed to mediate an end to the fighting, President Wilson recognized Carranza's very successful forces as the de facto government. Whether this abandonment by his former supporter drove Villa beyond reason is unclear. Whatever the cause, Villa's men stopped a train in Chihuahua and shot 15 Americans. Then Villa sent troops across the border into Columbus, New Mexico, to acquire arms. Instead they terrorized the village, shouting "Death to the gringos!" burning the town, and killing 18 residents.

Some in the U.S. Senate called for the occupation of all of Mexico. Instead, Wilson sent a punitive expedition under General Pershing to execute Villa. Violating Mexican sovereignty, Pershing searched for many months but left without ever setting eyes on Villa. The expedition cost the United States $130 million and a good deal of Mexican ill will.

Although Villa was somewhat contained in Chihuahua, the Carranza government had other uprisings to control. The most important was Zapata's. Carranza sent an army of 30,000 against Zapata's 20,000 and attempted to return confiscated estates to wealthy hacendados. The army managed to fight Zapata back into the confines of the state of Morelos, but later Zapata drove out the federal forces and organized an independent government with its own land commission.

## The Constitution of 1917

The first chief controlled much of Mexico, yet the situation was far from peaceful. Carranza also needed a constitutional convention in order to bring about a new legal framework to legitimize his government and his own election as president. Others supported the convention, but from it they intended to incorporate the goals and aspirations of the many peoples who had fought in the Revolution.

Hoping to revive the Constitution of 1857 with a few minor changes, Carranza convened 200 national delegates in Querétaro on December 1, 1916. They were far from representative. Delegate qualifications were so restrictive that relatives of Madero could not attend. All Zapatistas and Villistas were barred, and 80 percent of the delegates were from the middle class and only a third represented the military. Half were well educated and many were young. Even with a stacked convention, Carranza suffered a devastating defeat: under the leadership of Obregón, his minister of war, radical amendments were made to the constitution.

With their nation still suffering from civil war, the delegates struggled for two months to hammer out a constitution that would permit, and even mandate, fundamental social change. The most astounding amendment, Article 27, concerned land reform. Twenty-five hundred words in length, it comprised half the constitution and was an exposition on the relationship between private and public property, on individual rights versus the public good. In a section that alarmed all foreign corporations, it eliminated all monopolies on water and mineral resources and, reverting to the Spanish law that Díaz had repealed, it gave the nation rights to such natural resources. It made the communal Indian *ejidos* inalienable and limited the size of estates. It provided for land redistribution to be paid for by government bonds. And it restricted foreign ownership to those who agreed to be treated like Mexicans: no foreign interventions were to be allowed on their behalf.

Article 123 protected workers and destroyed debt peonage. A minimum wage was mandated, adequate to provide for education, "lawful pleasures," and the subsistence needs of workers. Work hours and a day of rest were also mandated, as was government insurance in times of unemployment, retirement, sickness, and death. In addition, the rights to organize, bargain collectively, and strike were granted by this amendment. It was an amendment that protected Mexican workers to the same degree as in industrial nations.

Many of the amendments included clauses that limited the role of the church. Huerta's considerable support from the church had revived anticlerical sentiments among the revolutionaries. All church properties were proclaimed government property, without compensation. Monastic orders were outlawed. Priests were not permitted to vote. Important mandates for universal and free primary education stipulated that only secular schools would be constitutional. Freedom of religion was granted; the Catholic Church would no longer be the sole religion permitted in Mexico.

For the first time the social concerns of most Mexicans and most revolutionaries were formulated. Institutions that had crippled the state in the past were weakened: the church, foreign interests, and haciendas. The Constitution of 1917 provided a legal framework for the government that, though amended, continues to this day. It would take two decades to implement.

## The Carranza Presidency, 1917–1920

Even Carranza never openly challenged the constitution—perhaps because the first chief did not wish to acknowledge his humiliating political defeat at a hand-picked convention. The constitution also legitimized his election to a four-year term as president in March 1917. The constitutional president simply ignored the rest of the provisions.

Carranza's election did not usher in the end of the military phase of the revolution; rather his policies continued the social violence and fighting. He did nothing to implement change, and he was properly criticized for his failure to conform to the constitution. Instead of setting up the commissions that would have implemented a minimum wage, he fought the unions. Strikes, organized by the anarchist Casa del Obrero Mundial, plagued industry. Because organized labor had supported Carranza, he had subsidized the various unions and permitted them to be armed. But with the economy disrupted and foreign powers complaining, he banished the Casa del Obrero and disbanded their armies. When the rail workers declared a strike, he conscripted the workers into the army. Despite his efforts to weaken the unions, however, in 1918 the first national organization, the Regional Confederation of Mexican Workers (CROM), was formed.

In regard to land reform his performance was equally regressive. He actually gave back communal *ejido* lands to the Porfiristas. Further, he

The Trench, *mural (c. 1930) by José Clemente Orozco in the National Preparatory School, Mexico City*

was relentless in his pursuit of Zapata. The army killed thousands of innocent civilians in its search for the rebel leader and burned crops and killed cattle to starve even more. The Zapatistas responded in kind, blowing up a civilian passenger train. Zapata wrote a letter to Carranza:

> It never occurred to you that the Revolution was fought for the benefit of the great masses ... you have given or rented our haciendas to your favorites ... and the people are mocked in their hopes.
>
> ■
>
> Emiliano Zapata, 1919 (Meyer & Sherman 1983, 548)

Carranza responded with an elaborate plot to assassinate the revolutionary hero. On April 10, 1919, his plot succeeded: Zapata was shot point-blank in an ambush. His body was displayed to convince the Zapatistas and the peasants for whom he had struggled so long that their leader was, in fact, dead.

## The End of Military Revolution: 1920
When Carranza's presidential term ended, the revolution had ravaged Mexico without accomplishing its primary social objectives. Carranza had also undermined its liberal political objectives by instituting martial law and rigging elections. He didn't dare openly challenge the no reelection clause of the constitution; he did try, however, to subvert it by nominating one of his puppets to run against Álvaro Obregón, the minister of war.

Patience ran out with Carranza. Generals from around the country declared against him; regions declared independence. It was Obregón who finally chased him out of office. Carranza's presidency ended with the corruption and violence typical of the period: he fled with all the public treasury he could carry, allegedly 20 train cars' worth; he was captured en route to Veracruz and shot.

## The Devastation of War

> Thinkers ... prepare the Revolution; bandits carry it out. At the moment no one can say with any assurance: "So-and-so is a revolutionary and What's-his name is a bandit." Tomorrow perhaps it will be clearer.
>
> ■
>
> The Flies, Mariano Azuela, 1918

A decade of civil war devastated the people, countryside, and economy. As armies of tens of thousands moved back and forth across the land, they took with them whatever crops were in the fields and drove the cattle along as provisions. Revolutionaries burned haciendas and destroyed mills. Any crops they missed could not be harvested because the able-bodied were carried off with the armies. In the cities, fires raged, too; in Mexico City alone more than 50 elementary schools were burned down.

Payment, when it couldn't be avoided, was in chits or recently printed paper called "money." Each army printed currency as needed. Not only were different currencies used in the various regions, but they changed with the arrival of each new army, being exchangeable one day, but not the next—except for Zapata's coins, that is, which were minted from the silver of confiscated mines. There was an unending supply of money for the armies and inflationary prices for everyone else. Guadalajara reported that the price of corn and beans tripled in 1918.

Mexicans were hungry during the Porfiriato, but they were hungrier during the revolution. Even when the government attempted to fix food prices, its efforts were inadequate. Transport systems, especially the railroads, had been expropriated by the armies or destroyed in the fighting; slow grain distribution was one result. With the United States and Europe engaged in World War I, not enough foodstuffs could be imported to alleviate the problem. The amount of maize available per capita was the lowest since colonial times. In 1917 the government officially recognized a corn famine. Malnutrition was common. Food riots broke out in some towns. Others reported 100 deaths a day due to starvation. Even in 1918 when there weren't marching armies sweeping the land, food production was low.

## The War Economy

With the prolonged fighting, Mexico's economy should have stopped short. Instead, World War I gave it a boost. Yucatecan *henequén* was in high demand for cordage; profits from its trade stabilized the revolutionary government's finances into the early 1920s. Oil and metals, too, were in higher demand than ever because of the war. During the Mexican Revolution, foreign oil companies bribed the armies to protect their equipment and industry. Oil production boomed, and Mexico became the fourth largest supplier in the world. Production, often wasteful and exploitative—gasoline cost more in Mexico than abroad—increased from almost 4 million barrels in 1910 to almost 200 million in 1921. Although the mines, mostly foreign owned, had suffered during

| Commodity Production, 1910–1920 | | | | | |
|------|------------|---------|---------|-------------|-----------|
| Year | Corn | Sisal | Copper | Oil | Silver |
| 1910 | 3,219,624 | 94,790 | 48,160 | 3,634,080 | 2,416,669 |
| 1912 | 2,062,971 | 139,902 | 57,245 | 16,558,215 | 2,526,715 |
| 1914 | 1,961,073 | 169,286 | 26,621 | 26,235,403 | 810,647 |
| 1916 | ** | 201,990 | 28,411 | 40,545,712 | 925,993 |
| 1918 | 1,899,625 | 140,001 | 70,200 | 63,828,326 | 1,944,542 |
| 1920 | ** | 160,759 | 49,192 | 157,068,678 | 2,068,938 |

In metric tons except oil in barrels; from John Womack in Bethell (1991, 133)
**-not available

the Huerta period, silver, zinc, and copper production under Carranza increased and even surpassed that of the Porfiriato—and prices had never been higher.

The Mexican government was kept afloat during World War I by its trade and by the taxes on extracted materials. But when its debts were reckoned, the nation couldn't have been in worse shape. Foreign debt was high even for Mexico: in 1923, it amounted to $750 million, three times higher than after the first round of fighting when Madero took office. Then, there was an additional $1 billion of foreign claims against Mexico for damage done to their companies during the Revolution. The domestic debt was no less impressive. All those army chits and paper monies and forced loans on businesses and the church became claims against the government. And the military was a continuing financial burden, with many soldiers and officers owed back pay. There were years in which the cost of the military was 70 percent of expenditures. Not even a war boom could finance so much debt.

## The Revolutionary Reconstruction, 1920–1940

*We too could produce a Kant or Hugo. We too could wrest iron from the bowels of the earth and fashion it . . . We could raise prodigious cities and create nations, and explore the universe. Was it not from a mixture of the races that the Titans sprang?*

■

*José Clemente Orozco (translated by Ramón Eduardo Ruiz)*

Mexico finally was about to embark on a period of political stability. Its leadership would be assumed by social revolutionaries such as Álvaro Obregón, Plutarco Calles, and Lázaro Cárdenas. Each president would lead Mexico toward social and economic changes as envisioned by the Constitution of 1917. Only Cárdenas wasn't from the north, however, and only he would understand the indigenous communities that dominated central and southern Mexico. With increasing political stability, Mexico created a national identity as well, one that esteemed its blending of races into a new culture and a mestizo people. As a new Mexico took shape, a few violent episodes occurred, but they did not succeed in ripping the nation apart. Mexico was well on the way to solving its conflicts without the military.

## President Álvaro Obregón, 1920–1924

Obregón (1880–1928) brought political ingenuity, not just military might, to the Mexican presidency. As one of the great military strategists of the revolution, Obregón had won many battles, including the decisive ones against Villa, with his Yaqui Indian soldiers and union supporters. He was a listener, a general who could sit and discuss strategy with his troops. He was a keen observer and chose his sides carefully and successfully. Although committed to social change and the implementation of the constitution, he was practical and knew how to compromise.

Knowing peace was imperative, Obregón granted an amnesty to all factions. He appointed Villistas and Zapatistas to his government. In exchange for remaining outside of politics, Pancho Villa was given a ranch and substantial pension. A Zapatista was put in charge of the Morelos troops that had once been the enemy. Other "generals" were bought off by well-paid positions in the army, but in an attempt to separate the government from the military, Obregón reserved most cabinet posts for civilians.

Obregón was the first revolutionary president committed to social reform. He was well aware of the simmering discontent of the peasants and organized labor who had received nothing after a decade of war. He had fought alongside them and heard their complaints. As a first step toward implementing the land reforms mandated in the constitution, he granted the Indians title to their lands that had been stolen. He also permitted peasants to keep the land they had occupied during the Revolution. Worried that agricultural production would be adversely affected if he moved too quickly on the haciendas before smaller enterprises got under way, Obregón's land redistribution was significant but tentative: on the whole, about 3 million acres returned to more than 600 villages. Not even the vast estates of the Terrazas clan were diminished in the process.

Obregón supported labor, as long as it did not attempt to disrupt the structure of the capitalist system. In collaboration with Luis Morones, the head of CROM, the government encouraged the growth of that union, even if it was not always so generous with more radical ones, especially when they had foreign leaders. During Obregón's term, CROM grew from 50,000 members to well over 1 million.

## The Mexican Vision: José Vasconcelos

For the first time in Mexican history, the government attempted to educate people of all classes. Obregón chose not to enforce strictly the anticlerical laws; it would have closed 20 percent of the schools, not to mention create political unrest. Instead he put a remarkable man in charge of education, José Vasconcelos (1882–1959). A man of letters, a lawyer by training and a self-taught philosopher, Vasconcelos desired a cultural identity for Mexico and inspired intellectuals and artists to collaborate with him in its creation. He conceived of a populist nationalism, a blending of all ethnic groups into a new 20th-century Mexican "cosmic race." This mixing of peoples would turn Mexico into a perfect mestizo nation.

The new Mexico needed education to incorporate all the peoples into the nation, from the rural Maya in the south to the mestizo miners in the north. The education budget increased from 15 million pesos in 1921 to 35 million in 1923. Under Carranza, education accounted for less than 1 percent of the federal budget; under Obregón it went up to 15 percent. The Vasconcelos budget more than tripled the amount spent by the Porfiriato.

Vasconcelos sent Peace Corps–style volunteers to live with village families and help them build schools. Then, the teachers would move in, as well as artisans and technicians to provide skills training and agricultural assistance. Determined to provide more than technical education to the poor, Vasconcelos published Spanish translations of the classics—Plato, Homer, and Dante—to stock the school houses.

Vasconcelos's vision of Mexico captured the Mexican spirit. Volunteers joined a campaign to go to the remotest areas to teach children and adults how to read. (The enormity of the undertaking can best be judged by the statistics: under Díaz, illiteracy was at least 80 percent; in 1934 it had been reduced only to 62 percent.) Artists joined in the educational campaign, too. Vasconcelos insisted that a Mexican identity required cultural nationalism and funded the Department of Fine Arts to sponsor painting, music, folk art, and songs. The walls of public buildings were given to artists such as Diego Rivera (SEE page 3) to paint with subjects relating to Mexican history and culture. From this was born Mexico's great muralist movement (SEE pages 188–190).

## Relations with the United States

Despite his popularity within Mexico, Obregón did not initially receive recognition from the United States under President Harding. There were matters to be resolved, such as the outstanding debt overdue since the Porfiriato and payment for damages to U.S. property during the Revolution. Furthermore, American corporations were alarmed about the constitutional restrictions on subsoil rights. Recognition would not be easily forthcoming.

The biggest oil companies had lobbied Harding and supported his election, so much so that their influence eventually was exposed as the Teapot Dome scandal. But in the interim, their business concerns became U.S. concerns. Looked at carefully, the Constitution of 1917 gave the Mexican government control over the very oil, silver, copper, and other natural resources that foreigners thought they owned. The United States wanted an exemption from the newly wrought Mexican constitution.

## The de la Huerta Rebellion

Obregón could not meet U.S. conditions. But in 1923, he was forced to seek U.S. support. The two strongmen of his administration were Plutarco Elías Calles, minister of the interior, and Adolfo de la Huerta, minister of finance. As Obregón's term approached its end, he declared support for Calles as his successor. Although Calles had been a general in the revolution in support of Obregón, most of his backing came from labor and Zapatista agrarians. Conservatives thought Calles was too radical. The military was unhappy with Obregón's reduction of the army, and there were other disgruntled groups who joined in encouraging de la Huerta to declare himself against Obregón. It was around the time of this tense juncture that Pancho Villa, having threatened to come out of political retirement, was assassinated.

Such powerful opposition in the past would have disrupted Mexico for untold years. This time it was quashed in a matter of a few months, but at a price. In return for U.S. recognition and support against the insurgents, Obregón conceded that the constitutional provisions in regard to natural resources would not be applied retroactively to properties exploited before 1917. At a critical moment, the United States blockaded the Gulf and sent munitions to Obregón. Obregón put down the uprising quickly and brutally. Seven thousand rebels were killed; their leaders, 54 of them Obregón's former supporters and friends, were rounded up and shot. The age of the caudillos was ending.

## President Calles: *Jefe Máximo*

When Obregón finally transferred his power to Calles, it was the first peaceful transition in almost half a century. Despite the brief violent outburst in 1923, Mexico was achieving a semblance of political stability. The economy was prospering after the post–World War I recession, and the treasury was in good shape. Although Obregón retired having gained considerable respect for his accomplishments, there were concerns that more progress had not been made toward implementing the constitutional reforms. Some, such as Vasconcelos, resigned from government. Others thought any progress was a worthy accomplishment.

Calles (1877–1945), a poor schoolteacher who had risen through the revolution to army general, governor of Sonora, and Obregón cabinet member, believed the primary role of his government was to get the Mexican economy working. With classic capitalist policies, he streamlined the government (the education budget dropped from 15 percent to 7 percent of the total), increased taxes on oil, and created a government surplus. The money went to creating financial and banking institutions that enabled Calles to begin much needed highway and rail construction, and agricultural improvements, such as irrigation. National industries were encouraged through protective legislation.

Luis Morones, the head of the most powerful union, CROM, was minister of industry, commerce and labor (1924–28). He was charged to set constitutional standards for labor—improved working conditions, minimum wages, pensions—but to do so while constantly mediating these matters with both business and workers. His efforts saved the Mexican textile industry and often were appreciated by other businesses that were protected from wildcat strikes. Unions that did not cooperate, rivals of Morones's CROM, ceased to be protected by the state.

## Oil Problems

An ardent nationalist, Calles repudiated Obregón's compromise with U.S. oil companies and insisted that the constitution be implemented in regard to natural resources. There already were signs that the oil wells had been wastefully exploited rather than managed for market demand and longevity. As Mexico threatened nationalization, the oil companies retaliated by decreasing production (by 42 percent in 1926–27) and investing in other countries like Venezuela. The pressure on Calles was unmistakable; oil duties fell from one-third of government revenues to one-eighth in 1927. As a further blow, the companies pulled their money out of the banks, causing a devaluation of the peso.

Because Mexico's economy had become so dependent on oil, which represented 70 percent to 76 percent of exports, it was easily disrupted and, worse, disrupted by foreign interests. Only 3 percent of the investments in the oil industry were Mexican. Mexican relations with U.S. banking and manufacturing concerns were good (for example, Ford, Colgate, British-American tobacco), but they could not replace oil revenues. The result was an empty treasury, unemployment, strikes, and nonpayment of interest on foreign debt. All this foreign retaliation, and the oil fields hadn't even been nationalized yet. The economic situation worsened with the Cristero Rebellion and sunk fully into the quicksand with the Great Depression of 1929.

## The Cristero Rebellion

As if Mexico were not confronting enough crises, Bishop José Mora y del Río granted a newspaper interview in which he adamantly attacked the anticlerical provisions of the constitution. This political attack in and of itself was in violation of the constitution, and Calles countered swiftly. Many of the anticlerical laws had not been implemented; now they were: foreign priests were deported, religious processions banned, monasteries closed. The church responded on July 31, 1926, by refusing to provide any religious services. For the first time since the conquest, not a single mass was performed in Mexico. There was no baptism, no Christian burial.

The stalemate continued between church and state for almost three years. Because the state owned the churches, they remained opened and most Mexicans, being devoutly Catholic, found solace in them. The clergy had hoped that their parishioners would instead rise in rebellion. Only a few did. Called Cristeros for their battle cry of "Viva Cristo Rey" ("Long live Christ the King"), they burned schools and killed teachers; they also attacked peasants who supported the government because they had received redistributed lands. In sum, it was another ugly episode in Mexican history. It was ugliest in the states of Michoacán and

Jalisco where, in 1927, the Cristeros dynamited a passenger train and then set it on fire so the survivors could not escape.

The U.S. ambassador Dwight Morrow negotiated a face-saving compromise between the church and Mexico. But before it could be implemented, a Cristero assassinated Obregón. Obregón, under an amendment to the constitution that permitted reelection after a term out of office and that extended the term to six years, had just been reelected. The outrage at the Cristeros ended the armed uprising.

## The Maximato, 1928–1934

It is believed that Calles and Obregón planned to alternate as president under the new constitutional amendment. But Obregón's campaign had brought out deeply held Mexican fears about reelection. After Obregón's assassination, Calles had no intention of giving up power—it was unclear who could have successfully replaced him at that time—but he thought it wiser to control the country from behind a puppet president. For this he was known as the Jefe Máximo (the Big Boss), and his extended term was the Maximato. The problems with the succession in 1929 also brought him to concentrate power in the hands of a single party, the PNR, or the Partido Nacional Revolucionario; the party would enable the state to transcend personality politics. Eventually it would become the PRI, or the Institutional Revolutionary Party that would control the government for the rest of the 20th century.

Calles was remarkable for the enemies he fought, because he believed they weakened the nation. He never backed down from the task of national integration and progress even when seriously challenged by foreign oil interests and the Catholic Church. But he did not resolve the problems involved with them, either, and they festered. Under the Jefe Máximo, elections once again were a political charade for a string of presidential puppets, but the government remained stable and power was concentrated in the PNR, a party open to many social forces, such as agrarian leagues and labor unions.

## Lázaro Cárdenas: The People's Hero 1934–1940

As his control over Mexican politics continued, Calles became increasingly cynical and corrupt. Like many before him, his personal wealth and that of his cronies became a major preoccupation, and his politics became more conservative after the depression put an end to so many of his programs. It seemed the initial energy imbuing the revolution and the idealism engaging the Mexican intelligentsia had been spent. Repeatedly in Mexican history, individuals born to humble circumstances were catapulted into power and succumbed to greed. Lázaro Cárdenas (1895–1970) should have been another *político* distorted by power. Instead he was incorruptible. At the moment history might have written the end of the revolution, Cárdenas became president.

Calles personally approved of the PNR's selection of Cárdenas as the presidential candidate. As a young man, Cárdenas had fought under Calles in the Mexican Revolution, became a general himself at the age of 25, then in 1928 became governor of the state of Michoacán where he was born. He was the first president of the revolution who was not from the north, but rather from a traditional indigenous state: he understood the importance of *ejido* lands to the peasants. Cárdenas also was a leader of the younger radical wing of the PNR, yet Calles thought he would be easy to control, given his reputation for loyalty and honesty. Instead, it would take Cárdenas only a year to defeat Calles's control of the presidency and one more year to force him into exile.

Although the results of his election were foreordained, Cárdenas campaigned diligently, traveling to small towns and factories and covering 1,800 miles, some of them on horseback. He campaigned on a platform formulated by the younger wing of the party, the "Six-Year Plan" that emphasized greater land distribution and agrarian assistance, more support of organized labor, the elimination of illiteracy, and less foreign dependence. The campaign educated him about the populace, and the platform gained him support, especially among peasants and workers. His election went smoothly and no caudillo or assassin disrupted his assumption of the presidency in 1934. In contrast to Calles's lavish lifestyle, Cárdenas cut his salary by half and gave up Chapultepec Castle, formerly Maximilian and Carlota's palace, as the presidential residence and made it into a museum. Throughout his presidency he received delegations of the people and patiently heard their concerns; he mandated one hour a day of free telegraph service for citizens wishing to communicate with him.

Cárdenas inherited a nation of pent-up frustrations. The economic impact of the 1929 depression had finally ended in 1934, but workers had suffered wage cutbacks and were engaged in escalating strikes and more radical politics. The agrarian movement had been abandoned by an increasingly conservative Calles; many peasants remained without land, and production of maize and beans had been falling since the already devastatingly low levels of the Porfiriato.

Meanwhile, Calles never stopped his attacks on the church, and the country festered with the conflict.

## Agrarian Reforms

In 1936 Mexico's agrarian policy appeared to be failing. Investments had encouraged mostly export crops, not the subsistence crops of the peasants. The depression, however, revealed the flaws in this export policy. Yucatán state with its *henequén* plantations, for example, was destitute. The peasantry was starving. Since the end of the revolution, less than 15 percent of cultivated land had been redistributed, and only 10 percent of the villages had been given *ejidos*. But Cárdenas, unlike his predecessors, made agrarian reform a hallmark of his presidency. In the quarter of a century before he took office, about 10 million hectares changed hands. Cárdenas alone redistributed 18 million hectares—about 49 million acres. The landless population fell from 2.5 million to less than 2 million. Forty-seven percent of the cultivated land belonged to *ejidos*.

Cárdenas not only gave traditional Indian villages land. He expropriated export crop haciendas and gave them to the peons working them: cotton in the north became the product of former peons, as did *henequén* in Yucatán. Cárdenas also took advantage of a healthy economy to pour resources into the *ejidos*, creating a special bank to extend credit to the communal lands to provide the infrastructure for success: irrigation, electrification, fertilizers, and seed. The *ejidos* were also encouraged to mobilize into organizations representing their interests, and the National Peasants Confederation (CNC) was formed.

Unfortunately, these experiments in collective commercial farming failed to be adequately productive (partially because they received no further support after Cárdenas's six-year term) and, with an explosion

| Land Distribution by Administration, 1915–1940 | |
|---|---|
| President | Percentage |
| Carranza | 1 |
| Obregón | 5 |
| Calles and the Maximato | 28 |
| Cárdenas | 66 |
| Based on Meyer & Sherman (1983, 599) | |

in the rural population, the amount of *ejido* land itself sometimes proved inadequate. But as a social reform, the success was unquestioned: the institution of the hacienda, a feudal legacy from the conquest, was finally destroyed. Anita Brenner described the changes in 1943:

> Before and after pictures of most Mexican villages would not show any great change. But once upon a time a stranger who happened to ride in would find deserted streets, closed doors, rustlings in the houses; famished dogs . . . if he dismounted, some elder with suspicion on his face, fear in his eyes, would inquire about his business. Today no one, not even the women and children, hides. Doors stay open . . . small boys tag along asking to act as guides. The women, if they get a chance, like to show the community prides . . . the public corn-grinder, run by an old car motor at the rate of a few pennies for the day's supply of dough; the pump, the school . . .

## Real Wages

Cárdenas also supported the labor unions. CROM was in disarray and politically discredited due to corruption. Cárdenas asked labor organizer Vicente Lombardo Toledano to organize another national union that could work with the government. Three thousand unions formed the Confederación de Trabajadores de México (CTM), which soon had more than a million members. Under Lombardo Toledano, CTM struggled to increase real wages. Although the average daily minimum wage was 1.6 pesos, it cost a head of household 4 pesos to support a family of four each day. Business resisted an increase in the minimum wage, but eventually a compromise of 3.5 pesos was reached. Real wages in Mexico had finally increased.

## Nationalization of Oil

> In how many of the villages bordering on oil fields is there a hospital, or school, . . . or even an electric plant fed by the millions of cubic meters of natural gas allowed to go to waste? . . . Who is not aware of the irritating discrimination governing construction of the company camps? Comfort for the foreign personnel; misery, drabness, and insalubrity for the Mexicans . . . Another inevitable consequence of the presence of oil companies . . . even more harmful than all those already mentioned has been their persistent and improper intervention in national affairs . . .
>
> ■
>
> Lázaro Cárdenas, March 18, 1938

Cárdenas implemented a policy by which companies that failed to comply with the constitution, especially when they could not resolve workers' strikes in accordance with it, would be confiscated. A number were. The most famous of these were the foreign oil companies, which had a long history of taking fortunes out of the country but giving little in return. Constantly interfering in Mexico's internal politics and seeking special favors, they were an obvious target of the country's new-found nationalism. Company policies toward Mexican workers had always been a problem: they were not given the better positions nor trained for management or technical jobs. Also, the companies did not respond seriously to union strikes and demands.

In 1938, the companies refused to settle a labor conflict in accordance with binding arbitration. They instead appealed the decision to the Mexican Supreme Court. Even after the court upheld the arbitration board, the companies failed to comply with the order. Cárdenas, claiming they had defied Mexico's law and sovereignty, nationalized the holdings of 17 U.S. and British oil companies—with compensation. For Mexicans it was an order for national respect. All classes rejoiced, even the archbishop encouraged support for the president, and the poor walked barefoot into the city to contribute coins and chickens—whatever would help pay for the expropriation.

The U.S. oil companies waged a newspaper campaign at home, claiming that Cárdenas's action was no less than theft and that Mexico's oil industry would collapse without foreign know-how. The world economy, they said, would suffer because Mexico was not technically

## OIL AND XENOPHOBIA

The nationalization of oil is no less an icon of Mexican consciousness than the Virgin of Guadalupe. Oil symbolized foreign dominance and discrimination against Mexican workers. In 1914, both U.S. and French investors owned more of Mexico than Mexicans; the total foreign holdings were triple that of Mexican holdings. Reacting to centuries of foreign intervention, the Revolution called for a Mexico for Mexicans. The expropriation of the petroleum industry finally satisfied the xenophobic Mexicans that their day had come. It was celebrated as Economic Independence Day with the commemoration of a monument in the capital.

competent to manage its own oil reserves. The sides angrily disagreed as to how much compensation was just: Mexico offered $10 million; the companies demanded $200 million. Fortunately for Cárdenas, Franklin D. Roosevelt had just become president on a platform of nonintervention in Latin America. The amount was settled peacefully between the two nations by a commission that agreed on $24 million as fair. Initially there was a drop in oil production, partly because of untrained workers and aging equipment. It did not take Mexico long, however, before it was outproducing the foreign companies.

## Church and Education

The younger generation of the PNR had emphasized education and the elimination of illiteracy as a six-year goal. Their kind of education had no room for the catechism—in fact, the government thought, the uneducated could not progress because they were superstitious rather than scientific in their approach to the world and its problems. This they blamed on the Catholic Church. Cárdenas did not want his educational program to stir up the fanaticism of the Cristeró Rebellion, however, and worked out a compromise with the church. The church would be forbidden under the constitution to run schools; but the curriculum of the schools would not attack either religion or the church.

Cárdenas increased the education budget to the highest it had ever been. The money for rural schools, half the budget, emphasized a practical curriculum—the reading teacher was accompanied by agricultural experts, midwives, home economics instructors, and artisans. The efforts did increase literacy, but because the population was increasing so rapidly, the funds were inadequate to be completely successful. In 1930 the population of Mexico was 16.5 million; in 1940 it had leaped to 20 million. Although the absolute number of illiterate individuals increased, the literacy rate nonetheless grew to 42 percent.

Not all of the government's efforts were welcomed. In the thinly populated region of Quintana Roo, some Maya had managed to live independently of government interference except for a few years at the end of the Caste Wars in 1901. But in the 1930s, the value of the resin in the native sapodilla trees, used to make chewing gum, increased on the international market. The government reasserted itself in the region, regulating schools and issuing licenses for bleeding the trees. The Maya, wishing to manage their own schools and work the land and its resources according to their traditions, challenged the government's right to interfere.

## Mexican Art and Society

*Even the smallest manifestations of the material or spiritual vitality of our race spring from our native midst.*

■

*1923 Manifesto of the Technical Workers, Painters, and Sculptors Union (Ashton 1990, 555)*

The Revolution of 1910 ushered in dramatic social changes. Contrasting the simplicity of Cárdenas's lifestyle with that of Díaz properly emphasizes some of the change. Instead of women in their embroidered Parisian dresses, one thinks of the artist Frida Kahlo dressed in indigenous clothing. Instead of champagne parties, one is reminded of university students volunteering, as teachers in Zapotec and Maya villages.

Revolutionary Mexico extolled its own traditions, its native peoples, and pre-Columbian past. Indians no longer were considered inferior as they had been since the Spanish conquest, rather, the destruction of their culture and their exploitation became major themes in the arts. The glories of their ancient history were revived and studied (SEE pages 3 and 51). An archaeology institute was established in 1925 to preserve and excavate pre-Columbian ruins. The ruins at Chichén Itzá in Yucatán, for example, were excavated in conjunction with the Carnegie Institute from the United States and restored in a manner to attract tourists to a Mexico now proud of its distinctive heritage. Sophisticates in the capital collected pre-Columbian artifacts and decorated their homes with rugs from Oaxaca, tiles from Puebla, and handpainted gourds from Michoacán. The Teatro de Bellas Artes, begun by Díaz in the Belle Epoque style, was furnished with art deco native designs.

A national culture was in the making and comprehended both urban dwellers and rural farmers. Mexicanness, or *mexicanidad,* encompassed folk art traditions as well as the paintings of the Mexican mural masters: Diego Rivera (1885–1957; SEE pages 3 and 51), José Clemente Orozco (1883–1949; SEE pages 111 and 173), and David Alfaro Siqueiros (1896–1974; SEE page 150). Encouraged by the public walls given them by the education minister José Vasconcelos, they created paintings that enabled all Mexicans, even those who couldn't read, to understand the grander themes of their history and culture. They depicted people who looked like most Mexicans, brown-skinned peasants and bureaucrats, rather than idealized Greek figures. They painted narratives about conquistadores and foreign capitalists, about Mexican heroes called Hidalgo and Zapata. These painters created works that constituted one of the greatest artistic periods in the Americas. The period boasted more than the paintings of the famous trio: many others contributed lasting works, such as Rufino Tamayo (1899–1991), whose reputation belongs a bit later in art history, Fernando Leal (1900–64), Jean Charlot (1898–1979), and Juan O'Gorman (1905–82). And there were other fine painters, such as Frida Kahlo (1907–54), Miguel Covarrubias (1904–57), and Francisco Goitia (1882–1960), who primarily confined themselves to canvas-size works. All these artists found inspiration in Mexico's rich history and artistic traditions, especially those from pre-Columbian times.

The revolution also inspired great works of music and literature. Carlos Chávez (1899–1978) was among Mexico's most distinguished musicians; he not only conducted the national symphony, but composed

## FRIDA KAHLO

Frida Kahlo (1907–54) represents the progress some women made in the early 20th century. She was educated at the capital's highly respected National Preparatory School during Mexico's most brilliant artistic period. Unlike the famous muralists, she painted smaller canvases that nonetheless captured the epoch's spirit of *mexicanidad*. Her work was greatly admired by the French surrealists, but only recently has it been fully appreciated in the United States.

Thinking about Death *(1943), a self-portrait by Frida Kahlo* (Courtesy of the Mexican Ministry of Tourism)

works such as *Sinfonía india* (1935) to be played with pre-Columbian instruments or their modern substitutes. And to reach out to the people he wrote more popular works such as *Llamadas* (1934). The famous revolutionary war novel *Los de abajo* (*The Underdogs*) was written in 1916 by Mariano Azuela who had traveled as a doctor with Villa's army. Martín Luis Guzmán (1887–1976) fictionalized his experiences as a university student who joined the Villistas in his 1928 *El águila y la serpiente* (*The Eagle and the Serpent*). These and other novels revealed the dehumanization of the long struggle and the personal corruption that too frequently accompanied success: as Azuela said, the underdogs merely replaced the "top dogs" in their violence and demagoguery. In his second novel, *La sombra del caudillo* (*The Shadow of the Political Boss*; 1929), Guzmán expressed disappointment in the strong-arm policies of Calles. Another novelist, Gregorio López y Fuentes, viewed a vaguely incomprehensible Mexico through Indian eyes in his 1935 novel *El indio*.

Apart from the artistic outpouring, life in Mexico was made easier by stability and modernization. In education, the rate of illiteracy fell from the 80 percent of the Porfiriato to 38 percent. Greater opportunities were offered to women, too; in the cities increasing, if small, numbers graduated from the universities (500 in 1930) and a league was formed for achieving the right to vote.

Running water and electricity, radio stations, paved roads for cars, trucks, and buses became commonplace, uniting city and village. Mexico remained predominantly rural, however, with 65 percent of its population living outside urban areas in 1940. Life in the countryside changed for the better. Village buildings were whitewashed and band-stands built along with schools. With more clinics and health volun-teers, life expectancy improved remarkably. Social reforms permitted former peons to travel freely and work in new locations. Migration to

| Infant Mortality | | Average Life Expectancy | |
|---|---|---|---|
| Year | Rate | Male | Female |
| 1910 | 450 per 1,000 | 30 years | 30 years |
| 1930 | 222 per 1,000 | 36.1 years | 37.5 years |
| 1940 | 125 per 1,000 | 40.4 years | 42.5 years |
| Based on Charles C. Cumberland and Fieldstaff Reports | | | |

the cities increased markedly: Mexico City's population jumped from 1910 by more than a million to 1,726,858 in 1940. Problems remained, including poverty, but the improvements were unmistakable.

## The End of the Revolution

Cárdenas's term ended without a single assassination attempt or rebellion. He resigned from the presidency in accordance with the no reelection clause of the constitution, just as every president after him would. He and his predecessors finally had achieved a nation that could settle its disputes within a legal and political framework. Cárdenas also reorganized the PNR into the Party of the Mexican Revolution (PRM), enabling it to officially embrace more diverse interests, including the new peasant and labor confederations, CNC and CTC. This trend toward consolidating the political forces under one powerful governmental organization, begun under Calles and continued for decades by the Institutional Revolutionary Party (PRI), has been called "one party democracy"—as well as, more recently, "one party dictatorship."

The church and state had defined their roles and Mexico, remaining primarily a devout Catholic society, also left its government to control matters of civic and public concern. The society had been demilitarized as well. The military absorbed less than 20 percent of expenditures by 1940 and had been professionalized: most of the disruptive caudillos had been killed in the many skirmishes or absorbed into the new party structure. Foreign businesses had learned to obey Mexican law. Peasants and workers had been organized and given a voice in politics.

The progressive restructuring of society had certainly not solved all the problems of Mexico. Poverty remained a painful reality, and centuries of racism could not be eliminated easily, even in the new mestizo nation. Yet the period of restructuring was ending. The impetus of the Mexican Revolution was about to give way to more moderate politicians who would consolidate the gains already made.

# 10

# THE INSTITUTIONALIZED
# REVOLUTION
# (1940–1988)

*Mexico . . . is changing at a rate approaching the vertiginous.*

■

*Lesley Byrd Simpson (1962, xvii)*

Building on the foundations of the revolution, Mexico entered a period of exceptional political stability and extraordinary economic growth and industrialization. The nation approached self-sufficiency in many important commodities and crops. New oil discoveries in the 1980s gave Mexico reserves comparable to the entire Persian Gulf; "petrodollars" brought greater economic and political independence as well as world stature: Mexico became a leader of the developing nations.

Mexico was transformed. The military and its budget were so reduced that more money was available for education and health care. Illiteracy was lowered significantly. Improved health services and the increased production of subsistence crops contributed to a growth in population that almost doubled every two decades. The middle class also doubled in size and, for a while at least, real wages grew. Industry attracted so many to the cities that by 1960 more people lived in urban areas than in the countryside for the first time in the nation's history.

Yet for all the changes in the modern period, Mexico was left with severe problems to overcome, including ones that were unknown in 1910 such as environmental pollution and overpopulation, as well as old ones, such as rural poverty and political corruption. The gap between the wealthy and poor widened even during periods of growth in the gross national product. The one-party state ruled by the

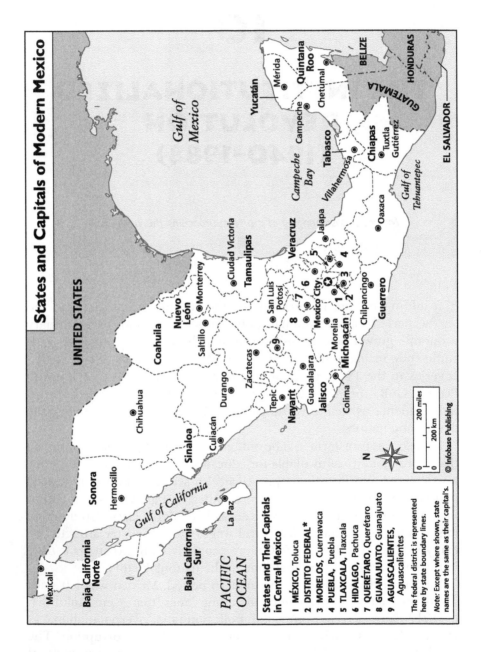

States and Capitals of Modern Mexico

**States and Their Capitals in Central Mexico**

1 MÉXICO, Toluca
2 DISTRITO FEDERAL*
3 MORELOS, Cuernavaca
4 PUEBLA, Puebla
5 TLAXCALA, Tlaxcala
6 HIDALGO, Pachuca
7 QUERÉTARO, Querétaro
8 GUANAJUATO, Guanajuato
9 AGUASCALIENTES, Aguascalientes

The federal district is represented here by state boundary lines.

*Note:* Except where shown, state names are the same as their capital's.

© Infobase Publishing

Institutional Revolutionary Party (PRI) since the time of Calles increasingly failed to respond adequately to demands for greater democratization. Despite the phenomenal gains in Mexico, the old problems lingered and contributed to an intellectual debate over whether the ideals of the Revolution of 1910 were furthered or undermined during the "institutionalized revolution."

## A Conservative Shift: 1940–1958

Following the reforms of Lázaro Cárdenas, the government shifted course. Cárdenas himself must have thought a period of consolidation was needed, because he supported the conservative General Manuel Ávila Camacho as his successor. President Ávila Camacho (1940–46) believed the revolution had been accomplished: all that was needed was evolution toward a more industrialized economy.

Ávila Camacho, a fighter in the revolution but not one of its heroes, was nicknamed "the unknown soldier." Mexico had achieved enough stability so that war heroes were not the only presidential candidates. Ávila Camacho, in fact, would be the last military president in Mexico. His successors were all civilians with experience in government, not war. Unlike many Latin American countries, Mexico controlled its militarism and decreased its military spending to the lowest in the hemisphere. Military spending dropped from 20 percent of the federal budget in 1934 to less than 10 percent in 1958.

## World War II: Relations with the United States

> Because of Mexico's immediate revolutionary past, it is something like a school for . . . many other Latin American republics; its moral leadership is beyond its size. Therefore it has had an enormous effect on the conduct of the war, for without its diplomatic work, the line-up of twenty-one American republics against the Axis could not have been achieved.
>
> ■
>
> Anita Brenner (1943, 105)

Although Mexican nationalism had been fueled by a distrust of the United States and an antipathy toward Spain and other European meddlers, Mexico did not hesitate to support the democratic powers against fascism. As early as Cárdenas's presidency, refugees from the Spanish civil war and Jews fleeing Nazi persecution were welcomed into the country. Under Ávila Camacho, Mexico organized Latin American countries in condemning warmongering among the Axis powers. When German submarines attacked two Mexican tankers in the Caribbean, Mexico formally declared war.

Mexico and the United States entered into a mutually supportive relationship during the war, encouraged by President Franklin Roosevelt's Good Neighbor policy. In 1943, Roosevelt became the first U.S. president to visit the interior of Mexico. The result was Roosevelt and Ávila Camacho's bracero (hired hand) program to provide Mexican contract labor to make up the labor shortages affecting American farms and factories. Mexico exported to the United States the zinc, copper, and other materials necessary for the war effort—without inflating the prices. And Mexicans fought in the war with the United States: an air squadron saw active combat in the Philippines, and Mexicans residing in the United States joined its army. This period of cooperation set a new tone for the nations' policies toward each other. When President Harry Truman visited Mexico City in 1952, he made a conciliatory gesture to Mexicans by laying a wreath at the monument to the Niños Héroes, Mexico's military cadets who had been killed by U.S. troops a century earlier.

## Mexicanization of Industry

World War II certainly gave Mexico's industrialization effort an early boost. The war provided a steady demand for Mexican products, and Mexico was forced to produce substitutes for items that formerly had been imported but no longer were available. But it was really the government's policies that created the nation's economic miracle.

Ávila Camacho's goal was to make Mexico self-sufficient in all the most important manufactured goods and, once the domestic goals were achieved, to export finished products. Mexican capital, Mexican industry, and Mexican raw materials would be used in this important endeavor. If foreigners wanted to invest, they were restricted to manufacturing industries rather than extractive ones. Even in manufacturing, foreign investments could not control a majority interest in any company: the so-called 51 percent rule. After World War II, the yields from Mexican investments were so satisfactory that U.S. and European investors were not deterred by such restrictions: Coca-Cola and Pepsi, General Motors and Ford, Dow Chemical, John Deere, Sears, and many others established themselves in Mexico.

Ávila Camacho's emphasis on industrial development and technological solutions would become the template for succeeding administrations. Not purely capitalist or socialist, the economic program was a uniquely Mexican mix, just as it had been under Cárdenas and others. The economy was too important to be left to private ownership, the lawmakers believed; government leadership was essential. Oil prices were controlled to fuel the national economy. If new equipment was needed, then government loans and tax breaks were made available. Fledgling businesses that were integral to attaining the goal of national self-sufficiency received tariff protections. When private enterprise failed to materialize, the government didn't avoid taking ownership of critical industries, not only oil and electricity, but also insecticide and fertilizer factories.

Mexico's industrialization efforts were successful into the 1980s. In Ávila Camacho's six-year term, the textile, food-processing, and chemical industries as well as breweries and cement factories developed rapidly. Electrical capacity jumped by 20 percent and tripled by 1952. Steel production increased from less than 100,000 metric tons in 1930 to more than 142,000 in 1946 alone. During President Miguel Alemán's term (1946–52), oil production doubled. By 1958 the gross national product had doubled. And Mexico did finally achieve self-sufficiency in iron, oil, and steel in 1964.

Throughout the initial phase of industrialization, Mexico's infrastructure was improved. Dams were built not just for electricity, but for land reclamation and irrigation as well. Oil pipelines and refineries were constructed. Alemán invested in massive public works that resulted in

| Agricultural and Industrial Production | | | | | |
|---|---|---|---|---|---|
| | Maize* | Cotton* | Steel** | Zinc* | Oil*** |
| 1930 | 1,377,000 | 38,000 | 102,859 | 124,084 | 39,529,901 |
| 1940 | 1,640,000 | 65,000 | 149,655 | 114,955 | 44,448,191 |
| 1950 | 3,122,000 | 260,000 | 332,631 | 223,510 | 73,881,472 |
| 1960 | 5,386,000 | 470,000 | 1,491,778 | 262,425 | 108,771,583 |
| 1970 | 8,997,000 | 398,000 | 3,881,201 | 266,400 | 177,599,055 |
| 1980 | 11,081,000 | 340,000 | 7,300,000 | 236,050 | 708,942,000 |

Based on Robert Ryal Miller (1985, 372–374)
*-metric tons     ** tons     *** barrels

7,500 miles of new highways. The Pan-American Highway linking the United States with Guatemala was completed along with a road linking the Pacific and Gulf coasts along the Isthmus of Tehuantepec. These roads encouraged not only commerce but tourism from the United States to the improved resort facilities at Acapulco and Puerto Vallarta. The irrigation and land reclamation works coincided with the Department of Agriculture's successful development of new, more fruitful plant varieties that created a "green revolution." During Alemán's term, corn yields increased from 300 kilograms per hectare to 1,300. The infrastructure laid the foundation for the later, more phenomenal periods of growth.

## Labor Policies

Economic growth led to a burgeoning middle class, and by 1958 there were 1.5 million industrial workers. The national income almost tripled: from 1940 to 1946 the per capita income rose from 325 to 838 pesos. These heartening figures, however, did not mean the gains were spread equitably throughout the population. They especially did not always work to the advantage of the lower classes.

Ávila Camacho's first act in regard to labor was to remove the progressive Lombardo Toledano as the head of CTM and replace him with the conservative Fidel Velázquez. A firmer hand on labor was considered necessary to accomplish the economic growth desired. Throughout the period, Velázquez did the bidding of the presidency more often than that of his constituents: he signed numerous documents that declared most strikes illegal. Without government support, most workers were afraid to strike. In 1958, the situation changed, however: the railway workers did strike. Initially, the government tried to co-opt the strike by granting some concessions. When the workers persevered, the government displayed its ability to bring them under control. The army was ordered to run the trains, the union leader was arrested (and replaced by the government), and thousands of strikers were jailed. The union leader was convicted of sabotage and imprisoned for 16 years.

Labor peace was achieved not only through coercion, but through persuasion as well. The government had become unsympathetic to labor, yet the ruling party, PRI, recognized the need to provide for workers' basic well-being—the devastation of the Revolution remained a vivid memory. Although labor did not share proportionately in the growing economy, the minimum wage maintained most of its purchasing power well into the 1970s. Unemployment was a serious problem, however: Population growth was so stupendous that the government found it impossible to create enough jobs to absorb the new workers. Alemán attempted to address the issue by using the healthy government treasury in massive public works projects.

Another significant labor effort began in 1943. Ávila Camacho created the Instituto Mexicano de Seguro Social (IMSS), a social security system to provide unemployment insurance and pensions, disability and death assistance, as well as health care benefits to workers and their families. The program began slowly, with less than 250,000 enrolled. Under President Adolfo Ruiz Cortines (1952–58), all workers were insured. The number of clinics increased from 42 to 226 and the number of hospitals from less than 20 to more than 100.

## Agrarian Policy

It is fair to say that during the first years of industrialization the agrarian revolution was abandoned. The emphasis on technology and industrialization seemed to exclude more human concerns. The more conservative presidents were concerned that land be efficiently used rather than justly distributed. Loans to buy tractors, government construction of dams for irrigation, and factories to produce fertilizer were the priorities. Whereas Cárdenas had distributed almost 50 million acres, Ávila Camacho distributed less than 12 million, and every acre went to small, privately owned farms, not the *ejidos*.

In the battle for productivity, policymakers showed a preference for the larger, private commercial farms that could supply the rapidly growing cities as well as contribute to the export capital of the nation. These policies favored the north, where the plains were most amenable to tractors and technology, and the nearby United States border made exporting more efficient.

In Mexico's central and southern regions, *ejido* farming became more productive by 1960. The government, however, remained dissatisfied: the *ejidos* constituted 43 percent of all crop land but produced only 40 percent of the crop value. The private farms were more productive per acre on a per capita basis.

Some economists have criticized the government assessment of the *ejido* program, and various administrations during the modern period have agreed. They contend that the lower harvest rates for *ejidos* resulted from government policies: only one-fifth of all tractors made their way to *ejido* land and, with the growing population, the figures per

# CORRUPTION

One of the most striking buildings of the new campus built for the National Autonomous University of Mexico (UNAM) in 1953, the library was covered with a mosaic mural by artist Juan O'Gorman. But inside there were only empty shelves: graft, unbridled during Miguel Alemán's presidency, had "diverted" the money for books.

*The library at the National Autonomous University of Mexico in Mexico City* (Courtesy of Infotour)

capita distorted the output. In addition, the most fertile land remained in private hands even after Cárdenas's redistribution because hacendados were permitted to select the plots they wished to retain. Apart from the issues of productivity, *ejido* farming guarantees the poor a subsistence: the basic crops are produced and consumed by peasants regardless of international market forces. Indeed, in 1960 more corn, wheat, and beans were produced on the *ejidos* than on all crop lands in the non-*ejido* system of the 1910 Porfiriato.

## Education under the Conservatives

Education remained important, but the more socialist, anticlerical curriculums of the revolutionary period were abandoned. The education minister Jaime Torres Bodet, a poet and scholar, did build more schools, libraries, and museums. More indicative of the times, however, was the volunteer program against illiteracy. Rather than paying more teachers, Ávila Camacho proclaimed the "Each One Teach One" program and set the proper example himself by setting aside one hour a day for tutoring. During the 1940s illiteracy was reduced from 58 percent to less than 43 percent, but the "voluntary" program lost its momentum when disgruntled government employees complained of being coerced into participating.

President Alemán constructed the impressive three-square-mile campus of the National Autonomous University of Mexico (UNAM). Planned by the mural artist Juan O'Gorman, its facades were covered with works by the great muralists Rivera and Siqueiros. A symbol of national progress and *mexicanidad,* the campus lacked basic library facilities and other educational necessities. It was much like the many

# WOMEN WIN THE VOTE

In 1954 Mexican women were finally granted the right to vote. The United Front for Women's Rights was founded in 1935, not only demanding the right to vote but organizing women's hospitals and child care centers. As the front's membership swelled to 50,000, it was asked by Cárdenas to join the official party that became the PRI. The front's absorption failed to result in the right to vote, even during the war years when growing numbers of women joined the workforce to fill the jobs vacated by men in the bracero program. After almost two decades, the PRI honored its commitment to universal suffrage, and in 1954 women were granted the right to vote. In 1974 it once again embraced women's issues by passing an Equal Rights Amendment to the constitution. In 1997 women represented a majority of the nation's registered voters and held 17 percent of the seats in the Chamber of Deputies and 16 percent in the Senate. By 2000 women held some of the most visible political offices, among them the mayor of Mexico City, the president of the Senate, and the head of one of the three major political parties. One out of three women worked, and some assumed nontraditional roles, from taxi drivers and bullfighters to movie direction. Also in 2000 women were permitted to volunteer for military service. Despite their growing presence in politics and the workforce, 26 percent of women workers earned less than the minimum wage in 2002.

new elementary schools in 1958 without teachers because salaries were too low. Less than 1 percent of rural children finished sixth grade.

## The Need for Change

As President Ruiz Cortines confessed at the end of his conservative tenure in 1958, masses of Mexicans had not sufficiently benefited from the economic miracle. They did receive, however, plenty of revolutionary rhetoric—including the change in the party name to Institutional Revolutionary Party (PRI) in 1946. Yet too much poverty, illiteracy, and social pain remained. One reason for this was the PRI's change in dynamics: the peasant and labor organizations had been supplanted in influence by business. Intellectuals, too, lost their influence. The party, less open to reconciling diverse interests, failed to implement policies that might have better distributed the increasing wealth, and it failed to even address the frightening population growth that also undermined any progress.

Public funds, estimated at well in excess of half a billion dollars under President Alemán, that could have been spent on social programs and education instead ended up in the foreign bank accounts of high-ranking members of government. Corruption became so notorious that the PRI had to bring in as president the colorless, but honest Ruiz Cortines to enhance its credibility.

## A Liberal Correction

In 1958 PRI candidate Adolfo López Mateos was elected over the National Action Party (PAN) opposition candidate by 90 percent of the vote! If any proof was necessary that the PRI had preempted democracy and that its nomination of a candidate was equivalent to election, it was such recurring statistics. Yet the PRI remained in control because it had the good sense to change course when necessary in order to accommodate a broad base of interests. In the case of President López Mateos (1958–64), the party had selected a candidate who would be one of the most popular in the postrevolutionary era. An energetic 47-year-old, the new president appealed to both intellectual youths and the masses with his promise to revive the ideals of the Mexican Revolution. He also promised democratic reforms that guaranteed at least limited representation by the opposition parties in Congress based on their percentage of the popular vote.

Declaring himself "on the extreme left within the constitution," the new president used his term to prove it. Taking advantage of a strong

| Urbanization: Percentage of Population in Cities | | | | | |
|------|------|------|------|------|------|
| 1910 | 1920 | 1930 | 1940 | 1950 | 1960 |
| 29.3 | 25 | 33.5 | 35 | 43 | 50.7 |

Based on *Mexico: Facts, Figures and Trends* (1968)

economy and healthy treasury, he invested in people, not just infrastructure. He distributed 30 million acres of land (only Cárdenas had distributed more) to both *ejidos* and private farmers and cleared new lands in the south to alleviate population pressures. He expanded the social security system, IMSS, and conducted successful public health campaigns against polio, tuberculosis, and malaria. He implemented a clause of the constitution requiring profit sharing with labor and thereby increased many workers' earnings by 5 to 10 percent.

# LAND EROJION IN THE JIERRA MIXTECA AND MIGRATION

Too many years of overgrazing by goats and sheep have eroded the Sierra Mixteca of Oaxaca into red "badlands." Land that produced agricultural surpluses in the 16th century now barely yields enough for subsistence. For decades many have been forced to find work elsewhere in the dry season in order to survive. As the population increased and the land could not yield more food, migration became wider ranging, with Mexico City the primary destination. There Mixtecs squatted in new slums or joined family members. The country was brought with them: roosters perched on roofs, and cornstalks grew in front yards. As the poverty and lack of arable land in the sierra continued, many Mixtecs made their way to the United States, particularly to California where approximately 100,000 Mixtec farm laborers constituted the state's largest Indian group in 2003. As the Mixtecs migrated, villages were transformed into places for women and the elderly but few working-age males. The Mixtec migration was repeated in poor villages throughout Mexico, transforming 20th-century Mexico from a predominantly rural nation to one in which just a quarter of the population lived in the countryside by 2006.

Education again became a priority. New schools were constructed quickly and in a cost-effective manner: the schools were prefabricated, the communities provided the land and the labor to assemble them. In order to attract more teachers to rural areas, their living quarters were included as part of the school construction. Free federal textbooks enabled more poor children to remain in school. The rate of illiteracy was further reduced from 80 percent in 1910 to 38 percent in 1960, but still the swelling population increased the absolute numbers of those who could not read or write: from 11,658,000 in 1910 up to 13,200,000 in 1960.

Like his predecessors, the president failed to implement any program to curb population growth. But he did attempt to rectify some of its worst impact on the cities. As rural farmers flooded urban areas, the cities could no longer provide adequate support services such as housing, running water, and sewerage. Shanty towns appeared on the outskirts of every city. López Mateos initiated a program of low-cost public housing. A slum in Mexico City was replaced with new units for 100,000 individuals.

On the international economic front, López Mateos encouraged French and British investments for the development of the new petrochemical industry, Petróleos Mexicanos (PEMEX). Yet he also purchased foreign interests in essential electric companies and bought out U.S. control of the burgeoning motion-picture industry, making Mexico the major distributor of Spanish-language films in the world. In a gesture typical of his presidency, López Mateos also guaranteed that movie tickets would remain affordable to the poor. Agricultural and industrial production continued to grow strongly and the foreign tourism industry, supported by luxury hotels in Acapulco and Puerto Vallarta, brought in almost twice as many travelers as under President Alemán.

## Renewed Conservatism: The Tlatelolco Massacre

President Gustavo Díaz Ordaz (1964–70) was probably the worst choice the PRI could have made for the 1960s. At a time when student activism led to demonstrations and police confrontations around the world, the PRI selected one of its most conservative presidents. When the nation demanded greater openness in the PRI, the new president annulled not only the victories of opposition parties but also the liberalizing reforms of his predecessor, López Mateos. Just when Mexico was receiving world attention in its preparation for the 1968 Olympics, it presented a government that would not easily tolerate public criticism and ruled more by coercion than persuasion.

*One of the modernization projects for the 1968 Olympic Games, the Mexico City subway system incorporated an Aztec temple uncovered during construction into one of its stations.*

In bidding for the 1968 Summer Olympic Games, the Mexican government hoped to find a global forum to show off the nation's miraculous economic progress. Side by side with the games, a cultural Olympics showcasing Mexican art and artisanship would add to the nation's prestige. The cost of constructing the stadiums and infrastructure for the games was excessive for a nation with so much poverty, or so the critics said. The total was estimated at between $150 million and $200 million, but the government argued that it was not money thrown away. A modern subway system, new housing, and sports facilities would remain, as would the money spent by visitors. The government implemented its plans, and everything was built on time. The games, too, were successful. The most troublesome events, however, happened before the Olympics began.

Against the background of the Olympic preparations, a public dispute between two schools in the capital erupted. The mayor responded by calling in a despised paramilitary police force, the *granaderos*. They dispelled the students with the excessive brutality for which they were known and in so doing politicized most students in Mexico City. When the *granaderos* were again called in during a student parade celebrating the anniversary of the Cuban Revolution, they provoked a riot using bazookas and barricades.

The situation continued to escalate. Students demanded that the mayor be removed and the *granaderos* disbanded. Failed negotiations led to the largest protest demonstration in Mexico's history on August 27: Half a million people marched from Chapultepec Castle to the main square of the government palace. The government, fearful that the students would attempt to disrupt the upcoming Olympics in October, greeted them with tanks. Undeterred, the students threatened further action. Díaz Ordaz ordered 10,000 troops to take over the campus of the National Autonomous University of Mexico (UNAM); 500 students were imprisoned. On October 2, just days before the games began, students planned a rally at the city's Plaza of Three Cultures in Tlatelolco. It was a peaceful rally, with about 5,000 participants, including children accompanying their parents. Army tanks arrived. The *granaderos* stormed in with tear gas. Someone fired shots from the rooftops into the crowd and at the army: terrorists, according to the government; the police, others said. It would take more than 30 years before the truth was revealed. The president, in fact, had ordered members of his secret service to shoot into the crowd in order to discredit the protesters. The snipers started the massacre, the police finished it with their machine guns.

Díaz Ordaz said there were only 43 deaths; the *New York Times* said several hundred. Two thousand were imprisoned. Mexico was shamed and Mexicans were stunned.

## Crisis with the PRI

The advances made during Díaz Ordaz's term in economic growth and education have been completely overshadowed by his repressive handling of the student demonstrations. The PRI never recovered from the tragedy at Tlatelolco. Mexicans were convinced that the party, out of touch with the nation's needs, only served the ambitions of its own politicians. Luminaries such as the poet Octavio Paz and the writer Carlos Fuentes condemned the government. Intellectuals abandoned the PRI, and dissident youth looked for more progressive parties to support. Others went underground: in 1969, on the anniversary of Tlatelolco, a terrorist group bombed government and newspaper buildings.

In the 1970s, many idealists simply dropped out of the political process, refusing to vote even though it was required. The abstention rate in 1979 was 50.8 percent. Student demonstrations and guerrilla movements proliferated. The PRI reaction to these tests of its power was the same as at Tlatelolco: violent repression, including illegal arrests, torture, and

| Presidential Election Results in 1970, by Party | | |
| --- | --- | --- |
| | PRI | PAN | Other parties combined |
| Percentage | 80.0 | 13.6 | 6.4 |

Based on figures from the Federal Election Commission, Mexico City, and Barry (1992, 33)

murder. The damage to the PRI was incalculable. Even today, Tlatelolco and the repression known as the *guerra sucia* (dirty war) that followed it inspire angry protests and government investigations.

The call for open elections and a broader-based government became a major issue in Mexican politics. Making the Mexican government more democratic was difficult. The government was, in fact, the PRI. The colors of the PRI were the same as the Mexican flag and appeared on electoral ballots. The PRI's control of the state apparatus was not technically illegal under the constitution, which permitted exceptionally centralized power in the office of the presidency. The autocratic party could not easily be removed either: the election apparatus was under its control, as was the television news. The newspapers could be influenced, because the government subsidized the cost of newsprint and hence financially controlled their ability to survive. There were alternative newspapers, and brutally critical ones at that, but their circulation was mostly among intellectuals. And there were opposition parties that gave the appearance of democracy to the electoral process; they just never were permitted to win. Congress did not serve as a check on the PRI or on the president, because the principle of no reelection applied to legislative office as well as to the presidency: the legislators never served long enough to develop an independent power base. The PRI president held absolute power for six years. The struggle for reforms would preoccupy Mexico for the rest of the century. And Tlatelolco became synonymous with the PRI's suppression of democracy.

## The Miracle Slows

When Luis Echeverría became president (1970–76), he exacerbated the alienation many already felt from the PRI. As minister of the interior under Díaz Ordaz, he was believed to be yet another party conservative and, worse, responsible for the Tlatelolco tragedy. His term was, in fact, notable for the political repression of guerrilla movements and the shadowy actions of the secret police. Yet Echeverría was a master of

PRI politics. He campaigned hard among the working classes and spent considerable time talking to people in rural areas about their needs. Although he did nothing to reform the PRI structurally, his own style made the party appear more broad based.

Echeverría had the misfortune to manage the economic miracle during a period of crisis. Economic growth slowed to under 4 percent, creating a recession from 1971 to 1972. U.S. policies under President Richard Nixon also adversely affected Mexico; they included a 10 percent surcharge on all imports and the elimination of the gold standard for the dollar. Because the peso had always been pegged to the dollar, the peso became unstable. Inflation did more damage. By 1973 the economy was in severe straits.

Echeverría's response surprised the private sector. He delineated a new economic policy of "shared development" that included a government coalition with workers and peasants, not just with the private business sector, thus proving himself to be one of Mexico's most progressive presidents in this century. He raised prices on electricity and gas, but protected workers by increasing their wages. Price controls were ordered on tortillas, beans, and other basic commodities to make them affordable to the poor.

Businesses complained, threatening to put their capital in U.S. banks. Echeverría lost his temper and launched into a speech against "the little rich ones" who were unwilling to strengthen Mexico for the next generation. Throughout his term, the president favored greater government intervention in the economy—and alienated the private sector. Echeverría even traveled throughout the Third World championing the need for developing nations to steer a course between capitalism and socialism and the importance of narrowing the gap between the rich and poor.

To revive the economy Echeverría lavished public monies on social programs. He doubled the production of oil, electricity, and steel—with borrowed money. He further regulated multinational corporations and attempted to lessen Mexico's reliance on the United States for exports and investment. He actively implemented the 51 percent Mexican control law and insisted that management, too, be mostly Mexican. He nationalized the tobacco and telephone industries and bought up smaller national companies to keep a strong Mexican corporate presence. (State-owned businesses increased from 86 to 740.) He invested in public works. The recession was left behind when the economy grew by over 5.5 percent annually. The problem was that inflation and the federal deficit grew even faster.

| Maize Cultivation and Population Increases | | |
|---|---|---|
| | Maize (in metric tons) | Population (in millions) |
| 1960 | 5,386,000 | 34.9 |
| 1970 | 8,997,000 | 48.2 |
| 1980 | 11,081,000 | 67.4 |
| Source: Statistical Abstract of Latin America | | |

## Maize Shortage

In 1970 maize production had increased 60 percent over that of 1960. Despite such phenomenal growth, the population had increased by 72 percent, so Mexico had to import 760,000 tons of corn to feed its people. Echeverría was disturbed that Mexico had failed to be self-sufficient in such a basic and, for Mexico, symbolic commodity. Unfortunately, it was only the most remarkable of the many foodstuffs that Mexico was forced to import. Echeverría made agriculture his priority, reinforcing it with 20 percent of the budget. Unlike his predecessors, he invested this money in the development of traditional farming communities and *ejidos*. Echeverría charged the agency CONASUPO with implementing an integrated program of credit, storage facilities, marketing advice, and price support for rural development and self-sufficiency in maize. The program, competing with older bureaucracies, was blocked from proper implementation which meant that it could never really succeed.

## Population

> *Here is the dilemma: either the developed Mexico will absorb and integrate the other, or the underdeveloped Mexico, by the sheer dead weight of demographic increase will end up strangling the developed Mexico.*
>
> ■
>
> *Octavio Paz (1972, 45)*

Control of population growth was also necessary to any program of self-sufficiency. Like his predecessors, the Catholic president initially resisted advocating any form of family planning. Instead he addressed the growing problems by spending public funds on housing and schools. By the middle of his term, however, he became the first president to support birth-control programs. His successor would follow suit, initiating public campaigns against large families. Posters in buses and television soap operas emphasized the importance of small families. Birth control was distributed at IMSS clinics.

Despite these efforts, which did eventually slow the birth rate, the population simply outstripped all efforts to keep up with it—in job creation, schools, and other necessities. A million young adults entered the labor force each year, yet the growth of the economy could not absorb them. In

## CIUDAD NEZAHUALCÓYOTL

On the outskirts of the capital, one squatters' settlement grew up along the edge of what had formerly been Lake Texcoco, a dreadfully dusty area in the dry season and a muddy one during the rains. By the 1980s the camp had an estimated population of 2 million. Many of its residents had come from the Sierra Mixteca of Oaxaca, so many that weekly communication with the home villages was made possible, not by the postal service, but rather by the comings and goings of the Nezahualcóyotl community. The sheer size of the slum forced the government to recognize it. Streets and schools were built, electricity and water and sewerage were provided. A municipal government was instituted, and the town was named for the pre-Columbian ruler and poet, probably his most unusual honor. Some claimed that Ciudad Neza, as it is more often called, was Mexico's unrecognized third largest city. Today it is the eighth largest, with a population of 1.1 million.

| Cities over 500,000 in 1980 | |
|---|---:|
| Mexico City | 12,000,000 |
| Guadalajara | 2,178,000 |
| Monterrey | 1,702,000 |
| Puebla | 771,000 |
| Ciudad Juárez | 680,000 |
| León | 596,000 |
| Tijuana | 542,000 |
| Based on Meyer & Sherman (1983, 691) | |

their search for work the unemployed migrated to the cities where they squatted on any available land. Mexico City became a megalopolis by 1980 with a population of 12 million: at least 5 million lived in poverty.

## Undocumented Workers

Population pressure increased migration across the U.S. border. Because the official bracero program instituted during World War II had terminated in 1964, Mexicans crossed the border as illegal aliens. Even before its termination, Mexican workers in the United States had been the target of resentment and racism. The increase in their numbers during the 1970s and 1980s caused some alarmists to claim there was a "silent invasion" of 8 to 12 million Mexicans into the United States. Studies in the mid-1980s, however, indicated only 1.5 to 3.5 million were in the United States at any one time. Those that were in the United States worked, many paid taxes, and few utilized available social services. Yet by the 1990s the numbers would increase and the hyperbole and tensions worsen, creating political problems between Mexico and the United States.

## Echeverría Ends Term

Echeverría never stopped trying to woo new groups. For the youth he lowered the voting age to 18 and ordered the release of jailed student dissidents, but they would never forgive him Tlatelolco no matter how revolutionary his policies: he still was pelted with rocks at the UNAM campus. He also negotiated the Equal Protection Amendment through the legislature and, with just days left in his term, distributed 250,000 acres to landless peasants in the state of Sonora. And in an unusual effort to let Mexicans comment on his successor—usually the PRI squabbled in private—he floated seven names to the public before making the final announcement that José López Portillo would be the next president of Mexico (1976–82).

## Petrodollars

López Portillo ascended to office much like his predecessors: he had worked in local politics, become active in the PRI, and taken a cabinet post that led to the presidency. He inherited a troubled economy with a large federal deficit, high inflation (up to 60 percent), and a trade deficit that, with imports outstripping exports by almost $3.5 billion, no longer could be balanced by foreign investment. At the end of his term, Echeverría had been forced to slow imports and make Mexican

| Oil Production, 1976–1980 | | |
|---|---|---|
| | 1976 | 1980 |
| Barrels per day | 800,000 | 2.3 million |
| Dollar earnings | $500 million | $6 billion |
| Based on Meyer & Sherman (1983, 679) | | |

products more competitive on the world market by devaluing the peso—twice. First, it was devalued by almost 40 percent; then, only a month later, it was devalued again. The peso, equivalent to $.08 for 20 years, suddenly was worth less than $.04. The shock sent capital to the security of foreign banks and shattered the view that the Mexican economy was safe for investment.

Yet López Portillo knew he had a historic opportunity to resolve Mexico's economic problems. In 1974 new oil reserves had been discovered in the southern states of Chiapas and Tabasco. At the same time the Arab oil embargo was causing oil prices to skyrocket. In 1980 the reserves were estimated to be at least 60 billion barrels and probably as many as 200 billion. Finding oil was equivalent to finding the proverbial pot of gold. Mexico was jubilant. It suddenly was a wealthy nation, a member of the haves rather than the have-nots. By 1980, its production had tripled and with rising oil prices, its earnings increased twelvefold.

There was immense foreign pressure on López Portillo to increase oil production. He resisted, arguing that the Mexican economy could withstand only a gradual increase and that its reserves should be used wisely, like a savings account for Mexico's future.

Nonetheless Mexico was the world's fourth largest producer by 1981. In 1982 petroleum comprised 78 percent of all its exports. The growing industry also alleviated unemployment: it absorbed 150,000 new workers each year and the expanding economy created almost 1 million jobs in 1979 alone. Although this growth contributed to rampant inflation, the economy still grew from 8 percent to 9 percent annually—more than in the miracle years of the 1960s.

## Independent Foreign Policy
Since World War II, Mexico had carefully nourished its friendship with the United States. Beginning with the López Mateos administration,

however, it increasingly took more independent stands in the international arena. Its foreign policy was formulated on a principle that sprang from Mexico's centuries of struggle against foreign domination: the principle of noninterference in matters of national sovereignty. Based on this principle, López Mateos did not follow the U.S. lead in breaking off diplomatic relations with Fidel Castro's Cuba. But it did support the United States in areas where its security was threatened, as in the case of the Cuban missile crisis. Echeverría more flamboyantly separated himself from many U.S. policies, organizing underdeveloped countries to make demands on the industrial nations and supporting the Chilean president, Salvador Allende, against U.S. interference. López Portillo, operating with the confidence of a major oil producer, felt free to disagree, too. As President Ronald Reagan increasingly involved the United States in Central American countries, such as El Salvador and Honduras, he found that López Portillo's support was not forthcoming. In fact, Mexico became a facilitator of the peace processes that finally occurred.

## Financial Troubles

Although Mexico had intended to avoid dependency on oil, its other exports, especially in agriculture, diminished—partly because prices for items such as sugar and coffee fell. And foodstuffs increasingly needed to be imported along with the machinery and goods required for industrial expansion. Despite the petrodollars, Mexico's trade deficit remained troubling, offset only by the willingness of foreign governments and banks to grant loans to the oil rich nation.

Once again Mexico attempted to become self-sufficient in food production. López Portillo, with the help of a World Bank loan and oil monies, invested billions of dollars in a new rural development effort. Initially good weather yielded encouraging results, like 30 percent higher grain crops, but the following years were plagued by drought.

## Debt Crisis

By the end of López Portillo's administration, the balance-of-payments deficit (resulting from more goods being imported than exported) approached a monstrous $12 billion. Government activism in agricultural and social development programs resulted in a budget deficit that grew phenomenally, from 7 percent of the gross domestic product (GDP) in the 1970s to 18 percent in 1982. Mexico borrowed money from foreign banks to finance its deficits. The total national debt climbed to $80 billion, and the inflation rate to 100 percent! Despite its good intentions, Mexico had succumbed to petroleum fever.

As an oil glut inundated the international market, prices fell, and Mexico's overreliance on petrodollars became a disaster. A world recession exacerbated matters. A devaluation was imperative to slowing imports and preventing capital flight to foreign banks. As under Echeverría, the peso had to be devalued twice and its value sunk from $.04 to little more than a penny. Suddenly Mexico could not meet its dollar debt repayments.

The U.S. Federal Reserve, fearing a default, put together an emergency plan. López Portillo, attempting to curb capital flight, nationalized Mexican banks—exempting only those that were foreign owned. He also imposed exchange controls on the peso to prevent any further devaluation. This was the final rupture in the economic alliance with the private and foreign sectors that had sustained Mexican growth for four decades. And it was the end of Mexico's dream of an easy future.

## A Severe Reversal

Mexico did not face its crisis alone. Foreign banks, the International Monetary Fund (IMF), and the World Bank all owned a piece of the Mexican debt problem. The new president, Miguel de la Madrid Hurtado (1982–88), would not be as free as his predecessors to manage the economy.

De la Madrid quickly demonstrated a more conservative bent than his predecessors. The Harvard-educated former minister of budget and planning represented the growing class of technocrats in the PRI elite. His training made him sympathetic to the demands of the IMF, and he quickly acceded to its conditions for a bailout on the debt. Many of these conditions eliminated the efforts, as inadequate as they were, to protect the poor. De la Madrid devalued the peso again, and it fell from 80 to 150 pesos to the dollar. He lifted the price controls on thousands of commodities (tortillas increased 40 percent in price, bread 100 percent), and depleted the resources of his predecessor's rural development program by targeting federal funds on increasing export production rather than domestic foodstuffs—again, at the instigation of the IMF. In all, de la Madrid cut public spending by one-third.

These actions encouraged the foreign banks and investment community, and they reinstituted their alliance with the private sector in Mexico. In this regard the changes were successful. Inflation slowed and nonpetroleum exports expanded until they comprised 70 percent of total exports by the end of the decade. Yet throughout the 1980s the economy contracted by 6 percent annually. Mexico renegotiated its debt, but to do so it committed 53 percent of the federal budget to repayments. Encumbered by such repayments, Mexico could not expect any economic growth for decades to come.

The political and social fallout was enormous. After the elation brought on by petroleum, Mexico was reduced to taking orders from foreigners about how to manage its affairs—an issue that brought back the most demoralizing moments in Mexican history. The left cried for a default on payments rather than accepting such an insult to the nation's sovereignty. Many Mexicans suffered, not just the poor, as food prices increased and the peso's value fell. Labor threatened massive strikes and demanded a government program of both price and wage freezes, but Fidel Velázquez (still in control of CTM) again managed to keep the workers in line. But the Mexican miracle of sustained economic growth was over.

## The Earthquake of 1985

As if matters were not bad enough, they were worsened by two catastrophes. One was a collapse of the oil market beginning in December 1985, with prices falling from almost $24 a barrel to less than $9. The drop was temporary, but the cost in revenues was over $8 billion. The other event started on the morning of September 19, 1985, when the capital was devastated by a tremendous earthquake that measured 8.1 on the Richter scale. The next day another hit, registering 7.3. Buildings collapsed, including many newer apartment buildings and Mexico's most advanced medical center. The death toll was estimated at between 7,000 and 20,000 people. Over 100,000 were left homeless or injured. Mexicans who could not find their loved ones gathered at the great pilgrimage plaza of the Virgin of Guadalupe seeking solace and information. Here, at the spiritual center of Mexico, emergency centers were established.

The earthquake disaster unified the Mexican people. While the government bureaucracy stumbled to respond, citizens' groups were saving lives. The government suffered a great blow in prestige while a grassroots movement was born, and it would multiply, creating new voices for political and social change. The Mexicans found solidarity, but their economy was succumbing to the continuing shock waves—the earthquake cost $4 billion in damages. More loans were necessary to enable Mexico to pay its debts, which rose to $96 billion.

## A New Course: Free Trade

Realizing that the nation's economic ills required radical surgery, de la Madrid set a new course in economic policy. He hoped a more open economy would enable Mexico to recover from its debt and rapidly privatized many government holdings, some of which were used as a collateral exchange for debt payments. Although the government retained control of oil, electricity, railroads, and telecommunication, their operations were made more efficient.

De la Madrid also withdrew the government from the private sector by lifting protective tariffs from many products and joining the international free trade GATT (General Agreement on Tariffs and Trade) in 1986. Instituting purer forms of capitalism into the Mexican government, de la Madrid hoped to jump-start the Mexican economy. This complete reversal of postwar economic strategies would become the hallmark of Mexican policy well into the 21st century.

## Moral Renovation

Hoping to ingratiate himself with the populace, de la Madrid initiated a policy of cleaning up corruption, or "moral renovation." Mexicans in the capital were subjected daily to demands for *mordidas* (or bribes; literally "bites") from traffic police—the chief of police built himself a house so large it was called "the Parthenon" by the press. The electorate's natural resentment had turned to disgust with the entire political system when President López Portillo and his cronies had too flagrantly enriched themselves while in office.

But Mexicans hoped that the president also meant to eliminate corruption in the electoral process itself, permitting opposition candidates to gain office. Their wishes were partly fulfilled when de la Madrid permitted the PAN, the conservative opposition party, to win important municipal elections in the north. Unfortunately, the record was made murky, and violent, when the PRI ousted a progressive candidate in Juchitán, Oaxaca, and insisted on total victory in the 1985 and 1986 gubernatorial elections. Citizens demonstrated against the corrupt practices of the PRI and received international attention when they blocked a bridge across the U.S. border.

Mexico ended decades of expansion and optimism with deep concern about its future. The PRI party dictatorship no longer would go uncontested. The protectionist economy seemed out of step with the international climate of free trade. The first steps made by President de la Madrid toward opening Mexico politically and economically became the foundation of future changes in policies.

## Modern Art and Culture

Mexico's expansion of education encompassed more than campaigns against illiteracy. Many secondary schools, art schools, and state universities also were founded or expanded in the modern period, and the highly esteemed scholarly institute the Colegio de México was begun. The result has been a modern period rich in literary journals, histories (Daniel Cosío Villegras's multivolume history of modern Mexico, published in the 1940s, remains a valued resource to scholars today), political essays, and a great diversity of intellectual life. In literature, Mexico can boast of two exceptional writers: the Nobel Prize–winning poet Octavio Paz (1914–98), whose *Labyrinth of Solitude* (1950), an essay on the Mexican character, was his most famous work, and Carlos Fuentes (b. 1928), an essayist and novelist who wrote, among other works, *Where the Air Is Clear* (1958) and *The Death of Artemio Cruz* (1964), both about the corruption of revolutionary values, and *The Old Gringo* (1984), again about the revolution. These Olympians do not stand alone in modern Mexican letters and literature. Gustavo Sainz's (b. 1940) novel *Gazapo* (1966) is considered a classic of Latin American literature. Elena Poniatowska (b. 1932) and Carlos Monsiváis (b. 1942) are internationally respected for the intellectual sweep of their writings on Mexico: Poniatowska for her essays on art as well as her novels, such as *Massacre in Mexico* (1975) based on the tragedy at Tlatelolco; and Monsiváis for the commentary on Mexican culture and politics found in his columns for the newspaper *La Jornada* and other journals. A younger generation of writers is flourishing and some have already gained fame, among them are two women: Angeles Mastretta (b. 1949), whose *Mexican Bolero* (1986) continues the Mexican tradition of historic fiction, and Laura Esquivel (b. 1950), whose novel *Like Water for Chocolate* (1989) follows the tradition of magical realism.

One scholarly field in particular has contributed to the national identity: anthropology. The National Institute of Archaeology and History (INAH) funded the excavation of major pre-Columbian cities such as Palenque in Chiapas, Monte Albán in Oaxaca, Uxmal in Yucatán, and the Aztec Great Temple (SEE page 59) revealed in the 1980s from under its cover of colonial buildings in Mexico City—and literally hundreds more. The INAH trained ethnologists who studied and recorded the customs of contemporary Indians and discovered Mesoamerican traditions surviving in many villages. The INAH also opened superb museums to display the magnificent sculptures excavated at the many ancient cities; none is more fabulous than the National Museum of Anthropology in Mexico City, designed by architect Pedro Ramírez Vásquez and opened in 1964. All this work has contributed to the now enormous understanding of Mexico's past and has been a source of pride to all Mexicans.

The traditions of the great muralists and themes of *mexicanidad* marked the postrevolutionary period. Although the first generation thrived well into the modern period and a second generation of painters continued to decorate the walls of town halls with regional history (SEE page 53), there was a shift to a more international style. The renowned Rufino Tamayo (1899–1991) is the foremost example of this change. His work often was monumental and inspired by Mexican themes, but the subject matter was not historical and the style not didactic. Rather, it is often in the genre called magical realism, a fusion of the fantastic and the real that also is apparent in the work of Frida Kahlo. When the revolutionary spirit insisted on a purely Mexican style, Tamayo rebelled by emphasizing the influences on his work from the entire world of art. Francisco Toledo's (b. 1940) work is most emphatically Mexican yet more surreal than magical. Other contemporary artists have worked both in realistic Mexican styles as well as abstract ones, such as Carlos Mérida (1891–1984), and many eschewed any hint of *mexicanidad* in their work, preferring international styles, such as the

Man Facing Infinity *(1971), mural by Rufino Tamayo in the Hotel Camino Real, Mexico City*

Opossum Family 2006, *wood carving by Moises Jiménez, an artisan continuing the tradition of his grandfather, Manuel Jiménez* (Courtesy Barry Scheinberg)

abstract sculptures of Pedro Coronel (b. 1931) and the avant-garde work of José Luis Cuevas (b. 1934). The variety is enormous, from the haunting photographs of Graciela Iturbide (b. 1942) to the narcissistic self-portraits of Nahum Zenil (b. 1947). They all have received international recognition through exhibits in world capitals. Mexico's artistic tradition has been rewarded by major exhibitions from Paris to San Francisco, but none was more comprehensive than the world tour of "Mexico: Splendors of Thirty Centuries," exhibited in the most prominent museums during the quincentennial of Columbus's voyage.

Artisans have also evolved in style. Many brought ideas from art school to embellish the traditions of their villages. The copper-ware of Michoacán was fused with silver and made into lovely, but purely impractical shapes. Others drew on the broader artistic environment, such as the animal woodcarvers of Oaxaca who have been so inspired by magical realism and the majolica ceramics of Guanajuato that incorporated Persian designs. Folk art reached such heights that many of its finest practitioners signed their works, such as the woodcarver Manuel Jiménez, the ceramicist Capelo, and the figurine maker Josefina Aguilar. Their work, often sold in art galleries, continues to attract international acclaim today.

Although much of the 1980s popular culture was overwhelmed by U.S. television programs and international rock, Mexico was the creator and exporter of its own popular culture. With Latin music globally popular, both traditional Mexican music (such as the song "La Bamba") and pop artists (such as Gloria Trevi, "the Madonna of Mexico") were major export items along with Mexican soap operas called *telenovelas*.

The Mexican film industry, a thriving if not always artistic medium, first received international notice when its stars showed up in Hollywood: Dolores del Río, Ricardo Montalban, and Anthony Quinn. But the motion pictures of Emilio Fernández (*Que viva México,* 1931) and Fernando de Fuentes (*Allá en el rancho grande,* 1936) brought Mexican movies to international attention, too. The industry grew rapidly in producing films for Spanish-speaking countries. Especially popular were movies with the comedian Cantinflas and famous mariachi stars, such as Jorge Negrete and Pedro Infante. Most recently the industry has regained its international standing with the success of films such as *Like Water for Chocolate* (directed by Alfonso Arau; 1992) and *El danzón* (directed by María Novaro; 1992).

## Decades of Accomplishment and Remaining Problems

By 1988 Mexico had progressed from a barely modernized nation to one with a complex economy of extractive and manufactured goods—processed foods, electrical machinery, petrochemicals, automobiles, textiles, and plastics took their place alongside livestock, coffee, and crude oil. Mexico's mining and agriculture remained important to the economy, just as they were in colonial times, but commerce and manufacturing were the two biggest contributors to the gross national product. The travel industry, initiated by Lázaro Cárdenas, attracted 4 million foreign tourists in 1980 who pumped $3 billion into the economy.

Socially the nation had made exceptional progress as well. A middle class, numbering in the millions and constituting 25 percent of the population in 1991, had been created and took a prominent role in politics. Literacy had increased from 20 percent in 1910 to 82 percent in 1990. The average caloric intake had doubled since 1910, and life expectancy had jumped from 30 to almost 67 years. These accomplishments were remarkable, especially when compared with those of other developing nations.

Yet, as in the past, overpopulation compounded the problems still to be overcome. In the four decades of the modern period alone, the population grew from about 20 million to over 81 million in 1990, with 70 percent living in cities—in contrast to 20 percent in 1910. Millions remained illiterate, unemployment was high, and many peasants did not have enough land to sustain themselves. By the late 1970s the economic miracle no longer sustained working-class wages: inflation (60 percent) finally outstripped wage increases (35 percent), and the minimum wage remained one of the lowest in the world (about $3.90 a day in 1991). In 1980 the gap between the rich and the poor had worsened: the poorest 20 percent owned only 3 percent of the national wealth; the richest 20 percent owned 54 percent. Much remained to be done.

Politically, Mexicans were increasingly alienated from their PRI-controlled government. In going from war heroes to technocrats as presidents, Mexico achieved a stupendous reduction in the role of the army in national affairs. The stability that enabled the economy to blossom must be attributed to the PRI's management of diverse interests while maintaining practically dictatorial control. Following a century of up-heaval, this, too, was an impressive accomplishment, especially since it was apparently achieved with only occasional episodes of repression. In a world where the choice for new nations is too often either tyranny or constant upheaval, Mexico seemed to have successfully found a middle course. As the period ended, however, Mexicans clearly were ambivalent about their government. The time for liberalization seemed to have come. Some, such as the guerrilla bands that robbed banks and kidnapped public figures in the 1970s, thought the time for another revolution was near. Even the PRI, under the leadership of its most recent presidents, agreed that profound changes were in order.

# 11

# THE MARCH TOWARD
# DEMOCRACY (1988-2000)

*This is a historic time. Everyone's clamoring for more democracy.*

■

*Carlos Salinas de Gortari, 1988 (Smith 1991, 393)*

The passage of the North American Free Trade Agreement (NAFTA) in 1993 represented the Mexican government's total abandonment of its protectionist management of the economy that had been in effect since the Revolution of 1910. So fundamental a reversal did NAFTA represent that many questioned whether its wholesale opening of the economy to U.S. and Canadian investors was not a return to the old Porfiriato gift of Mexico to foreign businesses. As one pundit put it, the only thing that is not negotiable in NAFTA is the virginity of the Virgin of Guadalupe (Barry: 1992). Others optimistically argued that NAFTA represented Mexico's chance to join developed nations as a technologically advanced country.

The years immediately following the ratification of NAFTA were not, however, preoccupied with monitoring its impact on the nation. Instead, the worst recession since the revolution knocked Mexico to its knees, threatening to affect financial institutions worldwide and undermining any expectations about Mexico's rosy future. Uprisings, political assassinations, and revelations of corruption on an unprecedented scale shocked the country and absorbed its energies. Amid all the sensation, quieter and more encouraging moves were made in the direction of democracy.

## President Carlos Salinas de Gortari, 1988–1994

In 1988 Carlos Salinas de Gortari faced the first serious political challenge of any PRI presidential candidate. The country was in recession;

its fortunes were managed by the IMF in order to meet debt repayments. Calls for democracy and more open politics intensified in Mexico as the PRI's increasing favoritism for business alienated its traditional support from populist groups. The PRI was divided over its response to the mounting criticisms, and the rifts became public, most noticeably when one of its respected members, Cuauhtémoc Cárdenas, abandoned the party.

Cárdenas, the son of Lázaro Cárdenas, one of Mexico's most beloved presidents and named in honor of the last great Aztec emperor, gained immediate appeal when he announced his presidential candidacy. He joined a coalition of progressive groups, the National Democratic Front (Frente Democrático Nacional [FDN]), which later became the Democratic Revolutionary Party (Partido de la Revolución Democrática [PRD]). Unlike Salinas, Cárdenas had held electoral office as governor of Michoacán and could speak to the masses of Mexicans who had suffered the most during the repeated fiscal crises since 1982. He was cheered by large crowds as he campaigned throughout the country; many believed he could win the election—if it was conducted fairly. Another candidate, Manuel Clouthier of the conservative PAN, was well financed by northern industrialists and courted the active support of the Catholic Church, which had been banned from politics since the Mexican Revolution. The PAN had gained popularity, not for its economic or social policies, but rather for its dramatic protests—hunger strikes and road blocks—against PRI-fixed elections.

## Calls for Democracy

Both opposition candidates campaigned for greater democracy, and both made the conduct of the election a primary issue. The international press scrutinized the proceedings. Nonetheless, the PRI once again claimed victory for its candidate. Charges of a rigged election were difficult to confirm: the government computers storing the ballot data conveniently broke down. But the race had been too hotly contested for the PRI to claim its usual 80 to 90 percent victory. Carlos Salinas de Gotari became president with only a slim majority amid charges of fraud.

From such an inauspicious beginning, Salinas presided over one of the most admired presidencies in recent memory. To counter public disgust over his "election," he initiated reforms, giving greater access to the media and restricting party financing: no longer would the PRI be financed by the national treasury. Also, the opposition parties won

| Presidential Election Results in 1988, by Party | | |
|---|---|---|
| | PRI | FDN/PRD | PAN |
| Percentage | 51 | 31 | 18 |
| Based on figures from the Federal Election Commission, Mexico City | | |

240 seats out of 500 in the chamber of deputies, forcing the PRI to negotiate with them over serious policy matters. The PAN won the governorship of Baja California in 1989, the first opposition gubernatorial victory in the PRI's 65-year history. Although Salinas's actions did much to assuage national and international opinions, they more deeply divided the PRI into two groups: the elite, foreign-educated "technocrats" involved in policy making and the elected politicos called "dinosaurs," who saw their patronage and power threatened by reforms and privatization.

## Economic Recovery

A consummate technocrat, the 39-year-old Salinas had, like his predecessor de la Madrid, been the minister of planning and budget. He seemed to prove the value of his two master degrees from Harvard University, one in economics and the other in public administration, when he managed to end the onerous debt payments (although $98 billion in external debts remained, it was reduced from 79 percent of the GDP to 29 percent) and stabilize the economy (inflation dropped from triple digits to 8 percent in 1994). The economy was expanding by a miraculous 4 percent in 1991, faster than any of the Group of Seven industrial nations. Per capita income increased somewhat for the first time in a decade, despite population growth.

The miracle had partially been accomplished by continuing de la Madrid's sale of government businesses to pay off the foreign debt: 400 state-owned businesses were privatized or shut down; banks, a television channel, and even the telephone company were no longer under party control, but owned by joint foreign and domestic corporations. The miracle continued because Salinas's fluency in the language of world finance—reduced inflation, deficit reduction, export promotion—brought an onslaught of foreign investment, especially in stocks and high-interest bearing bonds.

## NAFTA

Salinas convinced both the world and much of Mexico that the nation was on the fast track to modernity. Under the trade liberalization of GATT, foreign products poured into urban areas, and new technology such as cellular phones and bank ATMs became more readily available. Private investment fueled development. Superhighways spanned canyons and tunneled through the mountainous Sierra Madre. It was easy to believe that NAFTA would bring more of the same, speeding Mexico into the global market and "first world" status.

NAFTA and the Salinas modernization program required the jettisoning of the most fundamental principles of the revolution. The free market, it was said, demanded the abandonment of protected *ejido* land—the safety net for the poorest Mexicans. Now permitted to sell their communal lands, the poor in need would do so—and many did. Salinas also achieved a constitutional amendment eliminating the right of peasants to land for their subsistence. The land to grow maize and beans no longer would be available to them in desperate times.

Salinas also opened the economy further to foreign investors by lifting the 51 percent Mexican ownership rule and modifying the prohibition on foreign control of extractive commodities. Free trade and open markets stumbled over a few of the more charged symbols of Mexican identity, however—if only temporarily. In the case of maize, the Mesoamerican staff of life, even Salinas did not dare to make a change precipitously; he proposed phasing out tariffs protecting the grain over 15 years. And the oil industry, that former symbol of foreign exploitation, was to remain closed to investment, yet even this might be fudged for the petrochemical industry in the near future. Free enterprise and free trade in the style of the United States had become the economic commitment for Mexico's future.

## U.S. Borders

Despite Mexico's growing openness toward a stronger U.S. presence, the reaction in the United States was often tinged with financial fear. Many unions and environmental groups opposed NAFTA. As poverty and overpopulation increased illegal migration from Mexico, racism intensified in the United States. Some states passed laws making English the only official language. Border states like California agitated for protection from increasing numbers of illegal Mexican immigrants.

# VIRGIN OF GUADALUPE: SYMBOL OF MEXICAN FAITH

The church may sometimes find its newly permitted public profile a liability, at least in regard to the nation's patron saint. Monsigneur Guillermo Schulenberg, abbot of the revered Basilica of the Virgin of Guadalupe, saw his preference for fancy cars exposed in a political magazine. With public interest aroused, his remarks about doubting that the Virgin actually appeared in 1531 before the Aztec boy Juan Diego Cuauhtlahtoatzin also made the press. It caused such a stormy outburst from Mexicans that the abbot was forced to resign. The monsigneur, however, was not alone in his doubts about Juan Diego; some scholars doubt he ever existed. Yet the devotion in Mexico—and indeed in Latin America—to the Virgin of Guadalupe was recognized by Pope John Paul II in 2002 when he came to Mexico City to canonize Juan Diego as the first Indian saint in a ceremony that fused incense and organ music with Aztec drums and dancers.

While the two economies opened, ground sensors and night vision equipment were installed along the border and a $4-billion, seven-kilometer metal fence separated San Diego and Tijuana.

## The Church Finds Its Voice

Modernization seemed to sweep some Mexican fundamentals out the door. The long struggle during the Juárez reforms and the revolution to delineate the boundaries between church and state ended with the Constitution of 1917. No one had been eager to reopen this debate, although many administrations permitted Catholic schools to operate quietly. In a highly criticized move, Salinas, like his PAN opponents, championed greater freedom for the church and achieved constitutional amendments on its behalf. Not only does the church now actively comment on political affairs, from elections to the content of textbooks, but the religious are permitted to wear their vestments in public.

## Resurgence of Native Traditions

*I feel I am more Maya than ever . . . I have no desire to belong to another culture.*

■

*Pedro Meza (Foxx 1987, 209)*

The mestizo nation that was officially born with the Mexican Revolution embodied the ideals of two traditions and two races merging into one nation and one people. Racially, the desired mix was achieved in this country where the nonmestizo categories are most accurately described as "predominantly white" or "predominantly Indian." Culturally, national festivals, such as the Day of the Dead, incorporate pre-Hispanic ancestor worship into the very Catholic All Saints' Day. Yet many Indians are culturally distinct from mestizos; at least 10 million speak the language of their pre-Columbian forebears. The "mestizo ideal" overlooked the fact that these Mexicans cherish their pre-Columbian heritage and have no desire to lose it through assimilation, especially into a society that provides few opportunities for them.

In the most isolated villages indigenous groups continue to live in the most traditional manner. Nahuas still calculate their corn planting according to ancient traditions of the cyclical New Year. A vestige of an old solar calendar is still used in the Chiapas village of San Juan Chamula. Pre-Hispanic myths pervade the contemporary religious beliefs of the Mixtecs; Yucatec Maya sages, based on old myths, foretell the day when their ancestors will rule once again. These Mexicans also are among the poorest: as the millennium approached, they lived in homes without sewers (72 percent) or running water (48 percent), and their literacy rate (59 percent) was well below that for the nation as a whole (90 percent).

In 1992, the 500th anniversary of Columbus's voyage to the Americas, indigenous peoples organized within Mexico and throughout the hemisphere to present their concerns: they wanted the right to preserve their cultures while achieving greater economic parity. One result was an amendment to the Constitution of 1917: Mexico was designated as a multiethnic, not mestizo, nation. The hoped-for byproducts are that schools will become more multilingual and native cultures no longer will be treated as anachronisms in a mestizo world. It would take the 1994 Zapatista armed uprising, however, to make discrimination against Mexico's first peoples illegal.

*Two Mexicos: above, Mexico City skyscrapers; below, a Mexico City street vendor making* tlacoyos, *or flat corn-and-bean cakes* (Photos courtesy of the Mexico Ministry of Tourism)

## The Problems Overlooked

Salinas's agenda, especially concerning NAFTA, was not greeted with equanimity by all Mexicans. Intellectuals believed national sovereignty and *mexicanidad* were threatened. Small businesses knew their survival was at stake. Economists predicted millions of jobs would be lost in the first five years. Many became concerned that their country was up for sale. When U.S. vice president Al Gore defended NAFTA to U.S. citizens in a televised debate, his remark that NAFTA was an opportunity equivalent to the purchase of Alaska caused an uproar in Mexico.

Under Salinas, modernization ignored the basic needs of the citizenry and polarized Mexican society into the wealthy few and the

229

increasingly poor masses. Hoping to impress global investors with the strength and stability of the peso, Salinas overinflated it while holding down wages. To further expand the export-driven economy, he thought low wages were essential. (Fifty-one percent of manufactured exports were produced by maquiladoras, foreign businesses operating with cheap Mexican labor in order to send competitively priced goods into the United States.) The economy grew, but per capita income never increased enough to make up for the losses caused by the recessions during the 1980s. The purchasing power of the minimum wage declined 66 percent from 1982. The now grossly inadequate minimum wage, the lowest even among the more developed Latin American countries, became such a political issue in the United States—yet not for the PRI government—that NAFTA negotiations forced Salinas to increase it. However, at the beginning of 1997 it was still under $3.50 a day. A full-time job at minimum wage equaled poverty.

More than wages were depressed. Salinas developed new social services under his highly publicized solidarity program, yet the monies—

# OVERPOPULATION AND THE ENVIRONMENT

Family-planning efforts reduced the birth rate from 3.5 percent in 1970 to 1.8 percent in 1995. Statistics on fertility rates for 2000 showed the average family dwindling to just over 2.5 children in contrast to seven in 1965. Nonetheless, Mexico's population will continue to grow, albeit more slowly. Already it is the 11th most populous nation in the world. The car and industrial pollution in urban areas cannot be missed by the naked eye; smog has become a major health hazard requiring no-car days in the capital and the relocation of factories. Demand has depleted the water table so much that Ciudad Juárez is expected to run dry; in Mexico City the streets, built over the canals and lagoons of the Aztec city, have sunk 35 feet. In the countryside, overpopulation has forced families out of their communities in search of new farm land, and deforestation of 1.5 million acres each year has become a problem as potentially disastrous as it was to ancient Maya civilization. In response, an entirely new government agency, SEDUE, was created to prevent further disintegration of the environment, and citizen activist groups sprang up to monitor its progress. By 2008, however, the rate of deforestation had doubled.

mostly from temporary reserves resulting from privatization—were used selectively to neutralize opposition from both Cárdenas supporters and the "dinosaur" wing of the PRI. They did little to compensate for the 10 percent cutbacks in social programs at a time when continued population growth meant the government could barely keep up with the basic educational needs of the nation. For the first time in their history, public universities considered ending their open-door policy; primary schools required double shifts, but compensation was not always available for the teachers. The social security system, too, became overtaxed with state hospitals struggling to provide adequate care. At charity hospitals, people with broken bones could wait for weeks while the limited staff responded to more serious emergencies. Overpopulation had also resulted in land conflicts in some of the most indigenous, and poor, regions of Mexico. Little was done to resolve the disputes between peasants and ranchers or even between peasant and peasant.

## Trouble: Zapatistas

Despite these undercurrents, Salinas remained genuinely popular among the middle class and, of course, the elite. The president's confidence in his policies and the respect he received worldwide gave hope to many Mexicans that an era of prosperity and development would be theirs.

Then, on New Year's Day 1994, the day NAFTA took effect, Mexico was greeted by an armed uprising of 2,000 Maya Indians in the poor southern state of Chiapas. Their leaders, faces covered with ski masks, appeared in the world media saying that NAFTA was a death sentence for Indians. Calling themselves the Zapatista Army of National Liberation (EZLN), the Maya demanded land to farm and the return of the constitutional provisions protecting their right to land. They demanded greater democracy and the end to discrimination against them. They wanted schools and medical care. Said Carlos Aguilar, a Zapatista, "The peasants have awakened and realized that they had to do something in order for them to listen to us. Now the whole world is listening" (Holden: 1994).

Suddenly Salinas's promise of a modern Mexico crashed against the reality of a Mexico that had been completely ignored by the policies of two successive conservative administrations. In Mexico's indigenous states, such as Chiapas, 70 percent of the population lived below the poverty line. During the Salinas years extreme poverty increased by one-third.

The army was sent in to restore order, but Mexicans, ashamed of the abject poverty suffered by much of the peasant population, demanded negotiations, not war. Salinas adeptly avoided political catastrophe by unilaterally declaring a cease-fire. Negotiations began in earnest and resulted in the San Andrés Accords of 1996, which recognized Zapatista demands for indigenous rights. However, the government failed to submit the accords for congressional approval, and the conflict continued to fester, occasionally erupting in violence against the Zapatistas.

## Assassination

This shock was followed by another in Salinas's final year in office. His hand-appointed successor as the PRI presidential candidate, Luis Donaldo Colosio, satisfied many who had misgivings about Salinas's economic policies. Colosio had a political background that made him seem a progressive antidote to his two PRI predecessors: as minister of social development he was well known for his commitment to social programs; as an elected official, he was more attuned to the people than the technocrats. No one doubted that Colosio would be elected without the help of stuffed ballot boxes.

Despite democratic reforms and strengthened opposition parties, it looked as if Salinas had created so much support for the PRI and its new presidential candidate that the old political machine would once again be victorious. To further prove the PRI's commitment to an open election, Salinas invited international observers to monitor the election along with Mexican grassroots groups that had sprung up during the earthquake of 1985, such as Civic Alliance.

Colosio, however, was assassinated in March 1994 while campaigning in Tijuana. It was the first assassination of a presidential candidate or president in the PRI's history. Six months later, the PRI secretary general, José Ruiz Massieu, was gunned down. The combination of the Zapatista uprising and the political assassinations left Mexico profoundly shaken.

## President Ernesto Zedillo and Democratic Reforms

Unlike Colosio, the new candidate, Ernesto Zedillo, had never run for office. A PRI technocrat with a doctorate in economics from Yale University, Zedillo was politically awkward. The PRI won anyway, buoyed on a wave of Colosio sympathy. Cuauhtémoc Cárdenas ran again, but the PRI had done much to undermine the PRD; the left was

| 1997 Midterm Elections, by Party | | | |
|---|---|---|---|
| | PRI | PAN | PRD | Other |
| Old seats | 298 | 119 | 65 | 18 |
| New seats | 239 | 122 | 125 | 14 |

Source: Federal Elections Commission, Mexico City

in disarray and Cárdenas's campaign, lackluster. The PAN candidate, Diego Fernández de Cevallos, more popular after Mexico's historic first televised presidential debate, seemed to stop campaigning at a critical juncture—some claimed in collusion with the PRI. The PRI victory came with a healthy margin, because many Mexicans feared the unknown that would result from a PRI defeat. For the first time, they did not believe their votes were mere protests and local elections proved them right: the PAN racked up enough victories that by 1996 it represented about one-third of the population in municipalities, state governments, and

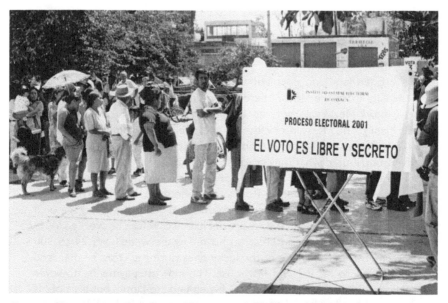

*El voto es libre y secreto (Your vote is free and secret). Election reforms, such as the secret ballot, under President Ernesto Zedillo resulted in a greater number of Mexicans voting. (Courtesy Partido de Convergencia, Oaxaca, Mexico)*

233

congressional delegations. These strides toward democracy culminated in 1996 when all parties agreed on a constitutional restructuring of the electoral process. Although the PRI "dinosaurs" continued their efforts to weaken these reforms, the 1997 midterm elections demonstrated that the PRI could no longer dictate who governed Mexico. For example, Cuahtémoc Cárdenas overwhelmingly defeated the PRI candidate in the mayoral election for Mexico City, the second most visible political office in Mexico. Also, despite the fact that the PRI had the only nationwide political machine, it lost majority control of the Chamber of Deputies for the first time in its history. The new opposition Congress had the power to force even more electoral reforms on the PRI government in time for the presidential election in 2000.

### La Crisis

While democracy made considerable advances under Zedillo, the economy almost collapsed. The fledgling president was immediately confronted with a fiscal crisis. Salinas, campaigning for the position of director of the World Trade Organization, had not seen fit to manage what would be a very unpopular devaluation of the peso. He left the

# A MIXTEC SUCCESS STORY

Eroded land and population pressures sent Isác López to Mexico City from the Sierra Mixteca as a young boy. Living with relatives in Ciudad Nezahualcóyotl, he attended school and, to contribute to the family's needs, sold chiclets on the public buses in the afternoon. While the rest of his family continued to struggle to make ends meet, they contributed what they could so that Isác could become a certified public accountant. For 15 years, Isác worked for major corporations in Mexico, such as Salinas y Rochas and Sheraton. In the 1990s, when interest rates had fallen under Salinas, he qualified for a mortgage on a new, two-story house in the resort of Huatulco, where he worked. With the crisis of 1995, the interest on his mortgage went from 24 to 100 percent. But Isác was one of the lucky ones during *la crisis:* he managed to hold on to his job and his house. The interest payments, however, affected the well-being not only of his immediate family, but also of his extended family who relied on him in times of trouble. In 1996, interest rates finally fell below 30 percent.

dirty work to the new president, who had not yet earned the confidence of foreign financial markets. It was mishandled: the Mexico peso went into a downward spin, and the nation was catapulted into its fourth recession since 1982 and its worst since the Revolution. It took an emergency bailout loan from the United States, with Mexican oil as collateral, to prevent complete collapse of the peso.

By mid-1996 there were signs of a fragile recovery, but Mexico was suffering still. Two million jobs and thousands of small businesses had been lost. To avoid a complete collapse of the currency, interest rates had been quadrupled, and the price of gasoline and utilities had been increased, as had the value-added tax. The cost of food increased as Zedillo eliminated subsidies for basic foods including tortillas. By 1997 Mexico City workers needed to labor almost twice as long (50 minutes) as in 1994 (27 minutes) to purchase a loaf of bread. Half the Mexican population was estimated to be living in poverty. The devastated middle class was angry: it was government lies and ineptitude that had done this to them. Salinas's popularity plummeted with the peso, as did world confidence in Mexican markets. Crime soared, as did migration to the United States: the average number of Mexicans establishing permanent residence in the United States during the 1990s rose to 227,000 annually, 10 times greater than during the 1960s.

## Oil and NAFTA

In 1998 the world economy was rocked by the Asian crisis, and oil prices started to plummet, threatening yet another fiscal crisis for Mexico. Although oil contributed only 12 percent to Mexico's export income, in contrast to a peak of 80 percent in 1982, taxes on PEMEX, the government monopoly, constituted 39 percent of the federal budget. Zedillo ruthlessly cut government programs in order to avoid deficits and a drop in the value of the peso. Further cuts were not needed, however, when his government used its position as the fifth largest producer of crude oil to organize a new cartel that included the OPEC nations along with Norway: oil prices rose.

Driven by NAFTA and Zedillo's fiscal austerity, Mexico's economy finally turned the corner, ringing up 7 percent growth in the GDP in 1998 alone. Exports to the United States grew from $60 billion in 1995 to $100 billion four years later. These exports demonstrated a new diversity: in addition to oil, machinery, clothing, fresh produce, glass, and electronic parts. In fact, manufacturing outstripped oil in importance and Mexico edged on China's position as the largest single

| Wages and Inflation | | | |
|---|---|---|---|
| | 1995 | 1997 | 1998 |
| Inflation | 52% | 17% | 14% |
| Minimum wage | −20% | −17% | 14% |

exporter of textiles. Inflation decreased dramatically, encouraging foreign investment that averaged about $11 billion annually and was increasing at the end of Zedillo's term. More than 3 million new jobs were created during his term. They were not enough to keep up with population growth, but the jobless rate was reduced and consumer spending increased. There were grounds for optimism.

## Corruption

At the time of Colosio's assassination, rumors were rampant about the PRI's possible involvement. With Ruiz Massieu's assassination, they became even more convoluted. The "dinosaurs" did it, some thought, in an attempt to end the liberalizing policies of Salinas. Salinas did it, others thought, because he wanted to run for a second term: his popularity was so great that some thought he could successfully amend the constitution, especially during a time of such crisis. Drug kingpins did it, others speculated, because they were being pursued by PRI prosecutors. As extraordinary as all these accusations seemed, they were widely held by the Mexican populace and press and were fanned into greater credibility by the television soap operas in which Salinas look-alikes played assassins.

More seriously, however, these speculations remained credible because the government failed to resolve the murders. In the incomplete process of untangling them, astonishing levels of corruption were revealed. Initially Ruiz Massieu's brother was appointed by Salinas to investigate the deaths, but he resigned in protest, saying political pressures from high within the PRI prevented an honest investigation. Once Zedillo took office he encouraged confidence in his administration by appointing an attorney general from outside the PRI. Soon thereafter Zedillo daringly permitted the arrest and imprisonment of Salinas's brother, Raúl, for collusion in the murder of Ruiz Massieu, his own brother-in-law.

The arrest of Raúl Salinas led to a series of revelations that even the most cynical Mexican would have thought impossible. After Salinas's arrest, the former attorney general Ruiz Massieu—hired to find his brother's murderer—fled the country and was arrested at a U.S. airport carrying a suitcase that contained large amounts of undeclared cash. Then, he was discovered to have millions of dollars in U.S. banks. Corruption was revealed to have touched everything, from the way tortillas are made to the sale of state-owned agencies, from protection of drug kingpins to murder. Corruption was always known to exist, but the Salinas scandal demonstrated a shocking degree of violence, even in regard to one's own family, and a scale of personal enrichment that made a farce of the PRI. The once popular Carlos Salinas was forced to join Hernán Cortés and Porfirio Díaz as among the most reviled figures in Mexican history. He sensibly sneaked out of Mexico; in 1997, he was living comfortably in Ireland, a country without an extradition treaty with Mexico.

Zedillo himself was tainted with PRI-style corruption when he proposed a bailout of failing banks in 1995. There was little doubt that the economic crisis had left many banks with a massive number of unpaid loans, but an independent audit discovered that much of the insolvency was due to fraud and political payoffs. In addition, the United States

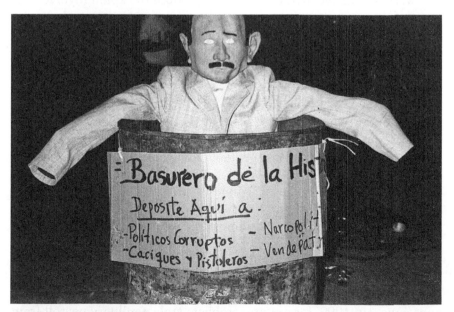

A garbage can in Mexico City stuffed with an effigy of Carlos Salinas de Gortari. The sign says, in part: "Trash can of history: Deposit corrupt politicians and narcopoliticians here." (Courtesy Diana Ricci)

in an undercover sting operation implicated some of Mexico's largest financial institutions for drug money laundering. One banker confessed to paying $25 million to the PRI for unspecified favors. Zedillo did not reveal the extraordinary cost of the bailout, nor did he fully answer allegations that he had received $5 million in donations from the banks for his 1994 campaign.

## Drugs and Politics

The amount of money that was discovered to have been squirreled out of the country was so great that outraged Mexicans believed corruption had bankrupted their nation. Not surprisingly, they felt personally robbed. Raúl Salinas alone had an estimated $300 million in European banks. He was charged with the additional crime of illicit enrichment, his government salary having been $190,000. Evidence mounted that kickbacks and favoritism were involved in the sale of government businesses. Many of the government plums went to members of Salinas's campaign finance committee; the number of Mexican billionaires soared from two to 24. Even given the privatization scandals, the stupendous prices offered, say for a television channel, were well above market value. The amount of capital involved led some of the more serious Mexican political scientists to conclude that drug money was welcomed by the Salinas administration. This too, shocked Mexico.

## Zedillo and the Military

Zedillo inherited the Salinas scandals, the Zapatista uprising, and the economic crisis, but as each unfurled during his term, they sparked other unsettling events. There were sporadic guerrilla outbreaks in 1996 by a group calling itself the People's Revolutionary Army (EPR), for example. The group was not a significant threat, yet its existence added to the general bewilderment: no one was certain whether these violent outbursts were staged by PRI dinosaurs, impoverished campesinos, or drug dealers. Mexicans were further unsettled by the rising rate of crime, much of it drug related and all of it seemingly unstoppable: drive-by assassinations became common in border cities and kidnapping gangs terrorized Mexico City. Some crimes were surprisingly audacious—in 1999, for example, robbers stole a military payroll from Zedillo's elite guard just two blocks from the presidential palace—and corrupt police were often implicated. Zedillo responded to the EPR, the

Zapatistas, drug trafficking, crime, and any and all threats to security by relying on the army. He even appointed a military commander as chief of police in Mexico City—an act quickly reversed by Cárdenas when he became mayor. Unfortunately, little was accomplished by this reliance on the secretive military in civic affairs. And concerns about the possible corruption of military commanders by drug lords would turn out to be completely justified.

## Mexico at the Millennium

Mexico reeled during the 1990s. During the 1994 election, pundits predicted either civil war or repression. Neither happened. During *la crisis*, they predicted a social explosion, and once again they were proven wrong. As the millennium approached, Zedillo appeared to have done much to put the country back on track.

His establishment of an autonomous central bank to control inflation and his tight fiscal policies regained investor confidence. In the last two years of his term, the economy was among the fastest growing in the world. Modern Mexico had survived its worst economic crisis without massive social upheaval. The PRI government, too, seemed to have learned its lesson from the Tlatelolco massacre of 1968 and avoided overreacting to protests: confronted with a disruptive 10-month-long student strike at the UNAM, Zedillo avoided violence by sending the police into the campus with only shields and batons and accompanied by human rights observers.

| Social and Human Development | | |
|---|---|---|
| | 1990 | 2001 |
| Literacy | 82% | 91% |
| Average schooling | 5.2 years | 7.2 years |
| Life expectancy | 67 years | 73 years |
| Infant mortality under five years | 46 per 1,000 | 29 per 1,000 |
| Per capita wealth | $2,180 | $4,460 |
| Wealth held by upper 20% | 53% | 57% |

*Although wealth was increasingly concentrated in a small percentage of the population, Mexico improved the basic health and education of its people during the 1990s.*

Despite continued progress in human and social development, much remained to be done to improve the welfare of the majority of Mexicans. Zedillo's bailout of the banks eventually cost taxpayers $120 billion at a time when educational and health resources were dwindling. By 2002 the social security system would face bankruptcy. NAFTA had exploited cheap Mexican labor, and government policies had kept wages low, so low that Mexican manufacturing workers in 1996 earned only 8 percent of their U.S. counterparts, in contrast to 22 percent in 1980. Mexico City workers were among the lowest-paid urban workers in the world. Many Mexicans could survive only by migrating; an estimated 6 million undocumented adults were working in the United States by 2000.

As the millennium approached, the presidential election of 2000 was foremost on everyone's mind. Mexicans seemed ready to shed the corrupt and autocratic PRI government, but were Zedillo's reforms enough to guarantee a truly democratic election? There was a much freer press, one willing to challenge the traditional authorities; an independent electoral commission had been established. Grassroots movements were increasingly tolerated: Civic Alliance had created a "corruption watch" in which participating citizens adopted a politician to monitor. With the death in 1997 of the PRI's labor leader Fidel Velázquez, splinter unions became stronger and more independent of the PRI. Politics had become more complex; the citizenry, more engaged. Yet the most important question remained: Would the PRI accept defeat?

# 12

## A MORE DEMOCRATIC MEXICO (2000–2009)

*The citizen's hour has come.*

■

*President Vincente Fox, 2005*

*We now have a chance of going from authoritarianism
to something that I hope is going to be democracy.*

■

*Lorenzo Meyer, historian, 1999*

On July 2, 2000, Vicente Fox Quesada was elected president of Mexico, the first in 71 years who was not a member of the PRI. The electoral process was transparently clean and democratic. As outgoing president Ernesto Zedillo graciously conceded Fox's victory to the nation, Mexicans spontaneously crowded into town squares throughout the republic to celebrate. In the weeks and months following, politicians from the various parties united to guarantee that the transition to a democratic government would not upset Mexico's political and economic stability. And it did not. The PRI dinosaurs cried foul, fought among themselves, and maligned Zedillo as a traitor. In the end, the truth was self-evident: PRI had been defeated. The independent Federal Elections Commission reviewed and certified the results. Fox had won. The victory was Mexico's.

The elections of 2000 ushered in democracy. Mexico not only became a government of shared power but also a more open nation. Today, the media are more critical. Strong grassroots organizations have proliferated and pushed their various agendas to the forefront of political affairs, quite often in ways authorities do not wish. Labor unions have multiplied, and although some of the largest remain co-opted by the government, more independent ones have become savvy in the art of protest.

Yet much remains to be done. Clean elections alone cannot remedy institutionalized corruption, a weak judiciary, drug violence, or the chasm between rich and poor. As the solutions to these complex problems are yet to be found, some voices have become more strident, growing into social movements that test the new democracy's commitment to human rights and its tolerance for change.

## The 2000 Campaign

The opposition parties had been so determined to end the PRI's one-party domination of presidential politics that they considered uniting behind one candidate to defeat the PRI's Francisco Labastida Ochoa. In the 1997 contests where the parties had formed such alliances, the PRI had been defeated, yet the PAN and the PRD represented opposite ends of the Mexican political spectrum. The PAN's probusiness platform, for example, recommended constitutional amendments to privatize the energy sector and to eliminate labor protections such as

*PAN candidate Vicente Fox Quesada campaigning for the presidency in 2000* (Courtesy Jorge Luis Plata)

the eight-hour day and the right to strike. And the PAN saw no reason for the strict separation of church and state. These positions were anathema to the PRD.

Not too surprisingly, the two parties could not agree on a candidate. The conservative PAN selected Vicente Fox, a former Coca-Cola executive and dynamic politician with a populist appeal. The PRD, allied with other progressive parties, relied on Cuauhtémoc Cárdenas once again. Although the two opposition parties fielded different candidates, some prominent members of the PRD joined an alliance behind Fox, who by the spring of 2000 looked increasingly like a winner. His maverick charm complemented by cowboy boots and an undoctrinaire attitude toward the PAN agenda gave him an early lead in opinion polls. He gained further popularity after the widely watched debates on television. For an increasing number of Mexicans, defeating the PRI became the priority, and they came to believe that Fox, with his promises to protect human rights and end corruption, was the candidate to do it. These advocates of the "useful vote" argued that the rest of the political agenda could be debated later.

The PRI selected Labastida, a candidate who first had to heal the divisions in his party between the Zedillo technocrats and the traditional politicians. He appealed to the technocrats by promising to rein in deficits, but at the same time he promised to improve the standard of living of most Mexicans by government spending, something the dinosaurs had long thought needed to be done. He promised affordable housing and crop and farm machine subsidies to appeal to the rural base of the PRI. However, in case that was not enough to gain victory, the PRI candidate played on citizen's fears by suggesting the nation would be destabilized without one-party government. The PRI still had enough resources to pull out all the stops for votes. (Indeed the party was later investigated for embezzling more than $100 million from the government-owned PEMEX.) In Yucatán, voters were given free refrigerators; in rural areas, government largesse was at its most generous with groceries delivered to poor homes as well as checks for schooling.

## The Democratic Victory

Most young, urban Mexicans found the PRI's continued domination of politics an embarrassment to their country. They wanted a democratic and more modern Mexico, and they voted overwhelmingly for change. With 75 percent of the population urban and 50 percent under 35

| Presidential Election Results in 2000, by Party | | | | |
|---|---|---|---|---|
| | PAN | PRI | PRD | OTHERS |
| President | 42.5% | 36.1% | 16.6% | 4.7% |
| Senate | 46 seats | 60 seats | 15 seats | 7 seats |
| Chamber of Deputies | 207 seats | 211 seats | 50 seats | 32 seats |
| State Governors | 7 | 19 | 5 | 1 |

*The PRI lost both the presidency and its majority in the Senate, yet it maintained a plurality in the Congress. By forming coalitions with the PRD, it was quite capable of blocking any legislative initiative by the PAN. As the goodwill of the historic election faded, President Vicente Fox found he could not control the Congress enough to get any major initiative enacted.*

Source: Federal Election Commission, Mexico City

years old, their votes determined the outcome on July 2, 2000. A new group of voters also turned out: Mexicans living in the United States were permitted to vote for the first time, but not by absentee ballot. Sensing their vote might be critical, thousands traveled by truck and bus, some for as long as 23 hours, to vote at special precincts established just across the border. Zedillo's electoral reforms, implemented against the desire of many in his own party, allowed everyone's vote to count. His own premature announcement that Fox was the likely victor prevented any attempts at fraud. Democracy was the victor.

## The Open Mexico

During the first years of the Fox presidency, Mexicans embraced their new government and reveled in its openness. The press, no longer subsidized by the PRI government, had never been freer—or more mocking of the establishment. One of the most popular journalists was Brozo the Creepy Clown, the TV persona of Victor Trujillo, who read the TV news each morning in a green wig and painted face. A newly established human rights commission reported to the nation on abuses, criticizing the government in the process. Freedom of information laws, passed by Congress, made the government more transparent. Commissions were established to investigate campaign finance abuses, and independent auditors routinely checked government accounts for fraud. These institutionalized checks on the government proved to be some of the most enduring reforms of the Fox era.

In 2002 the Supreme Court felt free to order the president to investigate some of the most sensitive scandals of previous administrations. The investigation revealed the government's shameful role in the Tlatelolco massacre of 1968 and the military's kidnapping and torture of citizens in the *guerra sucia* (dirty war) during the 1970s. And the first military trial in Mexico's history convicted two generals of collaborating with drug traffickers. However, human rights violations persisted. The police were believed to have a role in the horrible unresolved murders since 1993 of more than 600 young women along the border around Ciudad Juárez, but they were never prosecuted by the Fox government, despite intense international pressure. Digna Ochoa, a high-profile human rights lawyer who criticized the military, died suspiciously in 2001. Many believed the extremely secretive military should be subject to civilian review, but not Fox. In fact, as his term progressed, he exhibited less and less enthusiasm for structural reforms and human rights investigations, disappointing Mexicans who had expected more public accountability of past abuses by the PRI—not to mention the prevention of future violations.

## The Zapatista March

Few events better demonstrate the new political openness in Mexico at the beginning of Fox's term than his initiatives on the still-unresolved Zapatista conflict. And few better exemplify the political stalemate that repeatedly occurred in Congress during his presidency. Fox's first official act was to submit the San Andrés Accords of 1996 to Congress in support of a constitutional amendment for indigenous rights and autonomy. As a goodwill gesture for reopening the peace process, he released Zapatista prisoners and removed Mexican army units from Chiapas. Subcomandante Marcos, spokesman for the Zapatistas, refused to negotiate, however, until the five-year-old San Andrés Accords were enacted into law. To promote their passage, Marcos organized a Zapatista march to Mexico City, a caravan of unarmed Zapatista leaders and international supporters that traveled more than 3,000 kilometers and held rallies in 10 states before arriving in the main square of the capital. The march culminated in historic presentations by the rebel group before Congress. Fox embraced the march and guaranteed its safety, against the wishes of many in his own party who thought the Zapatistas should be arrested. The peaceful march was an international event, drawing extraordinary media attention and attracting thousands of people at rallies—an estimated 100,000 in Mexico City alone.

*The Zapatista march for indigenous rights as it passed through Oaxaca on the way to Mexico City.* (Courtesy Diana Ricci)

Unfortunately, the law Congress enacted in April 2001 amended the carefully negotiated accords in a way that forced the Zapatistas, as well as the National Indigenous Council, to reject it. The hoped-for peace negotiations never occurred. It was a bitter defeat for Fox, whose own party was partially responsible for the amendment.

## Political Gridlock

Fox came to office on a wave of optimism about the Mexican economy. In contrast to presidential transitions for the previous 20 years, the peso and prices remained stable and investment strong. Buoyed by an expanding economy in the United States, Mexicans hoped that Fox could actually live up to his ambitious campaign promises: a 7 percent growth rate, 1.35 million new jobs annually, and continued stability for foreign capital. Foreign investors looked forward to the privatization of PEMEX and the electric power industry. Despite his promised budget austerity, Fox said that health programs and education could be expanded through the "bonus" of eliminating corruption plus a new tax system.

However, the Fox presidency resulted in political gridlock. There was no consensus in Congress, where no single party had a majority. With few allies in the legislature and a PRI bureaucracy basically left intact, Fox needed more political savvy than he could muster to implement the changes Mexicans expected. Agencies sometimes undermined his own directives, and the Congress did not authorize most of his policies. When the privatization of electric power failed, he doubled the price of electricity, adversely affecting all Mexicans but particularly the poor. Furthermore, the two major items that were enacted into law, tax reform and indigenous rights, bore little resemblance to Fox's original proposals. Fox's proposed 15 percent tax on basic foods and medicines, for example, was transformed into a luxury tax by the more liberal parties.

## NAFTA Protests

When Fox was not being stymied by Congress, he was dealing with protesters. His enthusiastic support for free trade and NAFTA was sorely tested by the rural sector, which represented less than 4 percent of the nation's exports but 18 percent of the labor force. Under the provisions of NAFTA, various protections for the agricultural sector ended in 2003, when Mexican farmers and agribusinesses would have to compete with what they perceived as unfairly subsidized U.S. farm imports. In fact, subsidies in the United States had increased by 500 percent between 1994 and 2000, and by 2002 they made up 40 percent of farm income; yet in approximately the same time frame, Mexican farmers went from receiving just over 33 percent of their income from subsidies to only 13 percent. Also Mexico did not have the technology to compete with its favored trade partners, Canada and the United States, either in the number of tractors possessed or in cheap loans to buy them. Mexican farmers and agribusinesses demanded nothing less than the renegotiation of NAFTA. If that was impossible, they wanted enough government assistance to at least level the playing field. Without assistance, the farmers argued, Mexican poultry and pork producers would be eliminated and domestic grain production would plummet—and all because of illegal subsidies in the United States.

The most inflammatory issue concerned the threat to the nation's 3 million maize farmers. Unlike most other products, NAFTA protected maize, permitting limits on the amount imported until 2008. Yet such

*Wall painted with graffito proclaiming NAFTA ("TLCAN" in Spanish) means death to the small farmer.* (Courtesy Lawrence Foster)

protections were rendered useless because Mexico was not producing enough maize for domestic consumption.

Fox maintained steadfast support for NAFTA, arguing that the treaty had benefited Mexico as demonstrated by its trade surplus with the United States. He nonetheless offered to take legal action to eliminate U.S. subsidies of crops, a corrective process permitted under the treaty but one that provided little chance of relief. He also claimed there really was no crisis in rural Mexico to worry about—despite the fact that by most estimates more than 70 percent of the rural population was living in poverty. His indifference provoked an angry response. The increasingly unified farming groups were joined by sympathetic labor unions and indigenous organizations. Under the banner of "The countryside can't take anymore," they took over government offices buildings, blocked highways near the northern border, and tied up many urban centers with their demonstrations. The PRI seized the opportunity to gain much-needed political support and argued that NAFTA should indeed be reconsidered for national security. Fox was forced to negotiate with the agrosector, and promised renewed assistance for the rural

# MAIZE INVAJION

| Domestic Maize Cultivation v. Imports (in millions of metric tons) | | | | | |
|---|---|---|---|---|---|
| | 1980 | 1992 | 1994 | 2000 | 2003 |
| Mexican | 11.1 | 14.0 | 15.0 | 15.5 | 19.0 |
| U.S. imports | .8 | 1.0 | 2.5 | 5.5 | 5.6 |

Sources: Mexican Ministry of Agriculture, U.S. Department of Agriculture, and UN Food and Agricultural Organization

*Without corn, there is no Mexico.*

■

*political slogan, 2008*

Maize is so fundamental to the Mexican diet and Mesoamerican identity that its production increased at the end of the 20th century against all odds. Yet Mexico became less self-sufficient as population growth and demand outstripped domestic production. Imports from the United States increased dramatically, and after the implementation of NAFTA in 1994, the price of corn plunged from competition with U.S. government-subsidized grains. Corn that cost $3.41 per bushel to grow in the United States was sold for $2.28, undercutting Mexican farm prices. As imports increased, so did the spread of genetically engineered species. By 2001 high-tech corn was growing in remote mountainous regions of Oaxaca, contaminating irreplaceable native varieties in the very land where corn was first domesticated. Globalization, it seemed, was undermining not only maize production but also the future viability of the grain itself. Mexicans, from scientists and bureaucrats to peasants and environmental activists, joined in a worldwide protest of biotech crops. Above all else, the threat to maize production fanned discontent with NAFTA.

Sources: Institute for Agriculture and Trade Policy and U.N. Development Program sector, including government support for fertilizers and seeds and cheaper loans for the purchase of equipment. The immediate crisis was averted, and Mexican corn production actually increased. But roughly half of Mexican producers were subsistence farmers, most of them indigenous peoples whose incomes fell drastically after the implementation of NAFTA. The distrust of NAFTA remained.

## Migration and Remittances

The rates of rural poverty in Mexico and barriers to employment of the poor worsened after the implementation of NAFTA, leading to an increase in migration to the United States. So many migrated, villages were notably empty of working-age males, and Mexico's population growth fell below 1 percent for the first time in the modern era. By 2002 one of every three adult Mexicans had lived in the United States, however briefly. Twenty-one million people in the United States had roots in Mexico, and only half had lived there for five years or longer. An estimated 6 to 7 million were there illegally in 2005. By the end of Fox's term, Mexico had become the biggest exporter of labor in the world. Mexicans living in the United States or Mexicans traveling back and forth between the two countries have had a huge impact on both societies, creating a transnational culture of rap and *ranchera* music, graffiti and Corona beer. The cultural impact on the United States has been so great—Mexican pop stars like Alejandro Fernández sell more records in the United States than at home—that writer Carlos Fuentes has called it the reconquest of the territory lost in the Mexican-American War.

The greatest impact on Mexico, however, has been economic. Immigrant remittances sent back to families in Mexico constitute one of the largest sources of foreign revenues, second only to oil exports and ahead of tourist dollars. Despite the recession in the United States and the low wages earned by most immigrants, Mexicans were able to save over $20 billion to send home in 2006. In some states, remittances exceed local budgets. Seventy-five percent of the money helps poor Mexicans survive, accounting for half the household income of the extremely poor. For some, it pays for a better home, a village water system, or fireworks at the village patron saint's celebration. There is now greater concern to harness the money to stimulate new businesses and sustainable economic growth.

Fox, more than any other president, championed migrants and called them national heroes for the personal risks taken crossing the border

# CLOSE-UP: MIXTEC TRANSNATIONALISM

The lack of arable land and poverty in the Sierra Mixteca of Oaxaca caused a major exodus to the United States, especially to California where approximately 250,000 Mixtec workers now constitute that state's largest Indian group. They are so numerous in the city of Fresno, for example, that radio programs broadcast in their native language of Mixteco, traditional festivals are celebrated in their new, if temporary, home, and the Oaxacan Indigenous Binational Front enables them to organize projects to help Mixtecs in both countries. Mixtec culture has rooted in both the United States and Mexico.

Migrantes 2007, *a few of the 2,501 life-size clay sculptures created by Mixtec artist Alejandro Santiago to represent the enormous loss of youths from villages like his in Oaxaca* (Courtesy Diana Ricci)

in order to help their families. His first major foreign policy initiative with the United States was for a more open border and immigration reform that included granting legal status to 3.5 million undocumented Mexicans working in the United States. Initially U.S. president George W. Bush was receptive, but the terrorist attacks on the United States on September 11, 2001, brought an abrupt end to the dialogue, much to the embarrassment of the Fox government. In subsequent years, U.S. anti-immigrant feeling became so intense that the Bush administration began the construction of a 698-mile barrier along the border.

## Political Confrontation

*Now more than ever before, citizens are taking the country's destiny into their own hands.*

■

*President Vincente Fox, 2005*

For many Mexicans, democracy meant that their voices could be heard, their needs answered. The new Mexico, however, had the same nonresponsive bureaucracy as the old. No respected institutions of arbitration or conflict resolution had been developed. Politicians, barred from running for reelection, were more responsive to their parties than to their constituents. As a result, demonstrations proliferated as the most obvious means for getting the government's attention. Grassroots organizations conducted sit-ins at state capitals and town halls demanding everything from better schools to sewer connections. Ranchers rode their horses into the venerable Mexican Senate building to protest pork prices. The traffic tie-ups caused by near continuous rallies led some states to consider moving their government offices outside the capital city and Fox abandoned the presidential palace on the Zócalo for all but ceremonial occasions.

To Fox's credit, he initially took the political activism as a healthy symptom of the new democracy. And he believed Mexicans, remembering the *guerra sucia,* would denounce him for any use of force. When there was a strike at the Volkswagen factory, he did nothing to intervene, despite his lack of sympathy for labor rights. When villagers from San Salvador Atenco protested—with machetes in hand—the confiscation of their *ejido* land for an expanded airport in Mexico City, he shrugged off the project rather than arrest the activists. And when a teachers' strike in Oaxaca grew into a confrontation with the state government, he at first claimed it was not appropriate for the federal government to intervene in local affairs.

By the end of his term, however, Fox's tolerance ended. Succumbing to business pressures, he turned against independent unions, even sending the military and Federal Preventive Police (PFP) to break up a strike of the National Mining and Metal Workers Union. The surprise police action was violent, killing two workers and wounding 73. After the PRI gained congressional seats in the 2003 midterm elections by depicting the PAN president as out of control, Fox reengaged the recalcitrant activists of Atenco, this time over a misunderstanding with flower vendors at a local market. After a day of violent confrontations

*Federal Preventive Police occupy the state capital of Oaxaca, 2006.* (Courtesy Michele Gibbs)

between the state police and the protesters, he permitted the PFP to join the local police in what turned into a retaliatory attack on the villagers. Two villagers were killed, including a 14-year-old innocent bystander; many hundreds were arrested; and some were sexually assaulted.

Fox was also under pressure to intervene in the turbulent situation in Oaxaca, where protesters, demanding the resignation of the corrupt PRI governor Ulises Ruiz, had occupied the capital city for five months, closing most government offices and taking over radio and TV stations. Drive-by shootings, said to be authorized by the state, had killed many protesters. After his party won the 2006 presidential election, Fox bent to pressures to resolve the problem before the end of his term. He sent in federal police, who continued to occupy the city for months, enabling the discredited governor to resume control. According to the new National Commission of Human Rights, arbitrary arrests and torture were widespread, and at least 18 individuals were killed during the protest.

Fox ended his presidency amid cries of human rights abuses and repression from both Mexicans and international human rights organizations, such as Amnesty International and the United Nations. In 2009 the Supreme Court agreed, ruling that the state had gravely violated the rights of Mexicans in both Atenco and Oaxaca; the labor situation with the miners' union continued to fester.

## The Fox Presidency

After six years in office, most believed Fox had been a better candidate than president. He never provided the leadership to transform Mexico and squandered the faith Mexicans had in the new democracy to such an extent that 59 percent did not vote in the midterm elections. Both political gridlock and a contraction in the U.S. economy severely undermined his optimistic economic goals, with an actual loss of hundreds of thousands of jobs and growth that averaged less than 2 percent annually.

The corruption bonus disappeared too, taking the promised social programs with it. The freedom of information laws and audits exposed fraud and kickbacks during former president Zedillo's bank bailout, but Fox refused to take any corrective action. His own excesses were revealed as well, from $9 million in illegal campaign contributions to funds siphoned by his wife from the National Lottery for her personal charity, not to mention suspicious tax write-offs for various corporations, including a waiver of $3.5 billion in taxes owed by Citibank from its purchase of Banamex, Mexico's largest bank. Practically bankrupt at the beginning of his term, Fox nonetheless found the resources during his presidency to pay for expensive homes and cars for his seven children and stepchildren and for the luxurious upgrade of his own ranch.

Politically, Fox never dismantled the PRI apparatus or exposed its wrongdoings with sufficient diligence. Instead, the disgraced former president Carlos Salinas de Gotari was permitted to return permanently from exile; his brother Raúl Salinas, initially convicted of planning his brother-in-law's murder and charged with enriching himself at the public expense, was released from prison on the grounds of insufficient evidence. Fox never attacked the network of influence peddling but instead seemed absorbed into it. Yet he institutionalized changes that made government more transparent and accountable, changes that would prove embarrassing not only to Fox but to politicians in all branches of government.

## Presidential Campaign 2006

The 2006 presidential campaign offered real political choices and the possibility of a progressive government for the first time in decades. From start to finish, the campaign was intense, engaging voter interest and, occasionally, voter outrage. It pitted the soft-spoken, Harvard educated Felipe Calderón Hinojosa of the PAN against the dynamic

254

Andrés Manuel López Obrador, also known as AMLO (for his initials), of the PRD and, as the vote would demonstrate, it pitted the wealthier north against the poor southern states. From the northern state of Michoacán, Calderón embraced the conservative agenda of privatizing energy resources, curtailing labor rights, and, like Fox, using free trade to reduce poverty. On the other side, AMLO championed new solutions to many of the problems that had plagued the Fox administration, such as renegotiating the terms of NAFTA that most harmed small farmers and investing in education and pension programs that would reduce poverty. Calderón, chosen only after Fox's preferred candidate was forced to withdraw on charges of corruption, was not well known. López Obrador was the prominent mayor of Mexico City, admired for his personal frugality—he lived in a simple apartment in Mexico City—as well as for his effective leadership. He had successfully implemented a new pension program in the capital, as well as having revived downtown Mexico City through joint public and private initiatives. When he left office in 2004 to run for the presidency, AMLO had an 80 percent approval rating.

The PRI never gained momentum in the presidential election. The selection of Roberto Madrazo, a member of the dinosaur wing that represented the kind of government Mexicans had hoped to eradicate in 2000, splintered the party into two factions in which one refused to support the candidate. In fact, Madrazo suffered a terrible defeat by not winning in a single state. Nonetheless, the PRI played a critical role before the official campaign began. The PRI, desperate to regain the presidency, and the PAN, determined to keep power, feared they could never compete with the popularity of López Obrador. Before the official selection of candidates, they plotted to disqualify AMLO by impeaching him for a minor crime. The dirty politics ended with a judicial dismissal of the complaint in 2004 but not before the tactic had outraged much of the nation—1 million Mexicans gathered in the main plaza of the capital to protest it—and threatened to tarnish Fox's reputation as a defender of democracy. Unfortunately, this episode was just the first round of dirty politics that plagued the presidential campaign of 2006.

Calderón's predictable platform could never have catapulted him ahead of López Obrador. His ad campaign, however, did. It depicted López Obrador, with his broad support from grassroots organizations and the poor, as akin to the radical populist President Hugo Chávez of Venezuela and a danger to the Mexican nation. These ads were eventually forced off the air by the election commission as defamatory, but not before they convinced some voters that López Obrador would

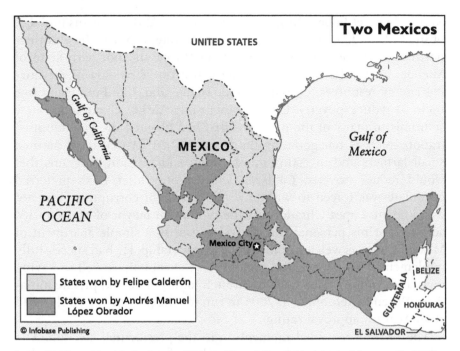

**Two Mexicos**

UNITED STATES

MEXICO

Gulf of California

Gulf of Mexico

PACIFIC OCEAN

Mexico City

States won by Felipe Calderón

States won by Andrés Manuel López Obrador

© Infobase Publishing

BELIZE

GUATEMALA

HONDURAS

EL SALVADOR

*In the 2006 presidential election, the PAN candidate, Felipe Calderón, won 16 states, the PRD's Andrés Manuel López Obrador won 15 states plus the federal district of Mexico City, and the PRI failed to win a single state. The vote divided Mexico into two geographic camps, with the north voting for Calderón and the south for López Obrador. The wealthier northern states, with their large, irrigated farms and manufacturing base, contrast so sharply with the subsistence farms and indigenous culture of the southern states that the World Bank (2008,6) has called them two worlds. The south includes the poorest states in Mexico, with inadequate educational and social services and few job opportunities. While the average income in northern cities such as Nuevo León can be more than $17,000, it is under $3,500 in rural states such as Oaxaca.*

bring instability to Mexico. The PRD candidate also damaged his own popularity through bad decisions, such as not participating in the first televised debate. His absence was all the more notable for an empty chair left on the stage throughout the debate. He appeared at the next debate but the damage had been done. He held only a slight lead in the final days of the election.

The election was a cliff-hanger. Both candidates declared victory. The close vote required absolute public confidence in the election commission's integrity; unfortunately, it was discovered that several million ballots had not been included in the preliminary count favoring Calderón. Once counted, these ballots narrowed the vote to just a .58 percent margin between the two. In an election in which almost

42 million Mexicans cast their votes, Calderón had just over 243,934 more votes than López Obrador. AMLO called for a total recount based on what he saw as evidence of fraud and, if not a recount, then a new election, owing to the illegal campaign practices of the PAN. While the Federal Election Tribunal reviewed his requests, hundreds of thousands of AMLO's supporters occupied the main square and streets of Mexico City to await the results. They would wait for more than two months.

With their nation's history of fraudulent elections, the majority of Mexicans wanted a recount to dispel any doubts about the legitimacy of the new president. When the tribunal ordered only 9 percent of the ballots recounted, there was widespread disappointment. The tribunal also ruled that the PAN had indeed risked the legitimacy of the election with its tactics: Mexican law prohibits a president from campaigning, yet Fox did; third party ads are illegal too, yet business organizations paid $19 billion in such ads in support of the PAN. Nonetheless, the tribunal claimed it could not decide whether these illegal methods were responsible for Calderón's narrow lead. The judges declared the election legal and Felipe Calderón the winner.

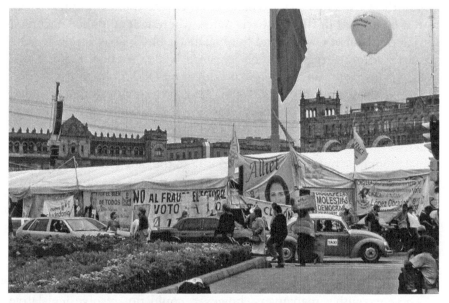

*Downtown Mexico City was transformed into an encampment of Andrés Manuel López Obrador's supporters during the deliberations of the election tribunal in 2006.* (Courtesy Diana Ricci)

## Peace or Protest

The tribunal's decisions did not end the controversy. Thirty percent of Mexicans believed the election was fraudulent; many others had doubts about the tribunal's verdict. However, most Mexicans simply feared the unrest that might result from AMLO's protests if they persisted. Although the sit-in was peaceful, it was happening at the same time as the social protest in Oaxaca challenged the legitimacy of that state government. The combination of the two created unease about the stability of the political order, even among some in AMLO's party. López Obrador and his followers did evacuate the capital peacefully but not until two weeks after the tribunal's decision and not before vowing to establish a parallel presidency to prevent the "illegitimate" Calderón from governing. They disrupted Calderón's public appearances so effectively, in fact, that pundits wondered if Mexico was heading for a presidency by television only.

## The New Presidency

On December 1, 2006, Calderón took the oath of office as opposition legislators attempted to steal the podium from him. He rushed through the presidential oath in a record four minutes, while senators and deputies of the various parties exchanged blows. At the same time, social unrest continued in the southern states, where federal police occupied the state capital of Oaxaca and the Zapatistas in Chiapas supported the struggles in other regions, such as San Salvador Atenco. Despite this inauspicious beginning, the new president quickly took control.

During the first months, Calderón issued proclamations that sounded much like the platform of López Obrador, with poverty initiatives and health care for newborn babies—he even cut his own pay, though not as much as AMLO had proposed. He not only preempted some of AMLO's social programs, but he also replaced him in the news so effectively that AMLO had to pay for TV coverage, and even then it was for a pre-dawn program. Unlike Fox, Calderón immediately demonstrated that he would rule with a firm hand. He selected an attorney general who had previously used violence against demonstrators, and he quickly ordered the arrest of the spokesman for the Oaxaca protestors. He deployed the Federal Preventive Police and army to maintain order wherever it seemed challenged.

These executive maneuvers, however, could not resolve legislative gridlock. No party had won a majority in either the Senate or Chamber of Deputies. Most of the PRD legislators initially refused to recognize

| 2006 Congressional Elections, by Party | | | |
|---|---|---|---|
| Percentage of Seats | | | |
| PRI | PAN | PRD* | Other |
| Senate | 25 | 41 | 28* | 6 |
| Chamber | 21 | 42 | 31* | 6 |

*Figures are for the three-party alliance supporting AMLO in the 2006 election
Source: Federal Election Commission, Mexico City

Calderón as the legitimate president, effectively isolating themselves from positions of power. However, the PRI, the one party that had truly been rejected in the election, was eager to regain power through an alliance with the PAN. In his determination to get his reforms passed by Congress, Calderón associated himself with some of the most corrupt leaders of the PRI, such as Governor Ruiz of Oaxaca and Governor Mario Marín of Puebla, who was implicated in the illegal arrest of the journalist Lydia Cacho after she exposed his friend's pederast ring. It was a high price for Calderón to pay, especially when he was accused of intervening on behalf of these politicians, as when criminal charges were dismissed against Marín. Yet Calderón accomplished what Fox could not, securing passage of some of his reforms on taxes, social security, and the judiciary during his first year in office.

## War on Drugs

*This is a permanent fight.*

■

*Felipe Calderón, president of Mexico (McKinley, 2007)*

It was not until two months after his inauguration that the protests subsided sufficiently for Calderón to preside at the official presidential palace. His first proclamation from the palace was to declare war on the drug cartels. Fox and Zedillo had also attacked the drug cartels, but with only modest success. Calderón promised that the transshipment of drugs from Colombia to the United States no longer would go through Mexico, and he convincingly backed up his

259

| Military Expenditures | | |
|---|---|---|
| 1983–1992 | 1998–2007 | 2008 |
| *In billions of U.S. dollars* | | |
| Annual Average $1.5 | $3 | $10.7 |
| Source: World Bank, 1999; El Proceso, 2008; Prensa Latina, 2009 | | |

promise by doubling the military budget and creating a combined force of more than 36,000 federal police and military troops. Calderón even reviewed the troops in military dress, the first time for a Mexican leader in 100 years. As the new forces set up checkpoints throughout the nation and occupied northern cities where the cartels operated, trucks filled with troops toting automatic weapons became a common sight in Mexico.

Critics argued that militarization would cause violence and turn the country into another Colombia, and they proposed instead a strategy focused on intelligence and money laundering. The Human Rights Commission worried that the military was not trained for police work. In fact, the commission received more than 1,000 complaints of human rights abuses and torture in less than a year. Others argued that it was a problem best resolved within the United States through control of drug consumption. Yet as Calderón's war quickly resulted in arrests of drug barons and confiscation of record amounts of drugs, weapons, and money, Mexicans felt more secure. Calderón's popularity jumped above 60 percent. A year after his election, he was trouncing AMLO in the polls, even though more Mexicans than ever (45 percent) believed the presidential election had been fraudulent.

## PEMEX Reform and Democracy

Calderón's biggest legislative challenge was to reform the government-controlled oil company PEMEX. The company had been a symbol of Mexican economic independence since Lázaro Cárdenas expropriated foreign oil companies in 1938 under the constitutional provision that natural resources belong to the nation. PEMEX profits made up 40 percent of the annual government budget, but in recent decades the government had invested little in the company, depleting its known oil reserves without searching for new wells and relying on U.S. refineries rather than building its own. Everyone agreed that PEMEX needed to be reformed in order to remain productive, but every other aspect of reform was controversial.

Fox had argued that the company should be privatized, but such a reform required an amendment to the Constitution of 1917—a move well beyond the support Fox could muster in Congress. Not even Calderón could swing the two-thirds majority required for a constitutional amendment. The opposition, led by López Obrador, who had sworn he would never permit the privatization of PEMEX, argued that Mexico itself had the ability to upgrade PEMEX. Calderón submitted his reform legislation in 2008, just before the end of the legislative session, in an apparent effort to gain passage with limited examination of the details. His plan permitted international investments in every aspect of PEMEX, but he claimed this did not require a constitutional amendment. He had clearly underestimated the opposition. AMLO mobilized his supporters, using female brigades called Adelitas after the women who fought in the Revolution of 1910 (SEE page 168), to block the streets around Congress while the PRD coalition of parties, called FAP (Broad Progressive Front), took control of both the Senate and Chamber of Deputies to prevent consideration of the legislation. The PAN and PRI tried meeting elsewhere but were again blocked by the Adelitas, as the police hesitated to use violence in arresting the women. A PAN-affiliated group took out TV ads calling the opposition fascists; another claimed democracy was endangered; and yet others called for using whatever force was necessary to stop the Adelitas. Mexico's political process was once again in chaos.

The impasse was resolved only when the most basic FAP demands were met: There would be more than two months of open discussion about the reform package, not just by politicians but by engineers and constitutional law experts. And the debate would be televised. During the unusually inclusive and open congressional discussion, the Zócalo filled with interested citizens watching the proceedings on a large screen installed for the purpose. At the end, the FAP wanted to conduct a national referendum that was opposed by the other parties; it had to settle instead for a cumbersome and poorly funded series of state referenda. It was the first use of the referendum process in Mexican history. Only 25 of 34 states (including the federal district) agreed to participate in the nonbinding vote. Voter turnout was too low for the results to be convincing, even if an average of 80 percent rejected the reform. Opinion polls, however, confirmed that a majority of Mexicans opposed Calderón's reform. In the midst of such public disapproval, the congressional vote was delayed until a later session. But Calderón eventually negotiated with the FAP, and the three parties joined in passing a weaker version of the reform legislation that satisfied most everyone except López Obrador.

## Foreign Trade

The Fox and Calderón terms saw the fulfillment of the neoliberal policies of presidents Zedillo and Salinas, not just in their efforts to privatize government-controlled industries, but also in their reliance on foreign investment and free trade to fuel the economy. More than a dozen trade agreements followed NAFTA and opened up trade with more than 40 countries. By 2008 Mexico had signed more agreements than any other country in the world, many of them with developed nations, such as Japan, and it pursued other agreements with nations such as China. Mexico's exports increased impressively, and, in most years, foreign investments increased as well. The diversity of trade partners provided some protection against recessions in the United States, the principal importer of Mexican goods (80 percent). By 2007 the United States accounted for one-half of foreign investments in Mexico, but European investments had increased to one-third. The variety of industries increased as well—petrochemicals but also aircraft, Corona beer but Nissan cars too.

Unlike NAFTA, most of the new trade agreements were passed with little protest. Fox's Puebla to Panama Plan (PPP), however, had to be suspended for its controversial impact on the environment and indig-

| Exports | | |
|---|---|---|
| 1986 | 1996 | 2006 |
| *In millions of U.S. dollars* | | |
| Total | 21,804 | 96,000 | 250,292 |
| Oil | 6,307 | 11,654 | 39,124 |
| Agriculture | 2,098 | 3,592 | 6,986 |
| Manufactures | 12,888 | 80,305 | 202,865 |
| Source: World Bank 2007 | | | |

enous lands. One of the most ambitious agreements, the PPP proposed not only the integration of commerce but also the modernization of southern Mexico, Central America, and Colombia. In 2008 Calderón revived the plan under the new name of Proyecto Mesoamérica, but it remained unclear whether it would result in the hydroelectric dams and massive highway complexes that could transform rural southern Mexico. Other trade agreements have already transformed much of Mexico's business culture, closing small and medium-size businesses that, without government loans or support, could not compete against companies such as Hewlett Packard or Wal-Mart. Wal-Mart has become the largest private employer in Mexico, at the expense of many local supermarkets; Hewlett Packard, on the other hand, pulled out of Mexico, but not before bankrupting many Mexican technology companies.

## The Stalled Economy

*How has it happened that a country with all the opportunities to expand its economy goes in the opposite direction?*

■

*Ilán Semo, journalist (2008, 4)*

Mexico maintained tight fiscal controls under the Fox and Calderón administrations, creating a stable peso and, for the first time in three decades, inflation rates lower than 10 percent. Lower interest rates enabled middle-class Mexicans to stretch their wages through bank loans and credit cards. Millions buy imported goods at malls, enjoy cell phones, and purchase new cars and even homes. Despite this expanding consumerism, economic growth has stagnated. And despite the billions in remittance money sent back from the United States and the record high oil prices contributing to the economy, growth was sluggish during Fox's term and the first two years of Calderón's. Mexico could boast the ninth-largest economy in the world in 2001, but by 2007 it had fallen to 12th place. Mexico is the largest exporter in Latin America and has the second-largest economy after Brazil, yet in 2007 and 2008 its growth was the slowest: Its internal growth rate was only half that for the region and less than one-third of Peru's.

Mexico has failed to achieve the sustained 5 percent annual growth expected from a free-market economy. Economists give numerous reasons for the currently stalled economy. Mexico had relied on

| Economic Indicators 2001–2008 | | | | |
|---|---|---|---|---|
| | 2001 | 2003 | 2005 | 2007 | 2008 |
| GDP Growth (%) | –.03 | 1.4 | 2.8 | 3.4 | 1.3 |
| Inflation (%) | 6.4 | 4.5 | 4.0 | 4.0 | 6.2 |

Source: IMF (2008), Banco de México (2009)

maquiladoras to generate the 800,000 new jobs needed annually, but, in fact, they created only 100,000. Mexico relied heavily on its cheap labor to attract investment, but it made no effort to integrate the maquiladoras with Mexican suppliers and services. Nor did it sufficiently invest in education to produce a more skilled and valuable workforce. As a result, industries could easily take advantage of opportunities in other countries. In 2002, for example, Mexico lost 542 manufacturers and a total of 320,000 jobs to cheaper labor markets, particularly China. Even with exceptional foreign investments in 2007, unemployment increased. Those industries that remained and even expanded, such as Ford in 2008, often did so only when wage cuts were accepted by workers.

In his 2009 budget Calderón finally addressed the need to provide tax supports and opportunities to small Mexican businesses, but the conservative government's failure to invest sufficiently in education and training, as well as infrastructure, has been cited as a major detriment to the economy. Such public investments are needed to modernize Mexico and improve the workforce and generate jobs. In recent years, booming Brazil invested four times the rate of Mexico; China invested even more. In response to the criticism, Calderón initiated an infrastructure plan that includes a commercial port in Baja California, a new oil refinery, hospitals and prisons, as well as the modernization of resorts, airports, and highways.

Monopolies, most created when government businesses were privatized, are another problem, as they inflate prices and discourage innovation. Although Calderón has promised to introduce legislation to break up these sectors, they remain. The telecommunications giant Telmex, for example, was still charging some of the highest phone prices in the world in 2008, making the cost of doing business in Mexico uncompetitive. Bureaucratic corruption is also perceived as rampant, with bribes to public officials adding $43 billion annually to the cost of doing business (CEI Consulting and Research 2005).

## Poverty and Joblessness

*For Mexico to realize its true potential, it must first help those living marginally to achieve their true potential.*

■

*Robert Zoellick, president of World Bank (2008,1)*

One of the greatest obstacles to economic growth is poverty. Although Mexico had Latin America's highest average per capita income at $7,870 in 2007, it also ranked among the 16 nations with the worst income inequality in the world: The 10 percent of households earning the least—some living on less than $2 a day—controlled only 1.2 percent of the nation's wealth; the highest 10 percent—including the third-wealthiest man in the world, Carlos Slim—controlled 37 percent. More than 40 percent of Mexicans live in poverty, and only half the working-age population has regular employment. Employment does not guarantee well-being, unfortunately. Only one in four workers receives the health and pension benefits guaranteed by law, and salaries have not gained over inflation since 1995.

The government, with encouragement from international organizations such as the World Bank, has increased funding for antipoverty programs, especially for the extremely poor, who face mounting barriers to education and employment. The innovative Oportunidades program provides direct financial payments and support services to families, but only if the children remain in school and go for regular health checkups. The program has lessened malnutrition while improv-

| Inflation and Wages | | | |
|---|---|---|---|
| | 2000 | 2006 | 2008 |
| | | *In pesos* | |
| Tortillas per Kilo | 4 | 6 | 10 |
| Minimum Daily Wage | 38 | 51 | 53 |

ing education, especially in the percentage of girls who enroll in high school. The program has been deemed so successful that it has been copied around the world, including in New York City. Another successful program, developed by nonprofit organizations, offers microcredit to poor women in the hope that a little financial boost of $50 or so might be enough to launch an income-generating project, such as raising chickens, selling tortillas, or sewing for neighbors. The lenders also organize support groups to help the women pay back the loans as well as learn more about nutrition or social problems. Inventive and promising, these programs need to be expanded for greater impact. Oportunidades, for example, serves the extremely poor, who constitute only 18 percent of those living in poverty.

## Cultural Openings

A new generation of Mexican artists and writers is defining itself in the age of globalization, leaving behind the tradition of *mexicanidad*. In architecture, for example, the colorist principles of Luis Barragán continue to have their impact long after his death in the work of Ricardo Legoretto, but at the same time a younger generation, represented by Enrique Norten of TEN Arquitectos and his design for the Visual and Performing Arts Library in Brooklyn, New York, has grasped on modernist principles that make their work international rather than Mexican. The conceptual works of artist Gabriel Orozco (b. 1962) are part of an international aesthetic, not a Mexican one. Indeed a retrospective on his work will be exhibited in New York City and in Europe in 2009 but not in Mexico. Even writers, such as the group calling themselves El Crack, have turned their focus away from Mexico to find international success: Jorge Volpi's prize-winning thriller *In Search of Klingsor* (2002) is a good example. In the new cinema, Mexican screenwriters and directors are pursuing careers in the United States, for example, Guillermo del Toro with his animated *Hellboy* film series (2006–08), Alejandro González Iñárritu's *21 Grams* (2003) and *Babel* (2006), and Alfonso Cuarón's *Harry Potter and the Prisoner of Azkaban* (2004) and *Children of Men* (2006). All three Mexican directors were nominated in 2007 for multiple Academy Awards. However, when these new directors turn their cameras on Mexico, the satirical and critical results seem to be inspired by the new openness of Mexico, such as González Iñárritu's *Amores perros* (1999); the more gentle *Y tu mamá también* (2002) by Cuarón; and

*Fraude: México 2006* (2007), Luis Mandoki's provocative film about the 2006 presidential election.

## Violence

*Mexican society lives in fear. The perception of vulnerability in front of the double violence of organized crime and those who pretend to fight it (the Army and the police) is growing immeasurably.*

■

*Jenaro Villamil, journalist (Proceso, 2008)*

The war on drugs eventually unleashed a surge of violence. As cartel leaders were arrested and transshipment routes disrupted, the cartels fought each other for control. And as the troops occupied cartel strongholds in northern cities, the gangs fought back with assault weapons and grenade launchers smuggled into Mexico from the United States. The confrontations between the army, police, and the narco-traffickers escalated, leaving more than 6,000 dead in 2008—a number greater, in fact, than that of U.S. military casualties in Iraq. Some of the president's most trusted advisers were assassinated with the assistance of policemen who had been bribed to join the cartels. Five hundred police were killed by the gangs, many because they refused to cooperate. The dead included journalists trying to cover the cartels and even ranchera singers who apparently sang the wrong tune. The assassinations were often bizarre, involving decapitations and torture. The dead also included innocent families caught in the cross fire. On September 15, 2008, the violence escalated when two grenades were tossed into a crowd celebrating Mexican independence in the Morelia town square. Eight innocent citizens were killed.

The cartels engage in more than drug trafficking. They traffic in kidnappings as well. By 2008 Mexico ranked with Iraq and Colombia in number of kidnappings. For the wealthy, bodyguards, armored cars and bulletproof clothing such as $7,000 tuxedo shirts became a necessity. But not even the wealthy could protect themselves: In the summer of 2008, 14-year-old Fernando Martí, the son of a sporting-goods magnate, was kidnapped from his chauffeur-driven car and then killed, even after his father paid a $500,000 ransom. The evidence implicated a police kidnapping ring.

The boy's murder sparked fear that no one was safe. And it sparked outrage against the government, against its corruption and its incompetence. Although the government quickly arrested the police suspects in the Martí kidnapping, it could not diminish worries that the war on organized crime was failing. An estimated million Mexicans participated in peaceful marches throughout Mexico, demanding the government do its job of protecting the public—or resign. Calderón sidestepped the immediate crisis with a national summit of every major political leader to implement a plan for public safety. A flurry of arrests of corrupt officials followed, including Calderón's chief drug czar, who was accused of taking bribes from the Sinaloa cartel. However, the kidnappings continued, as did the drug violence.

## Impunity

*Impunity is destroying us.*

■

*Alejandro Martí, father of murdered kidnapping
victim (Televisa, August 12, 2008)*

The problem was not just the government's failure to control organized crime, however. It was its willingness to permit an entrenched system of political cronyism and corruption to operate with impunity. Only 16 percent of Mexicans believe the government works for their benefit, and the government ranks among the institutions least trusted by the people (Consulta Mitofsky, 2008 & 2009). Thanks to the freedom of information act, the Mexican public has become increasingly informed about government abuses, from embezzlement and environmental destruction to bribery. Legislative committees might be appointed to investigate such abuses but rarely issue reports, not on the renovations to Fox's ranch or the PEMEX contracts benefiting the family business of Calderón's closest adviser. Mandated audits of government agencies reveal funds for new teachers going to politicians instead and government windfalls from oil profits offsetting taxes for the largest private corporations rather than social programs. Violations of human rights are officially recognized by the Supreme Court, for example, yet not prosecuted, even when they involve murder, such as the death of protesters in Oaxaca. More is revealed but little is done. Most politicians do not even feign embarrassment when exposed, much less offer to resign. Those unfortunate enough to stand trial know they will not be convicted or punished. A 2008 reform requiring public and oral trials might reduce corruption in the judiciary, but the government has resisted implementing the new law. For now, most crimes in Mexico remain unsolved, and 98 percent result in no punishment whatsoever.

## Mexico in the Twenty-first Century

*The past isn't past and the work remains to be done.*

■

*Lorenzo Meyer, historian (2008).*

In 2010 Mexico will celebrate the bicentennial of its independence from Spain. Despite its hard-won political autonomy and decades of stability, Mexico approaches its bicentennial embattled by drug violence. While charges of Mexico being a "failed state" are widely dismissed as exaggerated, the violence worsened in 2009 when 8,000 troops were sent to impose martial law in the border city of Ciudad Juárez. Fear of violence on both sides of the border brought together the new president of the United States, Barack Obama, and Calderón to discuss joint efforts to root out the problem in each country, curtailing drug consumption and gun smuggling as well as drug transshipment. The collaboration brought hope that a short-term solution could transform the war into a more manageable law-enforcement problem.

Mexico will also celebrate the centennial of the 1910 revolution in 2010, even though many ideals of that civil war have been discarded by recent governments. The protectionist economy that was the hallmark of postrevolutionary Mexico has already been dismantled, with more than 1,000 government companies privatized over the 25 years since the presidency of Miguel de la Madrid. The economy now has been transformed to compete in the global markets of the 21st century. Over the same period, Mexico struggled against the PRI dictatorship, also instituted after the revolution, and finally defeated it in 2000. The rejection of the old regime, both economically and politically, brought great hope to Mexicans for a more developed nation and democratic government. Unfortunately, Mexico has not yet demonstrated that it can fully satisfy these expectations and, even before the global financial crisis began in 2008, the vast majority of Mexicans expected the country to be worse off by the end of Calderón's presidency.

World events in 2009 will make it very hard for Mexico not to sink into an economic crisis, much less improve on its past performance.

Owing to the hardening of U.S. immigration policies, Mexicans are returning home, and remittance money, so important for the subsistence survival of poor families, is already decreasing. Global pressures also have affected exports and foreign investment at a time when Mexico is dependent upon them for economic growth. And, with oil prices falling, PEMEX, the government's cash cow, must find the resources to drill for new oil wells in order to sustain production levels. As this book is being prepared, Mexico has been forced by the global financial crisis to stabilize the peso with an IMF loan and has borrowed $1.5 billion from the World Bank to pay for Oportunidades, its basic antipoverty program. Mexicans can only hope that the country's low foreign debt and conservative fiscal management will help them survive this crisis without a devastating crash.

There have been real political gains, resulting in a more open and politically diverse government, yet the old political networks remain, having been left in place by Fox and exploited for a legislative majority by Calderón. Many believe that the PRI has been legitimized by this alliance. In fact, the old party, by controlling most state treasuries, can still get out the vote in its favor, especially when there is a low turnout. Although the PRI suffered a terrible defeat in the 2006 presidential election, it has gained in congressional and state elections in off-year elections and is positioning itself for more wins in the 2009 midterm elections and even for the presidency in 2012.

The PRI has not disappeared. Nor has its politics of impunity. The militarized response to the war on drugs worries many human rights organizations. However, Mexico could not easily return to the old authoritarianism. It is now a more democratic nation, with checks and balances among the branches of government and diverse political parties—not just one—negotiating for control. The Mexicans themselves are perhaps the most significant force for democracy. They have formed hundreds of civic organizations to make the too often insular govern-

| PRI Domination at the State Level 2006 | | | |
|---|---|---|---|
| | PRI | PAN | PRD |
| State Governorships by Party | 18 | 9 | 5 |
| Percent of Population Governed | 56 | 23 | 21 |
| Source: Consulta Mitofsky, Spring 2008 | | | |

ment hear their complaints—even when this involves a confrontation with the federal police. These groups have pushed the government into national summits and open legislative debates. It is hoped that their efforts, in addition to free elections and greater transparency in government, will result in the development of less corrupt and more responsive government. The 21st-century democratic order is flawed, but it is at least a beginning for a better Mexico.

# Appendix 1

## Basic Facts About Mexico

### Official Name
Estados Unidos Mexicanos

### Government
Under the Constitution of 1917, Mexico is a federal republic with a centralized government dominated by the office of the presidency. The presidential term is six years with no reelection. There is a bicameral federal congress composed of the Senate and the Chamber of Deputies; legislators may serve only one term. The judiciary forms a third branch of government; judges are appointed by the president.

There are many parties, but the PRI (Institutional Revolutionary Party) governed Mexico during most of the 20th century. Recent electoral reforms have strengthened opposition parties such as the conservative PAN (National Action Party) and the progressive PRD (Democratic Revolutionary Party). In the 2000 election the PRI presidential candidate was defeated for the first time in more than 70 years, and the opposition parties gained a majority of the congressional seats in both houses. In the 2006 presidential elections PAN candidate Felipe Calderón Hinojosa won a narrow victory over PRD candidate Andrés Manuel López Obrador, by a margin of only .58 percent.

### Political Divisions

#### States
Thirty-one, plus the federal district which includes the capital.

#### Capital
Mexico City

# Geography

## Area

Covering 761,604 square miles, Mexico is four times the size of Spain. Mexico is the 13th largest country in land area in the world and the fifth largest in the Western Hemisphere, after Canada, the United States, Brazil, and Argentina.

## Boundaries

To the north, the United States and the Gulf of Mexico. To the east and south, the Caribbean Sea, Belize, and Guatemala. To the west and south, the Pacific Ocean.

## Topography

Mountains (Sierra Madre Occidental) run from the northwest to the southeast near the Pacific coast. Another chain (Sierra Madre Oriental) runs near the Gulf coast. South of Mexico City the mountains become the Sierra Madre Sur.

Arid plateaus lie between the mountain chains with altitudes ranging from 6,500 to 8,000 feet. Coastal regions are tropical. One peninsula marks the west (Baja California) and another in the east (Yucatán). There are 5,785 miles of coastline

There are few navigable rivers. The most important riverine systems are in the southeast with the Grijalva, Usumacinta, and Coatzacoalcos rivers draining into the Gulf. The Balsas River, draining into the Pacific, is the most important in the central plateau. The Río Bravo (Rio Grande) defines the border with the United States.

Forty-five percent of the land is arid, and 26 percent is forest and woodland.

## Highest Elevation

Citlaltépetl (Pico de Orizaba), at 18,696 feet, is the third highest mountain in North America.

# Demographics

## Population (2008 est.)

With 110 million people, Mexico is the 11th most populous country in the world.

## Largest City

Mexico City; the metropolitan area has a population of 19.2 million.

## Language

Official language: Spanish, spoken by 95 percent of the population. Indigenous languages: Sixty-six distinct languages and hundreds of dialects are spoken by approximately 10 percent of the population over five years old. Nahuatl (in central Mexico), Yucatec Mayan, Zapotec (in Oaxaca), and Mixtec (in Oaxaca) are among the most prevalent.

### Ethnic Groups

Mestizo; 60 percent

Indian or predominantly Indian: 30 percent, divided among 62 officially recognized indigenous groups

White: 9 percent

Others: 1 percent

### Education

Literacy: 91 percent of total population (male, 92 percent; female, 90 percent)

Compulsory schooling: 10 years

Primary completion rate: 99 percent

### Health

Infant mortality: 19 deaths per 1,000 live births

Life expectancy: 76 years

### Religion

Roman Catholic: 89 percent

Protestant: 6 percent

Other: 5 percent

## Economy

### GDP, 2007 est.

$1.35 trillion; the 12th largest in the world and the second-largest in Latin America after Brazil.

### Economic Sectors (2007)

Services: 70 percent of GDP

Industry: 26 percent of GDP

Agriculture: 4 percent of GDP

### Most Important Sources of Foreign Revenues

Oil and petroleum export products

Remittances

Tourism

Agroexports

Manufactured export goods

Minerals

# APPENDIX 2

## CHRONOLOGY

### Pre-Columbian Mexico

| | |
|---|---|
| pre-10,000 B.C.E. | Peopling of the Americas from Asia. |
| ca. 5000 | Extinction of mammoths. |
| ca. 3000 | Farming. |
| ca. 2000 | Sedentary villagers. |
| ca. 1200 | Rise of Olmec civilization and other Early Preclassic cultures. |
| ca. 400 | Protoclassic cultures: the first cities. The rise of Teotihuacán, Monte Albán, and Maya cities such as El Mirador. |
| 250–900 C.E. | Classic period flourishing of Teotihuacán, Monte Albán, and southern lowland Maya. |
| 900–1200 | Terminal Classic and Early Postclassic horizon. Trade routes and population centers shift to cities such as Chichén Itzá, El Tajín, and Tula. |
| 1200–1521 | Aztecs gradually dominate much of Mesoamerica. A few other regional cultures, such as the Mixtec, flourish. |

### Spain in North America

| | |
|---|---|
| April 22, 1519 | Hernán Cortés anchors his ships off the Veracruz coast. |
| June 30, 1520 | The Noche Triste. |
| 1521 | Spanish conquistadores defeat Aztec at Tenochtitlán. |
| | Mexico becomes the colony of New Spain and governed by Spain until 1821. |
| 1523 | Arrival of the first Franciscan missionaries. Alvarado conquers Guatemala and El Salvador. |

| | |
|---|---|
| 1527–37 | Spaniards struggle to conquer the Maya of the Yucatán while most of Central America is pacified. |
| 1528 | Spaniards explore Florida, and Cabeza de Vaca returns overland through Texas into Mexico. |
| 1533 | Founding in Mexico City of the first university in the Americas. |
| 1535 | Antonio de Mendoza, the first viceroy of New Spain, arrives. |
| 1538 | De Soto explores from Florida to beyond the Mississippi River. |
| 1540–42 | Coronado explores Arizona and New Mexico. |
| 1542 | New Laws promulgated by Spain: Indian slavery prohibited. Cabrillo explores California coast. |
| 1565 | Legazpi colonizes the Philippines: China trade initiated. |
| 1571 | Inquisition instituted in New Spain. |
| 1610 | Oñate founds a colony in Santa Fe. |
| 1681 | Padre Kino and the Jesuits attempt to establish missions in Baja California. |
| 1697 | The last Maya stronghold of Can Ek capitulates to Spain. |
| 1700 | Charles II dies, last of the Spanish Hapsburgs. Bourbons rule the colonies. |

## Struggle for Independence

| | |
|---|---|
| September 16, 1810 | Miguel Hidalgo's cry for independence (Grito de Dolores). |
| 1811 | Hidalgo executed. José María Morelos continues the struggle. |
| 1815 | Morelos executed. |
| 1821 | Enlightened constitution in Spain; Mexican conservatives join in call for independence. Spain signs treaty granting independence. |

## Independent Mexico: Years of Chaos

| | |
|---|---|
| 1822 | Agustín de Iturbide crowned emperor of Mexico. The monarchy lasts seven months. |

| 1823 | Central American countries secede from Mexico. |
| 1824 | Mexico becomes a federal republic under its first constitution. |
| 1833–55 | The age of Antonio López de Santa Anna in Mexican politics. |
| 1835 | Texas declares its independence from Mexico. Santa Anna leads the Mexican attack on the Alamo. |
| 1845 | The United States annexes Texas. |
| 1846–48 | The Mexican-American War. The United States marches into Mexico City and defeats Santa Anna. Under Treaty of Guadalupe, Mexico loses half its territory to the United States. |
| 1847–49 | Maya Caste Wars in the Yucatán. |
| 1853 | Santa Anna sells southernmost Arizona and New Mexico to the United States in the Gasden Purchase. |
| 1855 | Liberals chase Santa Anna out of government. |
| 1857 | The Laws of Reform. New Liberal constitution separates the church and state; limits church property and restricts privileges of military. |
| 1858–61 | Reform War: Liberals v. Conservatives; reforms v. nonreforms. |
| 1860 | Benito Juárez becomes Mexico's first Indian president. |
| 1862 | French, Spanish, and British forces blockade port of Veracruz demanding payment of loans. |
| May 5, 1862 | Mexicans defeat French troops at Puebla (Cinco de Mayo). |
| 1863–67 | French install monarchy in Mexico under Maximilian at the invitation of Mexican conservatives. Juárez withdraws his government to the north. Struggle culminates in French defeat and execution of Maximilian. |
| 1867 | Constitutional republic restored. |
| 1872 | Benito Juárez dies. |

## The Porfiriato and the Mexican Revolution

| 1876–1910 | Porfirio Díaz rules Mexico. |
| 1910 | Centennial of Mexican independence. Francisco Madero calls for free elections. |
| | Mexican Revolution begins. |

| | |
|---|---|
| 1911 | Díaz forced into exile in France. Madero elected president of Mexico. |
| 1913 | Madero assassinated by Victoriano Huerta. Venustiano Carranza, Pancho Villa, and Emiliano Zapata fight Huerta. |
| 1914 | Wilson sends U.S. troops to blockade Veracruz against Huerta. |
| | Huerta defeated; flees. |
| | Factionalism among revolutionaries. |
| 1917 | Constitution of 1917 promulgated, instituting land reform and labor rights. |
| | Carranza elected first constitutional president. |
| 1920 | Álvaro Obregón becomes president, demilitarizes politics and initiates social reforms. |
| | José Vasconcelos, minister of education, begins muralist movement. |
| 1924–34 | Plutarco Elías Calles elected president; becomes strongman of Mexico. |
| 1926–29 | Cristero Rebellion. |
| 1929 | Calles founds National Revolutionary Party, forerunner of today's PRI and political system of party dictatorship. |
| 1934–40 | Presidency of Lázaro Cárdenas and period of land and social reform. |
| 1938 | Cárdenas expropriates foreign oil companies. |
| 1940 | Cárdenas leaves office peacefully, the first president to be neither exiled nor assassinated since the revolution. |

## The Institutionalized Revolution

| | |
|---|---|
| 1940–46 | Presidency of Manuel Ávila Camacho. |
| 1942 | Mexico declares war on the Axis powers. |
| | United States and Mexico agree on the Bracero Program for Mexican contract labor in the United States. |
| 1946–52 | Miguel Alemán's presidency. |
| | Ruling party renamed Institutional Revolutionary Party (PRI). |
| | New campus built for National Autonomous University of Mexico (UNAM). |
| 1952–58 | Presidency of Adolfo Ruiz Cortines. |

| 1954 | Women granted the right to vote. |
| 1958–64 | Presidency of Adolfo López Mateos. |
| 1964–70 | Presidency of Gustavo Díaz Ordaz. |
| 1968 | Tlatelolco student massacre. |
| | Olympic games held in Mexico City. |
| 1970–76 | Presidency of Luis Echeverría. |
| | First policy on population control. |
| | *Guerra sucia,* the repressive government response to guerrilla movements. |
| | Nationalization of many businesses, including state takeover of banks. |
| 1974 | Passage of Equal Rights Amendment for women. |
| 1976–82 | The oil boom and presidency of José López Portillo. |
| 1977 | Important electoral reforms to increase representation by opposition in Congress. |
| 1982 | Mexico's foreign debt crisis. |
| 1982–88 | Presidency of Miguel de la Madrid marked by foreign bank's interference in economy due to debt crisis. Promises for "moral renovation" and political reforms prove disappointing. |
| 1985 | Earthquake devastates Mexico City. |
| 1986 | Mexico liberalizes trade policies by joining GATT; privatization of industries begin. |

## The March toward Democracy

| 1988 | Presidential election hotly contested by opposition parties. The PRI's claim of victory results in massive demonstrations. |
| 1988–94 | Presidency of Carlos Salinas de Gortari. |
| | Austerity programs continue, coupled with free market and free trade policies. |
| 1989 | First opposition governor elected in more than 50 years. |
| | Constitutional amendments permit greater electoral reform. |
| | Mexico's foreign debt reduced. |
| 1992 | Constitutional amendment recognizing that Mexico is a multiethnic society. |
| 1993 | NAFTA signed by Mexico, the United States, and Canada. |

| 1994 | The Zapatista uprising in Chiapas. |
| | Assassinations of the PRI presidential candidate, Luis Donaldo Colosio, and the head of the PRI, José Ruiz Massieu. |
| 1994–2000 | Presidency of PRI candidate Ernesto Zedillo, after internationally monitored elections. Immediate peso devaluation devastates economy and morale of nation. |
| 1995–96 | Investigations into assassinations lead to arrest of Raúl Salinas, former president's brother. |
| | Opposition parties make great gains in midterm elections under new reforms. |
| 1996 | Sporadic rebellions intensify role of military. More electoral reforms approved. |
| | Indigenous rights recognized in San Andrés Accords signed by President Zedillo and Zapatista leader Subcomandante Marcos but not ratified by Congress. |
| 1997 | Opposition parties in lower house of Congress win slim but historic majority in July elections and take control of Mexico City from the PRI. |
| | Death of PRI labor leader Fidel Velázquez. |
| 1998 | Mexico negotiates a new oil cartel. |
| 1998–2000 | Period of rapid economic growth. |

## A More Democratic Mexico

| 2000 | Election of Vicente Fox Quesada, the first non-PRI president in 71 years. |
| | PRI loses majority control of Senate for first time. |
| 2000–2008 | Period of economic globalization yet stagnation. |
| 2001 | Zapatista march for indigenous rights. |
| 2002 | Investigations into the Tlatelolco massacre of 1968 and the *guerra sucia* implicate the government. |
| 2003 | NAFTA protests. |
| | Increased migration from countryside to the United States. |
| 2004 | Passage of freedom of information laws. |
| 2005 | Mexico becomes world's largest exporter of labor. |
| 2006 | Intensely contested presidential election results in victory for the PAN's Felipe Calderón, and the |

PRD candidate establishes a government in opposition.

Violent government responses to social protests in Oaxaca and Atenco.

2007    President Calderón achieves labor and tax reforms; militarizes war on drug cartels.

2008    PEMEX reforms approved after open debates and first public referenda.

Kidnappings and drug violence challenge Mexico.

Judicial reform laws passed but not implemented.

2009    President Calderón and U.S. president Barack Obama implement "Project Gunrunner" to stem violence from drug war.

The PRI predicted to gain in midterm elections.

Mexico accepts new IMF and World Bank loans to stave off impact of global financial crisis.

Swine flu crisis creates fears of pandemic.

# APPENDIX 3

## BIBLIOGRAPHY

Alamán, Lucas. *Historia de México, 1808–1849.* 5 vols. 2d ed. México, 1942.

Ashton, Dore. "Mexican Art of the Twentieth Century." In *Mexico: Splendors of Thirty Centuries.* New York: Metropolitan Museum of Art, 1990.

Azuela, Mariano. *The Flies.* In *Two Novels of Mexico.* Translated by Lesley Byrd Simpson. Berkeley: University of California Press, 1956.

———. *The Underdogs.* Translated by E. Munguía. New York: New American Library, 1963.

Barry, Tom, ed. *Mexico: A Country Guide.* Albuquerque: The Inter-Hemispheric Education Resource Center, 1992.

Benavides, Alonso de. *The Revised Memorial of 1634.* Translated and edited by Frederick W. Hodge et al. Albuquerque: University of New Mexico Press, 1945.

Borah, Woodrow, and Shelburne F. Cook. *The Aboriginal Population of Central Mexico on the Eve of the Spanish Conquest.* Berkeley: University of California Press, 1963.

Brenner, Anita. *The Wind that Swept Mexico.* Austin: University of Texas Press, 1971.

Burkhart, Louise M. "The Cult of the Virgin of Guadalupe in Mexico." In *South and Meso-American Native Spirituality.* Edited by G. H. Gossen. London: SCM Press, 1993.

Calderón de la Barca, Fanny. *Life in Mexico: The Letters of Fanny Calderón de la Barca.* Edited by Howard T. Fisher and Marion H. Fisher. Garden City: Doubleday, 1966.

CEI Consulting & Research. *Diagnostic on the Impact of Fraud and Corruption on Small and Medium Sized Companies.* Mexico City: CEI Consulting, 2005.

Chance, John K. "Colonial Ethnohistory of Oaxaca." In *Supplement to Handbook of Middle American Indians,* Vol. 4, *Ethnohistory.* Edited by Victoria Reifler Bricker and Ronald Spores. Austin: University of Texas, 1986.

285

Charlot, Jean. *Mexican Art and the Academy of San Carlos, 1783–1915.* Austin: University of Texas Press, 1962.

Consulta Mitofsky. "Elections 2009: Mexico Governorships and Legislatures by Party." Available online. URL: consulta.com.mx. Updated spring 2008.

———. "Evaluación del Gubierno de Felipe Caderón." Available online. URL: consulta.com.mx. Updated March 2009.

Cook, Sherburne F., and Woodrow Borah. *Essays in Population Study.* 2 vols. Berkeley: University of California Press, 1971–73.

Cortés, Hernán. *Letters from Mexico.* Translated and edited by Anthony Pagden. New Haven, Conn.: Yale University Press, 1986.

*Crónica mexicana.* México: Editorial Leyenda, 1944.

Cumberland, Charles C. *Mexico: The Struggle for Modernity.* London: Oxford University Press, 1968.

Daniken, Erick von. *Chariots of the Gods.* London: Souvenir Press, 1969.

Davis, Nigel. *The Aztecs.* London: Macmillan, 1973.

Denevan, William M., ed. *The Native Populations of the Americas in 1492.* Madison: University of Wisconsin Press, 1976.

Díaz del Castillo, Bernal. *The Discovery and Conquest of Mexico 1517–1521.* Edited and translated by A. P. Maudslay. New York: Farrar, Straus and Giroux, 1956.

Durán, Diego. *Books of the Gods and Rites and the Ancient Calendar.* Ca. 1575. Reprint, Norman: University of Oklahoma Press, 1971.

Farriss, Nancy M. *Maya Society under Colonial Rule: The Collective Enterprise of Survival.* Princeton, N.J.: Princeton University Press, 1984.

*Fieldstaff Reports,* North America Series, vol. 2, no. 1 (July 1974).

Florescano, Enrique. *Memory, Myth, and Time: From the Aztecs to Independence.* Translated by Albert G. Bork. Austin: University of Texas Press, 1994.

Foxx, Jeffrey Jay, and Walter F. Morris, Jr. *Living Maya.* New York: Henry N. Abrams, 1987.

Gage, Thomas. *Travels in the New World.* 1648. Reprint, Westport, Conn.: Greenwood Press, 1981.

Garibay, Angel M., ed. and trans. *La literatura de los aztecas.* Mexico City: Editorial Joaquín Mortiz, 1953.

González Casanova, Pablo. *Democracy in Mexico.* New York: Oxford University Press, 1972.

Guzmán, Martín Luis. *Memoirs of Pancho Villa.* Translated by V. H. Taylor. Austin: University of Texas Press, 1965.

Hammond, George P., and Agapito Rey, eds. *Narratives of the Coronado Expedition.* 1940. Reprint, Albuquerque: University of New Mexico Press, 1970.

Herrejón, Carlos. *Morelos, antología documental.* Mexico City: SEP, 1985.

Heyerdahl, Thor. *Kon-Tiki.* Chicago: University of Chicago Press, 1951.

Holden. Tom. "In Remote Mexican Village Roots of Rebellion Are Bared." *New York Times,* January 17, 1994.

Israel, Jonathan I. *Race, Class, and Politics in Colonial Mexico 1610–1670.* London: Oxford University Press, 1975.

Jones, Grant D., ed. *El manuscrito de Canek.* México: Instituto Nacional de Antropología e Historia, 1991.

Jones, Willis Knapp, ed. *Spanish American Literature in Translation.* New York: Frederick Ungar, 1966.

Katz, Frederick. "The Liberal Republic and the Porfiriato 1887–1910." In *Mexico since Independence.* Edited by Leslie Berthell. Cambridge: Cambridge University Press, 1992.

Keeler, Peter, trans. *Chilam Balam of Chumayel.* Unpublished, 1993.

Landa, Diego de. *Relación de las cosas de Yucatán.* Edited and translated by Alfred M. Tozzer. Papers of the Peabody Museum of American Archaeology and Ethnology. Vol. 18. Cambridge: Peabody Museum of Harvard University, 1941.

Las Casas, Bartolomé de. *In Defense of the Indian.* Edited and translated by Stanford Poole. DeKalb: Northern Illinois University Press, 1974.

————. *History of the Indies.* Abridged. Translated and edited by Andree M. Collard. New York: Harper Torchbooks, 1971.

León-Portilla, Miguel, ed. *The Broken Spears: The Aztec Account of the Conquest of Mexico.* Translated by Lysander Kemp. Boston: Beacon Press, 1962.

López de Gómara, Francisco. *The Life of the Conqueror by His Secretary.* Translated by Lesley Byrd Simpson. Berkeley: University of California Press, 1964.

McCarty, J. Hendrickson. *Two Thousand Miles through the Heart of Mexico.* New York: Phillips & Hunt, 1888.

McKinley, James C. "Mexico's Latest War on Drugs Gangs Is Off to a Rapid Start." *New York Times,* January 27, 2007.

"Mexicans Fear for Corn, Imperiled by Free Trade." *New York Times,* July 12, 1993.

*Mexico's Oil: A Compilation of Official Documents.* México: Gobierno de México, 1940.

Meyer, Jean: "Revolution and Reconstruction the 1920s." In *Mexico since Independence*. Edited by Leslie Bethell. Cambridge: Cambridge University Press, 1991.

Meyer, Lorenzo. "A Conversation with Lorenzo Meyer about Mexico's Political Transition: From Authoritarianism to What?" Available online. URL: http://www.indiana.edu/~jah/mexico/lmeyer.html. Updated January 1999.

———. "La polarización política persiste." Available online. URL: www.kikka-roja.blogspot. Updated July 10, 2008.

Meyer, Michael C., and William L. Sherman. *The Course of Mexican History*. 5th ed. New York: Oxford University Press, 1995.

Meyer, Michael C., William L. Sherman, and Susan M. Deeds. *The Course of Mexican History*. 6th and 7th eds. New York: Oxford University Press, 1999 and 2003.

Miller, Robert Ryal. *Mexico: A History*. Norman: University of Oklahoma Press, 1985.

Monaghan, John. *The Covenants with Earth and Rain: Exchange, Sacrifice, and Revelation in Mixtec Society*. Norman: University of Oklahoma Press, 1995.

Mongabay. Deforestation. Available online. URL: http://rainforests.mongabay.com/deforestation/2000/Mexico.htm. Updated 2006.

Motolinia, Fray. *History of the Indians*. Edited by Francis B. Steck. Washington, D.C.: Academy of American Franciscan History, 1951.

Needler, Martin. *Mexican Politics: The Containment of Conflict*. Westport, Conn.: Praeger, 1995.

Nuttall, Zelia, ed. *Codex Nuttall: A Picture Manuscript from Ancient Mexico*. New York: Dover Publications, 1975.

Paz, Octavio. *The Labyrinth of Solitude: Life and Thought in Mexico*. Translated by Lysander Kemp. New York: Grove Press, 1961.

———. *The Other Mexico: Critique of the Pyramid*. Translated by Lysander Kemp. New York: Grove Press, 1972.

Peden, Margaret Sayers, trans. *A Woman of Genius: The Intellectual Autobiography of Sor Juana de la Cruz*. Salisbury, Conn.: Lime Rock Press, 1982.

Poinsett, Joel R. *Notes on Mexico Made in the Autumn of 1822, Accompanied by an Historical Sketch of the Revolution*. New York, Frederick A. Praeger, 1969.

Prensa Latina. "Two-thousand Fold Increase in Mexico Military Expenditures." Formerly available online. URL: www.plenglish.com. Accessed January 6, 2009.

Proceso. "Military Expenditures in Federal Budget." Proceso. Available online. URL: proceso.com.mx. Updated September 17, 2008.

Quirk, Robert E. *The Mexican Revolution, 1914–1915: The Convention of Aguascalientes.* New York: Citadel Press, 1963.

Read, John Lloyd. *The Mexican Historical Novel, 1826–1910.* New York: Instituto de las Españas, 1939.

Roys, Ralph, ed. and trans. *Chilam Balam of Chumayel.* 1933. Reprint, Norman: University of Oklahoma Press, 1967.

Ruiz, Ramón Eduardo. *Triumphs and Tragedy: A History of the Mexican People.* New York: W. W. Norton, 1992.

Sahagún, Bernardino de. *General History of the Things of New Spain: Florentine Codex.* Ca. 1583). Translated by J. O. Anderson and Charles E. Dibble. 13 vols. Santa Fe, N.Mex.: School of American Research and University of Utah Press, 1950–82.

Santa Anna, Antonio de López de. *The Eagle: The Autobiography of Santa Ana.* Edited by Ann Fears Crawford, translated by Sam Guyler and Jaime Platon. Austin: University of Texas Press, 1967.

Semo, Ilán. "México a la luz y a la sombra de las cifras." In *La Jornada,* February 23, 2008.

Sierra, Justo. *The Political Evolution of the Mexican People.* Translated by Charles Ramsdell. Austin: University of Texas Press, 1970.

Simpson, Lesley Byrd. *Many Mexicos.* Berkeley: University of California Press, 1962.

Smart, Charles Allen. *Viva Juárez.* London: Eyre and Spottiswoode, 1964.

Smith, Peter H. "Mexico since 1946: Dynamics of an Authoritarian Regime." In *Mexico since Independence.* Edited by Leslie Bethell. Cambridge: Cambridge University Press, 1991.

Spores, Ronald. *The Mixtecs in Ancient and Colonial Times.* Norman: University of Oklahoma Press, 1984.

Stein, Stanley J., and Barbara H. Stein. *The Colonial Heritage of Latin America: Essays on Economic Dependence in Perspective.* Oxford: Oxford University Press, 1970.

Taube, Karl. *Aztec and Maya Myths.* Austin: University of Texas Press, 1993.

Tedlock, Dennis, trans. *Popol Vuh: The Mayan Book of the Dawn of Life.* New York: Simon and Schuster, 1985.

Thomas, Hugh. *The Conquest.* New York: Simon and Schuster, 1993.

United Nations Food and Agriculture Organization (FAO). "Trade in Agriculture, Fisheries, and Forestry." Available online. URL: http://www.fao.org/trade/stats_en.asp. Downloaded August 2, 2008.

United Nations Organization for Economic Co-operation and Development (OECD). *Health Data 2008: How Does Mexico Compare.* Available online. URL: www.oecd.org. Updated 2008.

———. *Income Inequality Poverty Rising in Most OECD Countries.* Available online. URL: www.oecd.org. Updated October 21, 2008.

Villamil, Jenario. "Analysis: Crisis de inseguridad." Proceso. Available online. URL: proceso.com.mx. Updated August 19, 2008.

Womack, John, Jr. "The Mexican Revolution, 1910–1920." In *Mexico since Independence.* Edited by Leslie Bethell. Cambridge: Cambridge University Press, 1991.

World Bank. *Country Partnership Strategy for the United Mexican States 2008–2013.* Available online. URL: http://go.worldbank.org/M82RL9YSNO.htm. Updated March 4, 2008.

———. Data & Statistics: Quick Reference Tables. Available online. URL: http://web.worldbank.org. Updated July 2008.

———. *Mexico Country Brief.* Available online. URL: http://web.worldbank.org. Updated 2007.

———. Poverty in Mexico—Fact Sheet. Available online. URL: http://web.worldbank.org. Updated 2008.

*World Factbook 2008: Mexico.* U.S. Central Intelligence Agency Publications. Available online. URL: www.worldfactbook.org. Updated October 9, 2008.

World Rainforest Movement. Deforestation. Available online. URL: www.wrm.org.uy/bulletin/Mexico.htl. Downloaded September 12, 2008.

Zahniser, Stephen. *Corn Trade during the NAFTA Era: New Twists to an Old Story.* Economic Research, U.S. Department of Agriculture Economic Research. Available online. URL: www.ers.usda.gov. Updated January 2006.

Zoellick, Robert. "Pobreza en Mexico." In *La Jornada,* May 6, 2008.

# APPENDIX 4

## SUGGESTED READING

Although this brief history is intended for nonscholars, more in-depth works are available on the many issues that could be discussed only cursorily. The following works in English include not only history and politics but also literature and art, anthropology, and ethnohistory.

### Books Spanning Major Periods

Babb, Sarah. *Managing Mexico: Economists from Nationalism to Neoliberalism.* Princeton, N.J.: Princeton University Press, 2006.

Beezley, William H. *Mexican National Identity: Memory, Innuendo, and Popular Culture.* Tucson: University of Arizona Press, 2008.

Bethell, Leslie, ed. *Mexico since Independence.* Cambridge: Cambridge University Press, 1992.

Brenner, Anita. *Idols behind Altars: The Story of the Mexican Spirit.* (1929) Reprint, Boston: Beacon Press, 1970.

Bricker, Victoria Reifker, and Ronald Spores, ed. *Supplement to the Handbook of Middle American Indians.* Vol. 4, *Ethnohistory.* Austin: University of Texas Press, 1986.

Brushwood, John S. *Mexico in Its Novel: A Nation's Search for Identity.* Austin: University of Texas Press, 1966.

Camín, Héctor Aguilar, and Lorenzo Meyer. *In the Shadow of the Mexican Revolution: Contemporary Mexican History, 1910–1989.* Austin: University of Texas Press, 1993.

Cumberland, Charles C. *Mexico: The Struggle for Modernity.* London: Oxford University Press, 1968.

Florescano, Enrique. *Memory, Myth, and Time in Mexico: From the Aztecs to Independence.* Translated by Albert G. Bork. Austin: University of Texas Press, 1994.

Frost, Elsa Cecilia, et al., eds. *Labor and Laborers Throughout Mexican History.* Tucson: University of Arizona Press, 1979.

Jones, Willis Knapp, ed. *Spanish American Literature in Translation.* New York: Frederick Ungar, 1977.

Krauze, Enrique. *Biography of Power: A History of Modern Mexico, 1810–1996.* New York: HarperCollins, 1997.

Léon-Portillo, Miguel, and Earl Shorris. *In the Language of Kings: An Anthology of Mesoamerican Literature—Pre-Columbian to the Present.* New York: W. W. Norton, 2002.

*Mexico: Spendors of Thirty Centuries.* New York: Metropolitan Museum of Art. 1990.

Meyer, Michael C., William L. Sherman, and Susan M. Deeds. *The Course of Mexican History.* Eighth edition. New York: Oxford University Press, 2007.

Ruiz, Ramón Eduardo. *Triumphs and Tragedy: A History of the Mexican People.* New York: W. W. Norton, 1993.

Sanderson, Susan W. *Land Reform in Mexico: 1910–1980.* Orlando, Fla.: Academic Press, 1984.

Simonian, Lane. *Defending the Land of the Jaguar: A History of Conservation in Mexico.* Austin: University of Texas Press, 1995.

Simpson, Lesley Byrd. *Many Mexicos.* Berkeley: University of California Press, 1967.

Smith, Bradley. *Mexico: A History in Art.* New York: Harper & Row, 1968.

Stevenson, Robert. *Music in Mexico: A Historical Survey.* New York: Thomas Y. Crowell, 1971.

Tuñón Pablos, Julia. *Women in Mexico: A Past Unveiled.* Translated by Alan Hynds. Austin: University of Texas Press, 1999.

## The First Peoples: Pre-Columbian Mexico

Adams, Richard E. W. *Prehistoric Mesoamerica.* 3d ed. Norman: University of Oklahoma Press, 2005.

Aveni, Anthony F. *Skywatchers of Ancient Mexico.* Rev. ed. Austin: University of Texas Press, 2001.

———. *Conversing with the Planets: How Science and Myth Invented the Cosmos.* Rev. ed. Boulder: University of Colorado Press, 2002.

Benson, Elizabeth P., ed. *Mesoamerican Sites and World Views.* Washington, D.C., Dunbarton Oaks, 1981.

Boone, Elizabeth H., ed. *Ritual Human Sacrifice in Mesoamerica.* Washington, D.C.: Dunbarton Oaks, 1984.

Christensen, Allen J., ed. and trans. *Popol Vuh: The Sacred Book of the Maya.* Norman: University of Oklahoma Press, 2007.

Coe, Michael D. *Breaking the Maya Code.* Rev. ed. New York: Thames and Hudson, 1999.

Coe, Sophie D. *America's First Cuisines.* Austin, Texas. University of Texas Press, 1994.

Davies, Nigel. *Voyagers to the New World*. Albuquerque: University of New Mexico Press, 1986.

Dillehay, Thomas D. *The Settlement of the Americas—A New Prehistory*. New York: Basic Books, 2000.

Freidel, David A., Linda Schele, and Joy Parker. *Maya Cosmos: Three Thousand Years on the Shaman's Path*. New York: HarperCollins, 1995.

Landa, Diego de. *Relación de las cosas de Yucatán*. Edited and translated by Alfred M. Tozzer. Papers of the Peabody Museum of American Archaeology and Ethnology. Vol. 18. Cambridge: Peabody Museum of Harvard University, 1941.

Scarborough, Vernon, and David Wilcox, ed. *The Mesoamerican Ballgame*. Tucson: University of Arizona Press, 1991.

Schele, Linda, and David Freidel. *A Forest of Kings: The Untold Story of the Ancient Maya*. New York: HarperPerennial, 1992.

Taube, Karl. *Aztec and Maya Myths*. Austin: University of Texas Press, 1993.

Wauchope, Robert. *Lost Tribes and Sunken Continents*. Chicago: University of Chicago Press, 1962.

## Diversity of Mesoamerican Civilization

Berrin, Kathleen, and Esther Pasztory, eds. *Teotihuacan: Art from the City of the Gods*. Thames and Hudson, 1993.

Blomster, Jeffrey P., ed. *After Monte Albán: Transformation and Negotiation in Oaxaca, Mexico*. Boulder: University of Colorado Press, 2008.

Clendinnen, Inga. *Aztecs: An Interpretation*. Cambridge: Cambridge University Press, 1995.

Coe, Michael D, and Rex Koontz. *Mexico: From the Olmecs to the Aztecs*. 6th ed. London: Thames and Hudson, 2008.

Coggins, Clemency C., and Orrin C. Shane III, eds. *Cenote of Sacrifice: Maya Treasures from the Sacred Well at Chichén Itzá*. Austin: University of Texas Press, 1984.

Culbert, T. Patrick, ed. *Classic Maya Political History: Hieroglyphic and Archaeological Evidence*. School of American Research Advanced Seminar Series. Cambridge: Cambridge University Press, 1996.

Diehl, Richard A. *The Olmecs: America's First Civilization*. London: Thames and Hudson, 2005.

Diehl, Richard A., and Janet Catherine Berlo, eds. *Mesoamerica After the Decline of Teotihuacan*. Washington, D.C.: Dunbarton Oaks, 1989.

Flannery, Kent V., and Joyce Marcus, eds. *The Cloud People: Divergent Evolution of the Zapotec and Mixtec Civilizations*. Clinton Corners, N.Y.: Percheron Press, 2003.

Foster, Lynn V. *Handbook to Life in the Ancient Maya World*. New York: Facts On File, 2002.

Kubler, George. *The Art and Architecture of Ancient America*. 3d ed. New Haven, Conn.: Yale University Press, 1993.

León-Portilla, Miguel. *Aztec Thought and Culture*. Translated by Jack Emory Davis. Norman: University of Oklahoma Press, 1990.

Martin, Simon, and Nikolai Grube. *Chronicle of the Maya Kings and Queens*. 2d ed. London: Thames and Hudson, 2008.

Miller, Mary Ellen. *The Art of Mesoamerica from Olmec to Aztec*. 4th ed. London: Thames and Hudson, 2006.

Miller, Mary, and Karl Taube. *An Illustrated Dictionary of the Gods and Symbols of Ancient Mexico and the Maya*. London: Thames and Hudson, 1997.

*The Olmec World: Ritual and Rulership*. Princeton: The Art Museum, Princeton University, 1996.

Pasztory, Esther. *Aztec Art*. Norman: University of Oklahoma Press, 1998.

Pohl, Mary, ed. *Prehistoric Lowland Maya Environment and Subsistence Economy*. Papers of Peabody Museum of Archaeology and Ethnology 77. Cambridge: Harvard University Press, 1985.

Sharer, Robert J., and Loa Traxler. *The Ancient Maya*. 6th ed. Stanford, Calif.: Stanford University Press, 2005.

Spores, Ronald. *The Mixtec Kings and Their People*. Norman: University of Oklahoma Press, 1967.

Townsend, Richard. *The Aztecs*. Rev. ed. London: Thames and Hudson, 2000.

Weaver, Muriel Porter. *The Aztecs, Maya, and Their Predecessors*. 3d ed. New York: Academic Press, 1993.

## The Age of Conquest

Carrasco, David, and Eduardo Matos Moctezuma, eds. *Moctezuma's Mexico: Visions of the Aztec World*. Rev. ed. Boulder: University Press of Colorado, 2003.

Cortés, Hernán. *Letters from Mexico*. Translated and edited by Anthony Pagden. New Haven, Conn.: Yale University Press, 2001.

Díaz del Castillo, Bernal. *The True History of the Conquest of New Spain*. Translated by A. P. Maudslay. Cambridge, Mass.: Da Capo Press, 2003.

Elliott, J. H. *The Old World and the New 1492–1650*. New York: Cambridge University Press, 1992.

———. *Imperial Spain 1469–1716*. New York: New American Library, 1963.

Hale, J. R. *Renaissance Exploration*. New York: W. W. Norton, 1968.

Hassig, Ross. *Aztec Warfare*. Norman: University of Oklahoma Press, 1995.

León-Portilla, Miguel, ed. and trans. *The Broken Spears: The Aztec Account of the Conquest of Mexico*. Expanded edition. Boston: Beacon Press, 2006.

López de Gómara, Francisco. *Cortés: The Life of the Conqueror by His Secretary*. Translated by Lesley Byrd Simpson. Berkeley: University of California Press, 1964.

Restall, Matthew. *Seven Myths of the Spanish Conquest*. Oxford: Oxford University Press, 2003.

Sales, Kirkpatrick. *Christopher Columbus and the Conquest of Paradise*. London: Tauris Parke, 2006.

Thomas, Hugh. *The Conquest*. New York: Simon and Schuster, 1995.

## The Founding of an Empire: 16th-Century Mexico

Aiton, Arthur S. *Antonio de Mendoza: First Viceroy of New Spain*. (1927). Reprint. New York: Russell and Russell, 1967.

Alvarado, Pedro de. *An Account of the Conquest of Guatemala*. Edited by Sedley J. Mackie. London: Melford House, 1972.

Bolton, Herbert E. *Coronado on the Turquoise Trail: Knight of Pueblos and Plains*. Albuquerque: University of New Mexico Press, 1990.

Bricker, Victoria Reifler. *The Indian Christ, The Indian King: The Historical Substrate of Maya Myth and Ritual*. Austin: University of Texas Press, 1981.

Cabeza de Vaca, Alvar Núñez. *Adventures in the Unknown Interior of America*. Translated and edited by Cyclone Covey. Albuquerque: University of New Mexico Press, 1983.

Clendinnen, Inga. *Ambivalent Conquests: Maya and Spaniard in Yucatán, 1517–1570*. 2d ed. Cambridge: Cambridge University Press, 2003.

Edgerton, Samuel. *Theater of Conversion: Religious Architecture and Indian Artisans in Colonial Mexico*. Albuquerque: University of New Mexico Press, 2001.

Elliott, J. H. *Empires of the Atlantic World: Britain and Spain in America 1492–1830*. New Haven, Conn.: Yale University Press, 2006.

Friede, Juan, and Benjamin Keen, eds. *Bartolomé de Las Casas in History: Toward an Understandings of the Man and his Work*. DeKalb: Northern Illinois University Press, 1971.

Gibson, Charles. *The Aztecs Under Spanish Rule: A History of the Indians of the Valley of Mexico 1519–1810*. Stanford, Calif.: Stanford University Press, 1976.

————. *Tlaxcala in the Sixteenth Century.* New Haven, Conn.: Yale University Press, 1952.

Greenleaf, Richard E. *The Mexican Inquisition of the Sixteenth Century.* Albuquerque: University of New Mexico Press, 1969.

Gruzinski, Serge. *Painting the Conquest: The Mexican Indians and the European Renaissance.* Translated by Deke Dusinberre. Paris: Flammarion, 1992.

Hassig, Ross. *Trade, Tribute, and Transportation: The Sixteenth Political Economy of the Valley of Mexico.* Norman: University of Oklahoma Press, 1993.

Kubler, George. *Mexican Architecture of the Sixteenth Century.* 2 vols. New Haven: Yale University Press, 1948.

Liss, Peggy K. *Mexico Under Spain, 1521–1556.* Chicago: University of Chicago Press, 1984.

Lockhart, James. *The Nahuas After the Conquest: A Social and Cultural History of the Indians of Central Mexico, Sixteenth through Eighteenth Centuries.* Stanford: Stanford University Press, 1994.

McAndrew, John. *The Open-Air Churches of Sixteenth-Century Mexico.* Cambridge, Mass.: Harvard University Press, 1965.

Phelan, John L. *The Millennial Kingdom of the Franciscans in the New World: A Study of the Writings of Gerónimo de Mendieta.* Rev. ed. Berkeley: University of California Press, 1970.

Ricard, Robert. *The Spiritual Conquest of Mexico.* Translated by Lesley Byrd Simpson. Eugene, Oreg.: Wiff and Stock, 2004.

Robertson, Donald. *Mexican Manuscript Painting of the Early Colonial Period: The Metropolitan School.* Norman: University of Oklahoma Press, 1994.

Sauer, Carl Ortwin. *Sixteenth Century North America: The Land and the People as Seen by the Europeans.* Berkeley: University of California Press, 1971.

Schurz, William L. *The Manila Galleon.* New York: E. P. Dutton, 1959.

Simpson, Lesley Byrd. *The Encomienda in New Spain.* 3d ed. Berkeley: University of California Press, 1982.

Spores, Ronald. *The Mixtecs in Ancient and Colonial Times.* Tucson: University of Oklahoma Press, 1984.

Wagner, Henry R. *Spanish Voyages to the Northwest Coast of America in the Sixteenth Century.* San Francisco: California Historical Society, 1929.

## The Colony of New Spain

Altman, Ida, and James Lockhart, eds. *Provinces of Early Mexico: Variants of Spanish-American Regional Evolution.* Los Angeles: UCLA Latin American Center Publications. Vol. 36. 1976.

Baird, Joseph Armstrong, Jr. *The Churches of Mexico: 1530–1810.* Berkeley: University of California Press, 1962.

Bakewell, Peter J. *Silver Mining and Society in Colonial Mexico: Zacatecas. 1546–1700.* Cambridge: Cambridge University Press, 2002.

Bennett, Herman L. *Africans in Colonial Mexico: Absolutism, Christianity, and Afro-Creole Consciousness, 1570–1640.* Bloomington: University of Indiana Press, 2003.

Cervantes de Salazar, Francisco. *Life in the Imperial and Loyal City of Mexico . . .* Translated by Minnie Lee B. Shepard. Austin: University of Texas Press, 1953.

Chevalier, François. *Land and Society in Colonial Mexico: The Great Hacienda.* Translated by Alvin Eustis, edited by Lesley Byrd Simpson. Berkeley: University of California Press, 1963.

Crouch, Dora P., Daniel J. Garr, and Axel I. Mundigo *Spanish City Planning in North America.* Cambridge, Mass.: MIT Press, 1982.

Farriss, Nancy M. *Maya Society Under Colonial Rule: The Collective Enterprise of Survival.* Princeton, N.J.: Princeton University Press, 1984.

———. *Crown and Clergy in Colonial Mexico, 1759–1821.* London: Athlone Press, 1968.

Foster, Nelson, and Linda S. Cordell, eds. *Chiles to Chocolate.* Tucson: University of Arizona Press, 1992.

Gage, Thomas. *Travels in the New World.* 1648. Reprint, Norman: University of Oklahoma Press, 1985.

Gerhard, Peter. *Pirates on the West Coast of New Spain, 1575–1742.* Glendale, Calif.: Arthur H. Clark Company, 1960.

Gibson, Charles. *Spain in America.* New York: Harper & Row, 1966.

Israel, Jonathan I. *Race, Class and Politics in Colonial Mexico, 1610–1670.* London: Oxford University Press, 1975.

Leonard, Irving. *Baroque Times in Old Mexico: Seventeenth-Century Persons, Places, and Practices.* Ann Arbor: University of Michigan Press, 1971.

Palmer, Colin A. *Slaves of the White God: Blacks in Mexico.* Cambridge, Mass.: Harvard University Press, 1976.

Paz, Octavio. *Sor Juana or, the Traps of Faith.* Translated by Margaret Sayers Peden. Cambridge, Mass.: Belknap Press, Harvard University Press, 1990.

Peden, Margaret Sayers, trans. *A Woman of Genius: The Intellectual Autobiography of Sor Juana de la Cruz.* Salisbury, Conn.: Lime Rock Press, 1982.

Stein, Stanley J., and Barbara H. Stein. *The Colonial Heritage of Latin America: Essays on Economic Dependence in Perspective.* Oxford: Oxford University Press, 1970.

Taylor, William B. *Drinking, Homicide and Rebellion in Colonial Mexican Villages*. Stanford: Stanford University Press, 1979.

Toussaint, Manuel. *Colonial Art in Mexico*. Translated and edited by Elizabeth W. Weismann. Austin: University of Texas Press, 1967.

Weismann, Elizabeth W. *Mexico in Sculpture 1521–1821*. Cambridge, Mass.: Harvard University Press, 1950.

## The Bourbon Reforms and Independence

Anna, Timothy E. *Spain and the Loss of the Americas*. Lincoln: University of Nebraska Press, 1983.

———. *The Fall of the Royal Government in Mexico City*. Lincoln: University of Nebraska Press, 1978.

Archer, Christon I. *The Army in Bourbon Mexico, 1760–1810*. Albuquerque: University of New Mexico Press, 1977.

———. *The Birth of Modern Mexico, 1790–1824*. Wilmington, Del.: Scholarly Resources, Inc., 2003.

Bannon, John F. *The Spanish Borderlands Frontier, 1513–1821*. Albuquerque: University of New Mexico Press, 1976.

Bobb, Bernard E. *The Viceregency of Antonio María Bucareli in New Spain, 1771–1779*. Austin: University of Texas Press, 1962.

Brading, David A. *Miners and Merchants in Bourbon Mexico, 1760–1810*. Cambridge: Cambridge University Press, 1971.

Charlot, Jean. *Mexican Art and the Academy of San Carlos, 1785–1915*. Austin: University of Texas Press, 1962.

De Volder, Arthur L. *Guadalupe Victoria: His Role in Mexican Independence*. Albuquerque: University of New Mexico Press, 1978.

Farriss, Nancy M. *Maya Society Under Colonial Rule: The Collective Enterprise of Survival*. Princeton, N.J.: Princeton University Press, 1984.

Fisher, Lillian Estelle. *The Background of the Revolution for Mexican Independence*. Gainesville: University of Florida Press, 1966.

Flores Caballero, Romeo. *Counterrevolution: The Role of the Spaniards in the Independence of Mexico, 1804–1838*. Translated by Jaime E. Rodriguez O. Lincoln: University of Nebraska, 1974.

Gálvez, Bernardo de. *Instructions for Governing the Interior Provinces of New Spain, 1786*. Edited by Donald E. Worcester. Berkeley, Calif.: Quivira Society, 1951.

Garner, Richard L. *Economic Growth and Change in Bourbon Mexico*. Gainesville: University Press of Florida, 1993.

Hamnett, Brian R. *Politics and Trade in Southern Mexico, 1750–1821*. Cambridge: Cambridge University Press, 1971.

Harris, Charles H., III. *A Mexican Family Empire: The Latifundio of the Sanchez Navarro, 1765–1867.* Austin: University of Texas Press, 1975.

Humboldt, Alexander von. *Political Essay on the Kingdom of New Spain.* Edited by Mary Maples Dunn. Norman: University of Oklahoma Press, 1988.

Katzew, Ilona. *Casta Painting: Images of Race in Eighteenth-Century Mexico.* New Haven, Conn.: Yale University Press, 2004.

Kicza, John E. *Colonial Entrepreneurs: Families and Business in Bourbon Mexico City.* Albuquerque: University of New Mexico Press, 1983.

Ladd, Doris M. *The Mexican Nobility at Independence 1780–1826.* Austin: University of Texas Press, 1976.

Lafaye, Jacques. *Quetzalcoatl and Guadalupe: The Formation of Mexican National Consciousness, 1531–1813.* Translated by Benjamin Keen. Chicago: University of Chicago Press, 1976.

Lieberman, Mark. *Hidalgo: Mexican Revolutionary.* New York: Frederick A. Praeger, 1970.

McAlister, Lyle N. *The "Fuero Militar" in New Spain, 1764–1800.* Gainesville: University of Florida, 1957.

Mörner, Magnus, ed. *The Expulsion of the Jesuits from Latin America.* New York: Alfred A. Knopf, 1965.

Motten, Clement. *Mexican Silver and the Enlightenment.* Philadelphia: University of Pennsylvania Press, 1950.

Poinsett, Joel R. *Notes on Mexico Made in the Autumn of 1822, Accompanied by an Historical Sketch of the Revolution.* New York: Frederick A. Prager, 1969.

Sprague, William F. *Vicente Guerrero, Mexican Liberator.* Chicago: University of Chicago Press, 1939.

Stein, Stanley J., and Barbara H. *Apogee of Empire: Spain and New Spain in the Age of Charles III, 1769–1789.* Baltimore: Johns Hopkins University Press, 2003.

Thomas, Alfred B., ed. and trans. *Teodoro de Croix and the Northern Frontier of New Spain, 1776–1783.* Norman: University of Oklahoma, 1968.

Timmons, Wilbert H. *Morelos.* 1963. Reprint, El Paso: Texas Western College Press, 1970.

## Years of Chaos

Anderson, William Marshall. *An American in Maximilian's Mexico, 1865–1866: Diaries of William Marshall Anderson.* Edited by Ramon Eduardo Ruiz. San Marino, Calif.: Huntington Library, 1959.

Anna, Timothy E. *The Mexican Empire of Iturbide.* Lincoln: University of Nebraska Press, 1990.

Barker, Nancy Nichols. *The French Experience in Mexico, 1821–1861: A History of Constant Misunderstanding.* Chapel Hill: University of North Carolina Press, 1979.

Bazant, Jan. *Alienation of Church Wealth in Mexico: Social and Economic Aspects of the Liberal Revolution, 1856–1875.* Cambridge: Cambridge University Press, 2008.

Berry, Charles R. *The Reform in Oaxaca, 1856–76: A Micro-history of the Liberal Revolution.* Lincoln: University of Nebraska Press, 1981.

Brack, G. M. *Mexico Views Manifest Destiny 1821–1846, An Essay on the Origins of the Mexican War.* Albuquerque: University of New Mexico Press, 1975.

Brading, David A. *Haciendas and Ranchos in the Mexican Bajío.* Cambridge: Cambridge University Press, 1978.

Bricker, Victoria Reifler. *The Indian Christ, The Indian King: The Historical Substrate of Maya Myth and Ritual.* Austin: University of Texas Press, 1981.

Cadenhead, Ivie E., Jr. *Benito Juárez.* New York: Twayne Publishers, 1973.

Calderón de la Barca, Fanny. *Life in Mexico: The Letters of Fanny Calderón de la Barca.* 1847. Reprint, edited by Howard T. Fisher and Marion H. Fisher. Garden City, N.Y.: Doubleday, 1970.

Charlot, Jean. *Mexican Art and the Academy of San Carlos, 1785–1915.* Austin: University of Texas Press, 1962.

Costeloe, Michael P. *Church and State in Independent Mexico: A Study of the Patronage Debate.* London: Royal Historical Society, 1978.

Cotner, Thomas E., and Carlos E. Castañeda, eds. *Essays in Mexican History.* Austin: Institute of Latin American Studies, 1958.

Hale, Charles A. *Mexican Liberalism in the Age of Mora 1821–1853.* New Haven, Conn.: Yale University Press, 1968.

Hanna, Alfred Jackson, and Kathryn Abbey Hanna. *Napoleon III and Mexico: American Triumph over Monarchy.* Chapel Hill: University of North Carolina Press, 1971.

Harris, Charles H, III. *The Sanchez Navarros: A Socio-economic Study of a Coahuilan Latifundio, 1846–1853.* Chicago: University of Chicago Press, 1964.

Haslip, Joan. *The Crown of Mexico, Maximilian and His Empress Carlota.* New York: Holt, Rinehart and Winston, 1971.

Henderson, Timothy J. *A Glorious Defeat: Mexico and Its War with the United States.* New York: Hill and Wang, 2007.

Jones, Oakah L., Jr. *Santa Anna.* New York: Twayne Publishers, 1968.

Monaghan, John. *The Covenants with Earth and Rain: Exchange, Sacrifice, and Revelation in Mixtec Society.* Norman: University of Oklahoma Press, 1999.

Ramírez, José Fernando. *Mexico during the War with the United States.* Edited by Walter V. Scholes and translated by E. B. Sherr. Columbia: University of Missouri Press, 1950.

Read, John Lloyd. *The Mexican Historical Novel, 1826–1910.* New York: Russell and Russell, 1973.

Reed, Nelson. *The Caste War of Yucatan.* Revised edition. Stanford, Calif.: Stanford University Press, 2001.

Rives, George L. *The United States and Mexico, 1821–1848: A History of the Relations between the Two Countries from the Independence of Texas to the Close of the War with the United States.* 2 vols. New York: Charles Scribner's Sons, 1913.

Ruiz, Ramón Eduardo, ed. *The Mexican War: Was It Manifest Destiny?* New York: Holt, Rinehart and Winston, 1963.

Santa Anna, Antonio López de. *The Eagle: The Autobiography of Santa Anna.* Edited by Ann Fears Crawford and translated by Sam Guyler and Jaime Platon. Austin: State House Press, 1988.

Sinkin, Richard N. *The Mexican Reform, 1855–1876: A Study in Liberal Nation-Building.* Austin: University of Texas Press, 1979.

Smith, George W., and Charles Judah, eds. *Chronicles of the Gringos: The U.S. Army in the Mexican War, 1846–1848.* Albuquerque: University of New Mexico Press, 1968.

Stephens, John L. *Incidents of Travel in Central America, Chiapas & Yucatán.* 2 vols. 1841. Reprint, New York: Dover Publications, 1969.

———. *Incidents of Travel in Yucatán.* 2 vols. 1843. Reprint, New York: Dover Publications, 1963.

Ward, Henry G. *Mexico in 1827.* 2 vols. London: H. Colburn, 1828.

## The Porfiriato Dictatorship

Anderson, Rodney. *Outcasts in Their Own Land: Mexican Industrial Workers, 1906–1911.* DeKalb: Northern Illinois University Press, 1976.

Bernstein, Marvin D. *The Mexican Mining Industry, 1890–1950.* Albany: State University of New York at Albany, 1965.

Charlot, Jean. *Mexican Art and the Academy of San Carlos, 1785–1915.* Austin: University of Texas Press, 1962.

Coatsworth, John. *Growth against Development: The Economic Impact of Railroads in Porfirian Mexico.* DeKalb: Northern Illinois University, 1980.

Cockcroft, James. *Intellectual Precursors of the Mexican Revolution.* Austin: University of Texas Press, 1981.

Cosío Villegas, Daniel. *United States versus Porfirio Díaz.* Lincoln: University of Nebraska Press, 1963.

Cumberland, Charles C. *Mexico: The Struggle for Modernity.* London: Oxford University Press, 1968.

Flandrau, Charles M. *Viva Mexico.* 1908. Reprint, London: Eland Books, 1985.

Friedrich, Paul. *Agrarian Revolt in a Mexican Village.* Chicago: University of Chicago Press, 1977.

Hannay, David. *Díaz.* 1917. Reprint, Whitefish, Mont.: Kessinger Publishing, 2008.

Joseph, G. M. *Revolution from Without: Yucatán, Mexico and the United States, 1880–1924.* New York: Cambridge University Press, 1982.

Kroeber, Clifton B. *Man, Land, and Water: Mexico's Farmlands Irrigation Policies 1885–1911.* Berkeley: University of California Press, 1984.

McCarty, J. Hendrickson. *Two Thousand Miles through the Heart of Mexico.* New York: Phillips & Hunt, 1888.

Sierra, Justo. *The Political Evolution of the Mexican People.* ca. 1902–06. Translated by Charles Ramsdell. Austin: University of Texas Press, 1981.

Thompson, Edward. *People of the Serpent: Life and Adventure Among the Mayas.* 1932. Reprint, New York: Capricorn Books, 1965.

Turner, John Kenneth. *Barbarous Mexico.* 1910. Reprint, Austin: University of Texas Press, 1969.

Tyler, Ron, ed. *Posada's Mexico.* Washington: Library of Congress, 1979.

Vanderwood, Paul J. *Disorder and Progress: Bandits, Police and Mexican Development.* Rev. ed. Wilmington, Del.: SR Books, 1992.

Weiner, Richard. *Race, Nation, and Market: Economic Changes in Porfirian Mexico.* Tucson: University of Arizona Press, 2004.

Weismann, Elizabeth Wilder. *Art and Time in Mexico: From the Conquest to the Revolution.* New York: Harper and Row, 1985.

Zea, Leopoldo. *Positivism in Mexico.* Translated by Josephine H. Schulte. Austin: University of Texas Press, 1974.

## The Revolution of 1910

Azuela, Mariano. *The Underdogs.* Translated by Sergio Waisman. New York: Penguin Books, 2008.

Bailey, David. *Viva Cristo Rey: The Cristero Rebellion and the Church-State Conflict in Mexico.* Austin: University of Texas Press, 1974.

Bernstein, Marvin D. *The Mexican Mining Industry 1890–1950: A Study of the Interaction of Politics, Economics, and Technology.* Albany: State University of New York, 1964.

Billeter, Erika, ed. *Images of Mexico.* Dallas: Dallas Museum of Art, 1987.

Brenner, Anita. *The Wind That Swept Mexico: The History of the Mexican Revolution.* 1943. Reprint, Austin: University of Texas Press, 1984.

Charlot, Jean. *The Mexican Mural Renaissance, 1920–1925.* New Haven, Conn.: Yale University Press, 1967.

Clark, Marjorie. *Organized Labor in Mexico.* Chapel Hill: University of North Carolina Press, 1934.

Clendenen, Clarence C. *The United States and Pancho Villa: A Study in Unconventional Diplomacy.* Ithaca, N.Y.: Cornell University Press, 1981.

Cockcroft, J. D. *Mexico: Class Formation, Capital Accumulation, and the State.* New York: Monthly Review Press, 1983.

Cumberland, Charles C. *Mexican Revolution: Genesis under Madero.* Austin: University of Texas Press, 1952.

———. *Mexican Revolution: The Constitutionalist Years.* Austin: University of Texas Press, 1972.

Dulles, John W. *Yesterday in Mexico: A Chronicle of the Revolution, 1919–1936.* Austin: University of Texas Press, 1961.

Guzmán, Martín Luis, ed. *Memoirs of Pancho Villa.* Translated by V. H. Taylor. Austin: University of Texas Press, 1970.

———. *The Eagle and the Serpent.* Translated by Harriet de Onís. Gloucester, Mass.: P. Smith, 1969.

Haddox, John H. *Vasconcelos of Mexico.* Austin: University of Texas Press, 1967.

Hall, Linda. *Alvaro Obregón: Power and Revolution in Mexico, 1911–1920.* College Station: Texas A and M University Press, 1981.

Hamilton, Nora. *The Limits of State Autonomy: Post Revolutionary Mexico.* Princeton, N.J.: Princeton University Press, 1982.

Herrera, Hayden. *Frida Kahlo: A Biography.* New York: Harper and Row, 2002.

Katz, Friedrich. *The Secret War in Mexico: Europe, the United States, and the Mexican Revolution.* Chicago: University of Chicago Press, 1981.

Lieuwen, Edwin. *Mexican Militarism: The Political Rise and Fall of the Revolutionary Army.* Albuquerque: University of New Mexico Press, 1968.

Link, Arthur S. *Wilson: Campaigns for Progressivism and Peace, 1916–1917.* ACLS Humanities E-Book, 2008.

López y Fuentes, Gregorio. *El India.* Translated by Anita Brenner. New York: Frederick Ungar, 1961.

MacKinley, Helm. *Mexican Painters: Rivera, Orozco, Siqueiros and Other Artists of the Realist School.* 1941. Reprint, New York: Dover Publications, 1989.

Niemeyer, Eberhardt V. Jr. *Revolution at Querétaro: The Mexican Constitutionalist Convention of 1916–1917.* Austin: University of Texas Press, 1974 and 1991.

Poniatowska, Elena. *Las Soldaderas: Women of the Mexican Revolution.* El Paso, Tex.: Cinco Puntas Press, 2006.

Reed, John. *Insurgent Mexico.* 1914. Reprint, New York: Simon and Schuster, 1969.

Ross, Stanley. *Francisco I. Madero: Apostle of Mexican Democracy.* New York: Columbia University Press, 1955.

Ruiz, Ramón Eduardo. *Mexico: The Challenge of Poverty and Illiteracy.* San Marino, Calif.: Huntington Library, 1963.

Rutherford, John D. *Mexican Society during Revolution: A Literary Approach.* Oxford: Oxford University Press, 1971.

Salas, Elizabeth. *Soldaderas in the Mexican Military: Myth and History.* Austin: University of Texas Press, 1990.

Sommers, Joseph. *After the Storm: Landmarks of the Modern Mexican Novel.* Albuquerque: University of New Mexico Press, 1968.

Sullivan, Paul. *Unfinished Conversations: Mayas and Foreigners Between Two Wars.* Berkeley: University of California Press, 1991.

Truett, John Kenneth. *Fugitive Landscapes: The Forgotten History of the U.S.-Mexico Borderlands.* New Haven, Conn.: Yale University Press, 2006.

Wasserman, Mark. *Capitalists, Caciques, and Revolution: The Native Elite and Foreign Enterprise in Chihuahua, 1854–1911.* Chapel Hill: University of North Carolina Press, 1984.

Weyl, Nathaniel, and Sylvia Weyl. *The Reconquest of Mexico: The Years of Lázaro Cárdenas.* New York: Oxford University Press, 1939.

Whetten, Nathan L. *Rural Mexico.* Chicago: University of Chicago Press, 1948.

Wilkie, James W. *The Mexican Revolution: Federal Expenditure and Social Change since 1910.* Berkeley: University of California Press, 1973.

Wolfskill, George, and Douglas W. Richmond, eds. *Essays on the Mexican Revolution: Revisionist Views of the Leaders.* Austin: University of Texas Press, 1979.

Womack, John, Jr. *Zapata and the Mexican Revolution.* New York: Alfred A. Knopf, 1968.

## The Institutionalized Revolution

Barry, Tom, ed. *Mexico: A Country Guide*. Albuquerque: The Inter-Hemispheric Education Resource Center, 1992.

Beacham, Hans. *Mexico: Architecture of Yesterday and Today*. New York: Architectural Book Publishing, 1969.

Billeter, Erika, ed. *Images of Mexico*. Dallas: Dallas Museum of Art, 1987.

Camp, Roderic A., ed. *Mexico's Political Stability: The Next Five Years*. Boulder: Westview Press, 1986.

Cline, Howard. *Mexico: From Revolution to Evolution*. New York: Oxford University Press, 1962 and 1968.

Cline, William R., ed. *International Debt and the Stability of the World Economy*. Washington, D.C.: Institute for International Economics and MIT Press, 1984.

Cornelius, Wayne A. *Politics and the Migrant Poor in Mexico City*. Stanford, Calif.: Stanford University Press, 1975.

Fuentes, Carlos. *The Death of Artemio Cruz*. Translated by Alfred MacAdam. Rev. ed. New York: Farrar, Straus and Giroux, 1991.

Galarza, Ernesto. *Merchants of Labor: The Mexican Bracero Story*. San Jose, Calif.: Rosicrucian Press, 1964.

Gallo, Ruben. *The Avant-Garde and the Technological Revolution*. Cambridge, Mass.: MIT University Press, 2005.

Gentleman, Judith, and Peter H. Smith, eds. *Mexico's Alternative Political Futures*. San Diego: Center for U.S.-Mexican Studies, 1989.

Goldman, Shifra M. *Contemporary Mexican Painting in a Time of Change*. 1981. Reprint. Albuquerque: University of New Mexico Press, 1995.

González Casanova, Pablo. *Democracy in Mexico*. 2d ed. Translated by Danielle Salti. New York: Oxford University Press, 1970.

Grayson, George. *Oil and Mexican Foreign Policy*. Pittsburgh: University of Pittsburgh Press, 1988.

———. *The Mexican Labor Machine: Power, Politics, and Patronage*. Washington, D.C.: Center for Strategic Studies, 1989.

Grindle, Merilee Serrill. *Bureaucrats, Politicians, and Peasants in Mexico: A Case Study in Public Policy*. Berkeley: University of California Press, 1977.

Hellman, Judith A. *Mexico in Crisis*. New York: Holmes and Meier, 1983.

Hodges, Donald C. and Daniel Ross Gandy. *Mexico 1910–1980: Reform or Revolution*. Rev. ed. London: Zed, 1983.

Johnson, Kenneth F. *Mexican Democracy: A Critical View*. 3d ed. Westport, Conn.: Praeger, 1984.

King, Timothy. *Mexico: Industrialization and Trade Policies since 1940*. New York: Oxford University Press, 1970 and 1982.

Lamartine Yates, Paul. *Mexico's Agricultural Dilemma.* Tucson: University of Arizona Press, 1981.

Langford, Walter M. *The Mexican Novel Comes of Age.* Notre Dame: University of Notre Dame Press, 1971.

Levine, Daniel B., Kenneth Hill, and Robert Warren, eds. *Immigration Statistics: A Story of Neglect.* Washington, D.C.: National Academy Press, 1985.

Levy, Daniel C. *University and Government in Mexico: Autonomy in an Authoritarian System.* New York: Praeger, 1980.

Levy, Daniel C., and Gabriel Székely. *Mexico: Paradoxes of Stability and Change.* Rev. ed. Boulder: Westview Press, 1987.

Lewis, Oscar. *The Children of Sánchez: Autobiography of a Mexican Family.* 1961. Reprint, New York: Random House, 1987.

*Mexico: Splendors of Thirty Centuries.* New York: Metropolitan Museum of Art, 1990.

Mora, Carl J. *Mexican Cinema: Reflections of a Society, 1896–2004.* 3d ed. Jefferson, N.C.: McFarland Company, 2005.

Morton, Ward. *Woman Suffrage in Mexico.* Gainesville: University of Florida Press, 1962.

Mosk, Sanford A. *Industrial Revolution in Mexico.* 1950. Reprint, New York: Russell & Russell, 1975.

Murphy, Arthur D., and Alex Stepick. *Social Inequality in Oaxaca: A History of Resistance and Change.* Philadelphia: Temple University Press, 1991.

Newell, Roberto G., and Luis Rubio F. *Mexico's Dilemma: The Political Origins of Economic Crisis.* Boulder: Westview Press, 1984.

Pastor, Robert A., and Jorge Castañeda. *Limits to Friendship: The United States and Mexico.* New York: Alfred A. Knopf, 1988.

Paz, Octavio. *The Labyrinth of Solitude and Other Writings.* Translated by Lysander Kemp. New York: Grove Press, 1994.

Poniatowska, Elena. *Massacre in Mexico.* Translated by Helen R. Lane. Columbia: University of Missouri Press, 1992.

Reynolds, Clark W. *The Mexican Economy: Twentieth-Century Structure and Growth.* New Haven, Conn.: Yale University Press, 1970.

Riding, Alan. *Distant Neighbors: A Portrait of the Mexicans.* New York: Vintage Books, 2000.

Ronfeldt, David, ed. *The Modern Mexican Military: A Reassessment.* San Diego: Center for U.S.-Mexican Studies, 1984.

Ross, Stanley R., ed. *Is the Mexican Revolution Dead?* Rev. ed. New York: Alfred A. Knopf, 1975.

Sainz, Gustavo. *Gazapo*. New York; Farrar, Straus and Giroux, 1968.

Sanderson, Steven. *The Transformation of Mexican Agriculture*. Princeton, N.J.: Princeton University Press, 1986.

Schlefer, Jonathan. *Palace Politics: How the Ruling Party Brought Crisis to Mexico*. Austin: University of Texas Press, 2008.

Smith, Peter. *Labyrinths of Power: Political Recruitment in Twentieth Century Mexico*. Princeton, N.J.: Princeton University Press, 1978.

Solís, Leopoldo. *Economic Policy Reform in Mexico: A Case Study for Developing Countries*. New York, 1981.

Vázquez, Josefina Zoraida, and Lorenzo Meyer. *The United States and Mexico*. Chicago: University of Chicago Press, 1986.

Vernon, Raymond. *The Dilemma of Mexico's Development: The Roles of the Private and Public Sectors*. Cambridge: Cambridge University Press, 1963.

Vogt, Evon Z. *The Zinacantecos of Mexico: A Modern Maya Way of Life*. New York: Holt, Rinehart and Winston, 1970.

Williams, Edward J. *The Rebirth of the Mexican Petroleum Industry*. Lexington, Mass.: D.C. Heath, 1979.

## The March toward Democracy

Bacon, David. *Communities without Borders*. Ithaca, N.Y.: Cornell University Press, 2006.

Barkin, David. *Distorted Development: Mexico in the World Economy*. Boulder: Westview Press, 1990.

Barry, Tom, ed. *Mexico: A Country Guide*. Albuquerque, N.Mex.: The Inter-Hemispheric Resource Center, 1992.

Bustamante, Jorge, and Wayne Cornelius, eds. *Mexican Migration to the United States: Origins, Consequences, and Policy Options*. San Diego, Calif.: Center for U.S.-Mexican Studies, 1989.

Camp, Roderic. *Crossing Swords: Politics and Religion in Mexico*. New York: Oxford University Press, 1997.

Castañeda, Jorge G. *The Mexican Shock: Its Meaning for the United States*. New York: New Press, 1995.

Cornelius, Wayne A., and Ann L. Craig. *The Mexican Political System in Transition*. San Diego, Calif.: Center for U.S.-Mexican Studies, 1991.

Cypher, James M. *State and Capital in Mexico: Development Policy Since 1940*. Boulder: Westview Press, 1990.

Foweraker, Joe, and Ann Craig, eds. *Popular Movements and Political Change in Mexico*. Boulder: Lynne Rienner Publishers, 1990.

Foxx, Jeffrey Jay, and Walter F. Morris, Jr. *Living Maya*. New York: Harry N. Abrams, 1987.

Fuentes, Carlos. *A New Time for Mexico.* Berkeley: University of California Press, 1997.

Ganster, Paul, and David E. Lorey. *The U.S.-Mexican Border into the Twenty-first Century.* 2d ed. Lanham, Md.: Rowman & Littlefield, 2007.

Haber, Stephen. *Industry and Underdevelopment: The Industrialization of Mexico, 1890–1940.* Stanford, Calif.: Stanford University Press, 1995.

Lorey, David. *The U.S.-Mexican Border in the Twentieth Century.* Wilmington, Del.: Scholarly Resources, 1999.

Lowenthal, Abraham F. *Partners in Conflict: The United States and Latin America in the 1990s.* Baltimore: Johns Hopkins University Press, 1990.

Lustig, Nora. *Mexico: The Remaking of an Economy.* 2d ed. Washington, D.C.: Brookings Institution Press, 1998.

McAnany, Emile G., and Kenton T. Wilkinson, eds. *Mass Media and Free Trade: NAFTA and the Cultural Industries.* Austin: University of Texas Press, 1997.

Menchaca, Martha. *The Mexican Outsiders: A Community of Marginalization and Discrimination in California.* Austin: University of Texas Press, 1995.

Monaghan, John. *The Covenants with Earth and Rain: Exchange, Sacrifice, and Revelation in Mixtec Society.* Norman: University of Oklahoma Press, 1999.

Morris, Stephen D. *Political Reformism in Mexico: An Overview of Contemporary Mexican Politics.* Boulder, Colo.: Lynn Reiner, 1995.

Oppenheimer, Andrés. *Bordering on Chaos: Mexico's Roller-Coaster Journey towards Prosperity.* Boston: Back Bay Books, 1998.

Rotella, Sebastian. *Twilight on the Line: Underworlds and Politics at the U.S.-Mexican Border.* New York: W. W. Norton, 1998.

Russell, Philip L. *Mexico under Salinas.* Austin, Tex.: Mexico Resource Center, 1994.

Sandstrom, Alan. *Corn Is Our Blood: Culture and Ethnic Identity in a Contemporary Aztec Indian Village.* Norman: University of Oklahoma Press, 1991.

Stoddard, Ellwyn R. *Maquila Assembly Plants in Northern Mexico.* El Paso: Texas Western Press, 1987.

Sullivan, Paul. *Unfinished Conversations: Mayas and Foreigners Between Two Wars.* Berkeley: University of California Press, 1991.

Weintraub, Sidney. *Transforming the Mexican Economy: The Salinas Sexenio.* Washington D.C.: National Planning Association, 1990.

————. *A Marriage of Convenience: Relations between Mexico and the United States*. New York: Oxford University Press, 1990.

Womack, John, ed. *Rebellion in Chiapas: An Historical Reader.* New York: New Press, 1999.

## A More Democratic Mexico

Bacon, Christopher M., ed. *Confronting the Coffee Crisis: Fair Trade, Sustainable Livelihoods and Ecosystems in Mexico and Central America.* Cambridge, Mass.: MIT Press, 2008.

Butler, Edgar W., James B. Pick, and W. James Hettrick. *Mexico and Mexico City in the World Economy.* Boulder, Colo.: Westview Press, 2001.

Egan, Linda. *Carlos Monsiváis: Culture and Chronicle in Contemporary Mexico.* Tucson: University of Arizona Press, 2001.

Levy, David, and Kathleen Bruhn. *Mexico: The Struggle for Democratic Development.* 2d ed. Berkeley: University of California Press, 2006.

Levy, Santiago. *Progress against Poverty: Sustaining Mexico's Progresa-Oportunidades Program.* Washington, D.C.: Brookings Institution Press, 2006.

Martínez, Oscar J. *Troublesome Border.* Rev. ed. Tucson: University of Arizona Press, 2006.

Martinez, Ruben. *Crossing Over: A Mexican Family on the Migrant Trail.* New York: Henry Holt, 2001.

Montemayor, Carlos, and Donald Frischmann. *Words of the True Peoples/Palabras de los seres verdaderos.* Austin: University of Texas Press, 2005.

Preston, Julia, and Samuel Dillon. *Opening Mexico: The Making of a Democracy.* New York: Farrar, Straus and Giroux, 2005.

Randall, Laura, ed. *Changing Structure of Mexico: Political, Social, and Economic Prospects.* Armonk, N.Y.: M. E. Sharpe, Inc., 2005.

Shadlen, Kenneth C. *Democratization without Representation: The Politics of Small Industry in Mexico.* University Park, Pa.: Penn State University Press, 2004.

# INDEX

Page numbers in *italic* indicate illustrations. Page numbers followed by *m* indicate maps. Page numbers followed by *c* indicate chronologies. Page numbers followed by *t* indicate tables.